"In his theological concern for t... Edwards stands at the end of a long theological tradition that reaches back to Augustine and beyond, even to the Scriptures themselves. In the last two centuries, however, this area of theological inquiry seems to have dropped off the radar for Christian theologians and practitioners, which may explain why students of Edwards's corpus of writings have not tackled the subject. Ortlund's study nicely fills this lacuna, for he rightly shows, from a multitude of angles, that beauty is the fulcrum of Edwards's thinking. A joy to read and to ponder!"

Michael A. G. Haykin, Professor of Church History and Biblical Spirituality, The Southern Baptist Theological Seminary

"Jonathan Edwards is widely known as a hellfire-and-brimstone preacher. Serious students, like Dane Ortlund, have long known he was much more. In this book Ortlund puts his careful research to good purpose as he demonstrates convincingly that the center of Edwards's concern was always and supremely beauty—in God, from God, and for God. Grateful readers will find this book highly informative on Edwards and deeply encouraging for the Christian life today."

Mark A. Noll, Francis A. McAnaney Professor of History, University of Notre Dame

"No one has taught me more about the dynamics of Christian living than has Jonathan Edwards. And no one has more clearly articulated the role of beauty in Edwards's understanding of the Christian life than has Dane Ortlund. If you're unfamiliar with Edwards, or if you wonder how beauty could possibly have any lasting effect in your growth as a Christian, this book is for you."

Sam Storms, Lead Pastor for Preaching and Vision, Bridgeway Church, Oklahoma City, Oklahoma

"What a delight to see a book on Edwards's conception of the Christian life. And how beautiful it is that it depicts the Christian life as ordered by and to the beauty of God. This book will help strengthen the fertilization of today's churches by Edwards's vision of God's triune beauty."

Gerald R. McDermott, Jordan-Trexler Professor of Religion, Roanoke College; coauthor, *The Theology of Jonathan Edwards*

"Edwards is profound, and this book breaks down the complexity into manageable portions around the theme of beauty, thus engaging readers in a fresh vision of the importance of Edwards's theology to contemporary living."

Josh Moody, Senior Pastor, College Church, Wheaton, Illinois; author, *Journey to Joy: The Psalms of Ascent*

"'The supreme value of reading Edwards is that we are ushered into a universe brimming with beauty,' writes Ortlund. I couldn't agree more. And one would be hard-pressed to find a more engaging introduction to this universe for the church. Even the final chapter, on ways in which we should *not* follow Edwards, offers crucial Christian wisdom. Ortlund's criticisms of Edwards hit the mark—and deserve consideration by Edwards's growing number of fans. I plan to use them with my seminary students in years to come. Please peruse this beautiful book. It's good for the soul."

Douglas A. Sweeney, Professor of Church History, Director of the Jonathan Edwards Center, Trinity Evangelical Divinity School

EDWARDS

on the Christian Life

THEOLOGIANS ON THE CHRISTIAN LIFE

EDITED BY STEPHEN J. NICHOLS AND JUSTIN TAYLOR

EDWARDS

on the Christian Life

ALIVE TO THE BEAUTY OF GOD

DANE C. ORTLUND

Foreword by George M. Marsden

WHEATON, ILLINOIS

Edwards on the Christian Life: Alive to the Beauty of God

Copyright © 2014 by Dane C. Ortlund

Published by Crossway
            1300 Crescent Street
            Wheaton, Illinois 60187

Cover design: Josh Dennis
Cover image: Richard Solomon Artists, Mark Summers

First printing 2014

Printed in the United States of America

Unless otherwise indicated, Scripture quotations are from the ESV® Bible (The Holy Bible, English Standard Version®), copyright © 2001 by Crossway, a publishing ministry of Good News Publishers. 2011 Text Edition. Used by permission. All rights reserved.

Scripture quotations marked KJV are from the King James Version of the Bible.

Trade paperback ISBN: 978-1-4335-3505-5
PDF ISBN: 978-1-4335-3506-2
Mobipocket ISBN: 978-1-4335-3507-9
ePub ISBN: 978-1-4335-3508-6

Library of Congress Cataloging-in-Publication Data

Ortlund, Dane Calvin.
  Edwards on the Christian life : alive to the beauty of God /
Dane C. Ortlund; foreword by George M. Marsden.
     pages cm. — (Theologians on the Christian life)
  Includes bibliographical references and index.
  ISBN 978-1-4335-3505-5 (tp)
  1. Edwards, Jonathan, 1703–1758. 2. Christian life.
3. Aesthetics—Religious aspects—Christianity. I. Title.
BX7260.E3O78   2014
230'.58092—dc23   2014002414

Crossway is a publishing ministry of Good News Publishers.

VP		29	28	27	26	25	24	23	22	21	20	19
16	15	14	13	12	11	10	9	8	7	6	5	4

To Granddad

As much as anyone I've known,
you were—and are much more now—
alive to beauty.

CONTENTS

SERIES PREFACE

Some might call us spoiled. We live in an era of significant and substantial resources for Christians on living the Christian life. We have ready access to books, DVD series, online material, seminars—all in the interest of encouraging us in our daily walk with Christ. The laity, the people in the pew, have access to more information than scholars dreamed of having in previous centuries.

Yet for all our abundance of resources, we also lack something. We tend to lack the perspectives from the past, perspectives from a different time and place than our own. To put the matter differently, we have so many riches in our current horizon that we tend not to look to the horizons of the past.

That is unfortunate, especially when it comes to learning about and practicing discipleship. It's like owning a mansion and choosing to live in only one room. This series invites you to explore the other rooms.

As we go exploring, we will visit places and times different from our own. We will see different models, approaches, and emphases. This series does not intend for these models to be copied uncritically, and it certainly does not intend to put these figures from the past high upon a pedestal like some race of super-Christians. This series intends, however, to help us in the present listen to the past. We believe there is wisdom in the past twenty centuries of the church, wisdom for living the Christian life.

Stephen J. Nichols and Justin Taylor

FOREWORD

Jonathan Edwards has become remarkably popular. In recent decades many thoughtful Christians have been finding his works to be immensely illuminating resources for exploring the depths of the riches of God's ways. Edwards was not just a theologian, but also a many-sided pastor, preacher, missionary, revivalist, and spiritual guide who was deeply involved in a major Christian awakening.

Books such as *Edwards on the Christian Life* are especially welcome as part of the current Edwards revival precisely because Edwards is so many-sided and complex. The essence of his theology needs to be distilled from his many writings and to be presented in practical terms for Christians today. Dane Ortlund does just that. Reading Edwards's own works can inspire Christians today, but often it is best to start with a more accessible introduction, such as the present one.

Edwards wrote with precision and care and is usually eminently clear. Yet, rather than using an economy of words, he often explained things by repetitions that explored all the nuances of the point he was making. He also did not write one systematic work that explains his whole outlook from beginning to end. So even though there are a few of his works, such as his sermon "A Divine and Supernatural Light" or his sermon series "Charity and Its Fruits," that anyone can immediately appreciate, it is helpful to have an overview that presents his outlook in an accessible way. It is all the more valuable that this overview is not just an academic summary but is here used as a guide for the contemporary Christian life.

Dane Ortlund rightly emphasizes that beauty is an overarching and integrating theme in Edwards's theology of the Christian life. This is in contrast to most of modern evangelical theology, in which beauty is rarely mentioned. One reason for this lack is that evangelicalism has often been shaped by practical emphases and techniques selected on the basis of what seems to work best for particular goals. Beauty typically seems abstract and impractical, something that might be associated with mysticism, contemplation, or perhaps the aestheticism of High Church liturgies and music.

In Edwards, by contrast, beauty is at the center of a practical dynamic. His outlook might be said to be a theology of active beauty. Beauty is first of all a quality radiating from the center of all reality. Edwards connects beauty closely with God's holiness and with God's love. At the center of reality are the persons of the Trinity, who perfectly manifest these qualities in the harmony of their mutual love. The creation of the universe is an expression of the overflowing of these dynamics. The highest beauty is perfect love, manifested to us in the sacrificial death of Christ on behalf of the undeserving. Beauty is thus an active power.

If we have eyes to see perfect beauty, it is like a magnet that draws us to it. And if we are drawn into the beauty of that holy love, then we too must respond to it in our loves and actions. Our deepest desires will be to love God and to love what God loves. So a life built around a response to God's beauty should be characterized by the traits of those who are being drawn into the loving fellowship of the triune God. Dane Ortlund, following Edwards, spells out practical dimensions of what that involves.

George M. Marsden

PREFACE

Thirty years after Jonathan Edwards died, Ezra Stiles, president of Yale, predicted that Edwards's books would soon enjoy "transient notice perhaps scarce above oblivion" and that "when posterity occasionally comes across them in the rubbish of libraries, the rare characters who may read and be pleased with them will be looked upon as singular and whimsical."[1]

Ezra who?

To me—and, according to any decent library's section on Edwards, to many others—it is a small price to pay to be viewed as "singular and whimsical" when reading and enjoying the writings of Jonathan Edwards. The supreme value of reading Edwards—by which I have in mind reading not for the sake of academic cleverness but for the sake of one's soul—is not historical insight or doctrinal sharpening or moral improvement, though these things happen. The supreme value of reading Edwards is that we are ushered into a universe brimming with beauty. Edwards walks us through the wardrobe into Narnia. We are given glasses—not sunglasses, which dim everything, but their opposite: lenses that brighten everything.

Much has been written on Edwards in recent years. Do we really need another book on the man? And yet, surprisingly little has been said at a nontechnical level that connects his theology of Christian living with the current state of the church. Even if much *had* been written on his theology

---

[1] Ezra Stiles, *Literary Diary*, quoted in Joseph A. Conforti, *Jonathan Edwards, Religious Tradition, and American Culture* (Chapel Hill, NC: University of North Carolina Press, 1995), 3. The original reference can be found in Franklin B. Dexter, ed., *The Literary Diary of Ezra Stiles, D.D. LL.D.*, 3 vols. (New York: C. Scribner's Sons, 1901), 3:275.

of the Christian life, those who have spent time with Edwards will agree that complaining about another Edwards book today is like complaining about another meal today. Regular nourishment doesn't get old.

The purpose of this book is to reflect on how a Massachusetts pastor three hundred years ago understood the Christian life and, upon this reflection, to be changed, so that we are slightly different people than we would otherwise be. Calmer, gentler, happier. A little brighter, to use Edwards's favorite metaphor. More beautiful. More *human*.

We are simply asking, then, under Jonathan Edwards's tutelage: What does it mean to live as a Christian? What *is* a Christian?

Edwards's answer exposes our misconceptions. To live as a Christian *at its core* is not to adhere to a set of morals, or to assent to right doctrine, or to champion a set of ethical causes, or to passively receive forgiveness of sins, or to attend church or give to the poor or say the right prayer or come from a godly family.

All these have value. But for Edwards, none of them is definitive of Christian living. The Christian life, he says, is to enjoy and reflect the beauty of God. Everything Edwards wrote on Christian living funnels down into this. All the obedience and giving and generosity and kindness and praying and Bible reading in the world, without a heart-sense of divine beauty, is empty. Even damning.

Our strategy will be to ask twelve questions about the Christian life and provide, from Edwards, corresponding answers. These will form the chapters of this book, with a final, thirteenth chapter diagnosing four weaknesses in Edwards's view of the Christian life. Twelve chapters identify what we can learn from Edwards; one chapter identifies what he could learn from us. In brief the twelve questions and answers are these:

1. What is the overarching, integrating theme to Edwards's theology of the Christian life?

   Beauty.

2. How is this heart-sense of beauty ignited? How does it all get started? What must happen for anyone to first glimpse the beauty of God?

   New birth.

3. Having begun, what then is the essence of the Christian life? What does seeing God's beauty create in us? What's the heart and soul of Christian living?

   Love.

4. How does love fuel the Christian life? What's the nonnegotiable of all nonnegotiables that will keep us loving? What does divine beauty give us?

   Joy.

5. And what uniquely marks such love and joy? What is the aroma of the Christian life? What in Edwards's portrait of the Christian life is most lacking in our own world today?

   Gentleness.

6. Where do I go to get this love, joy, and gentleness? How can I find it? What, concretely, sustains this kind of life through all our ups and downs?

   The Bible.

7. But as I go to the Bible, what do I do with it as I read? How do I own it, make it mine, turn it into this joy-fueled love?

   Prayer.

8. What then is the overall flavor of the Christian life? What is the aura, the feel, of following Christ in a world of moral chaos and pain?

   Pilgrimage.

9. As new birth, Bible, prayer, and all the rest go in, what comes out? What is the fruit of the Christian life?

   Obedience.

10. Who is the great enemy of Christian living? Who wishes above all to prevent loving, joyful, gentle lives?

    Satan.

11. What is the great concern of the Christian life? Toward what, supremely, should our efforts be directed as we walk with God?

The soul.

12. Finally, what does all this funnel into? When will we be permanently and fully and unfailingly alive to beauty? What, above all else, is the great hope of the Christian life?

Heaven.

So we will learn from Jonathan Edwards about the Christian life.

Some might be skeptical. Understandably so. How does a man who never typed an e-mail or drove a car or swung a golf club or watched a Super Bowl or blogged or tweeted or Skyped help me live my twenty-first-century Christian life? Not much if what matters essentially in Christian living is what we do. A lot if what matters essentially in Christian living is what we are. The way to make a wilting rose bush as healthy as the lush cherry tree next door isn't to glue cherries onto it but to plant that rose bush in the same rich soil. The point of this book is not mainly to encourage us to imitate Edwards's life externally. The point is to encourage us all to draw nourishment from the same rich soil of divine beauty that made Edwards's own life so abundantly fruitful.

"There is a brightness and glory in a Christian life," preached Jonathan Edwards. There was in his. I want there to be in ours. Edwards helps get us there.

I am grateful to Justin Taylor and Steve Nichols for inviting me to contribute this volume to this strategic series. What dear brothers these two men are. And Thom Notaro's editing was outstanding.

During the writing of this book I was helped more than words can say in living the Christian life by the Fight Night men at Wheaton College: Erik, Wade, Ian, Tanner, Dave, Ben, Adam, Bobby, and the two Marks. You men make me want to live well. You help me see the beauty of God.

This book is dedicated to my grandfather, Ray Ortlund Sr. (1923–2007), because he was for me a flesh-and-blood incarnation of the radiant beauty to which Edwards summons us. I love you, Gramps, and miss you. What Edwards preached, you were.

Above all, you, Stacey, have been the greatest earthly encouragement to me. (How are you more cheerful than ever after twelve years of living with me?)

What fun it will be to sit with Jonathan Edwards in the new earth some day, just the two of us, and say to him, to God's glory, "May I tell you how you helped me to live the Christian life? . . ."

VOLUMES IN

THE WORKS OF
JONATHAN EDWARDS

All sources abbreviated *WJE*, followed by volume and page numbers, are from *The Works of Jonathan Edwards*, ed. Perry Miller, John E. Smith, and Harry S. Stout, 26 vols. (New Haven, CT: Yale University Press, 1957–2008). Individual volumes are as follows:

Vol. 1   *Freedom of the Will*, edited by Paul Ramsey, 1957.

Vol. 2   *Religious Affections*, edited by John E. Smith, 1959.

Vol. 3   *Original Sin*, edited by Clyde A. Holbrook, 1970.

Vol. 4   *The Great Awakening*, edited by C. C. Goen, 1972.

Vol. 5   *Apocalyptic Writings*, edited by Stephen J. Stein, 1977.

Vol. 6   *Scientific and Philosophical Writings*, edited by Wallace E. Anderson, 1980.

Vol. 7   *The Life of David Brainerd*, edited by Norman Pettit, 1985.

Vol. 8   *Ethical Writings*, edited by Paul Ramsey, 1989.

Vol. 9   *A History of the Work of Redemption*, edited by John F. Wilson, 1989.

Vol. 10   *Sermons and Discourses, 1720–1723*, edited by Wilson H. Kimnach, 1992.

Vol. 11   *Typological Writings*, edited by Wallace E. Anderson and Mason I. Lowance Jr., with David Watters, 1993.

Vol. 12   *Ecclesiastical Writings*, edited by David D. Hall, 1994.

Vol. 13   *The "Miscellanies": Entry nos. a–z, aa–zz, 1–500*, edited by Thomas A. Schafer, 1994.

Vol. 14   *Sermons and Discourses, 1723–1729*, edited by Kenneth P. Minkema, 1997.

Vol. 15   *Notes on Scripture*, edited by Stephen J. Stein, 1998.

Vol. 16   *Letters and Personal Writings*, edited by George S. Claghorn, 1998.

Vol. 17   *Sermons and Discourses, 1730–1733*, edited by Mark Valeri, 1999.

Vol. 18   *The "Miscellanies": Entry nos. 501–832*, edited by Ava Chamberlain, 2000.

Vol. 19   *Sermons and Discourses, 1734–1738*, edited by M. X. Lesser, 2001.

Vol. 20   *The "Miscellanies": Entry nos. 833–1152*, edited by Amy Plantinga Pauw, 2002.

Vol. 21   *Writings on the Trinity, Grace, and Faith*, edited by Sang Hyun Lee, 2003.

Vol. 22   *Sermons and Discourses, 1739–1742*, edited by Harry S. Stout and Nathan O. Hatch, with Kyle P. Farley, 2003.

Vol. 23   *The "Miscellanies": Entry nos. 1153–1360*, edited by Douglas A. Sweeney, 2004.

Vol. 24   *The Blank Bible*, edited by Stephen J. Stein, 2006.

Vol. 25   *Sermons and Discourses, 1743–1758*, edited by Wilson H. Kimnach, 2006.

Vol. 26   *Catalogues of Books*, edited by Peter J. Thuesen, 2008.

CHAPTER I

BEAUTY

The Organizing Theme of Edwards's Theology of the Christian Life

To become a Christian is to become alive to beauty. This is the contribution to Christianity that Jonathan Edwards makes and no one has made better.

Augustine gave us a theology of will-transforming grace that liberates the Christian life by replacing our loves. Luther left us the utter settledness of God's favorable verdict over our morally fickle and despair-prone lives. Calvin gave us the majesty of God over every detail of the Christian's life. Owen brought us into the joy of loving communion with the triune God. Bunyan left us with hope and courage in battling through the ups and downs of the Christian journey. Bavinck's legacy is the restorative dimension to divine grace, grace opposed not to nature but only to sin. Spurgeon gave us in unparalleled language the gratuity of the gospel against a backdrop of an utterly sovereign Lord. Lewis expanded our imaginations in seeing the Christian life as a painfully joyous longing to be part of the larger story that makes sense of all things.

And Edwards has given us the beauty of the Christian life—first, the beauty of God, beauty that comes to tangible expression in Christ, and second, the beauty of the Christian, who participates in the triune life of divine love. Divine loveliness, enjoyed and reflected in his creatures:

this is Edwards's legacy.[1] Sinners are beautified as they behold the beauty
of God in Jesus Christ. That is Edwards's theology of the Christian life in
a single sentence. If Luther was a St. Paul, terse and punchy and emphasizing faith, Edwards was a St. John, calm and elegant and emphasizing
love.[2]

"What an honor must it be," preached Edwards, "to a creature who is
infinitely below God, and less than he, to be beautified and adorned with
this beauty, with that beauty which is the highest beauty of God himself,
even holiness."[3] This comes from a sermon entitled "God's Excellencies"
and therefore provides a good opportunity to clarify that, for Edwards,
God's "excellency" is another way of speaking of God's "beauty."[4] Edwards
makes this connection earlier in this very sermon when he speaks of "the
infinite excellency of Christ" as "delightful, beautiful, and pleasing."[5] We
today do not use the word *excellency*, but we do know what beauty is. So
this is the word we will use in an umbrella-like way to capture his vision
of Christian living.

Beauty in God

"The key to Jonathan Edwards' thought," writes George Marsden, "is that
everything is related because everything is related to God."[6] A book on the
Christian life in the thought of Jonathan Edwards must begin with God.
And the very first thing to be said about the Christian life is that for Edwards, beauty is what makes God *God*. "God is God, and distinguished
from all other beings, and exalted above 'em, chiefly by his divine beauty."[7]
Not sovereignty, not wrath, not grace, not omniscience, not eternity, but
beauty is what more than anything else defines God's very divinity. Edwards clearly believed in these other truths about God and saw all of them

---

[1] In stating this I am not arguing for divine beauty as a controlling theme or center to Edwards's theology
as a whole, though some have done so—e.g., Belden C. Lane, *Ravished by Beauty: The Surprising Legacy
of Reformed Spirituality* (New York: Oxford University Press, 2011), 170–210; see also the last paragraph
of Marsden's biography in George M. Marsden, *Jonathan Edwards: A Life* (New Haven, CT: Yale University
Press, 2003), 505; cf. also, on p. 266: "At the core of his vision of God was the beauty of God's irrepressible
love manifested in Christ." I am arguing simply for beauty as a controlling theme to Edwards's theology
of the Christian life, specifically. The two other thinkers in the church's history who come closest to
Edwards at this point are Augustine and Hans Urs von Balthasar.
[2] This is not to say Edwards was never hard on his people. But the hellfire Jonathan Edwards presented in
much American historiography is only a minor chord in the symphony of his vision of the Christian life.
[3] *WJE*, 10:430.
[4] Cf. John J. Bombaro, *Jonathan Edwards's Vision of Reality: The Relationship of God to the World, Redemption
History, and the Reprobate*, Princeton Theological Monograph Series (Eugene, OR: Pickwick, 2011), 58–74.
[5] *WJE*, 10:416.
[6] Marsden, *Jonathan Edwards*, 460.
[7] *WJE*, 2:298.

as upholding and displaying and connected to God's beauty. Yet none of them expresses who God is in the way that beauty does.

While we normally use the word *beauty* to speak of what is physically beautiful, Edwards uses beauty as a moral category.[8] Not only the eyes but also the soul has an aesthetic capacity. The beauty of God is not captured with a camera but enjoyed with the heart.

This is why, according to Edwards, to speak of God's holiness is virtually the same thing as to speak of his beauty.[9] Edwards refers in one 1730 sermon to God's "beauteous holiness."[10] Whenever he refers to God's beauty, a reference to his holiness is often not far behind. Beauty, to Edwards, is fundamentally a moral matter. One might still wonder, however—is not beauty an aesthetic matter, not a moral one? Yet here is the genius of Edwards's understanding of God and of the Christian life. The moral *is* the aesthetic. The holy *is* the beautiful. God does not happen to be beautiful and holy (for Edwards, you cannot have one without the other), but is beautiful in his holiness. This is not a collapsing of categories so as to eradicate all distinction between the moral and the aesthetic; rather it is to understand that supreme loveliness is found only in supreme holiness.

What then is holiness?

The "moral excellency of an intelligent being," says Edwards in *Religious Affections*, "when it is true and real, and not only external, or merely seeming and counterfeit, is holiness. Therefore holiness comprehends all the true moral excellency of intelligent beings: there is no other true virtue, but real holiness."[11] Two things are worth noting.

First, Edwards reverts back to the language of excellency, or beauty, in describing holiness. Thus he elsewhere speaks of "the holiness of God, which is his infinite beauty."[12] Holiness is "a flame infinitely pure and bright"[13]—once more Edwards reverts to the language of sight and heat. Second, he says that holiness "comprehends" all other virtues; "there is no other true virtue" outside holiness. Holiness is not one virtue standing alongside others—love, joy, peace, patience, and all the rest (Gal. 5:22–23). Each of these virtues is itself a particular manifestation of holiness. Edwards believes this is true of Christians (on which more below), but most fundamentally it is

---

[8] E.g., *WJE*, 2:264.
[9] E.g., *WJE*, 2:201, 257–60, 274; 13:330.
[10] *WJE*, 17:64.
[11] *WJE*, 2:255.
[12] *WJE*, 6:364.
[13] *WJE*, 4:336.

true of God. Holiness is the macro-category within which all virtue is sub-sumed. There is no virtue that is not also, at the same time, holy.

One reason for Edwards's close association of beauty and holiness is doubtless his own experience. Soon after coming to Northampton, he later recounted, "God has appeared to me, a glorious and lovely being, chiefly on the account of his holiness."[14] That God is holy is what made God beautiful to the young pastor.

Strikingly, Edwards speaks of divine beauty not only in terms of holi-ness but also in terms of happiness. I call this striking because our instinct even as believers is to set holiness and happiness over against one another. For Edwards, it is both or neither. The two rise and fall together. "Men are apt to drink in strange notions of holiness from our childhood," he said in a sermon preached at age nineteen, "as if it were a melancholy, morose, sour, unpleasant thing."[15] A dear friend recently e-mailed me and said in blessed honesty, "By far the greatest functional heresy I believe is that holiness is boring and lustful selfishness is fun."[16] If we were to let others peer into how our hearts are really functioning, that statement would ring true for just about all of us as we roll out of bed into another day. And it is a great triumph of the enemy that we would think so. For in truth there is nothing more thrilling, more solid, more exhilarating, more humanity-restoring, more radiantly joyous, than holiness.

In another sermon Edwards sets this as his central doctrine: "It is a thing truly happifying to the soul of men to see God."[17] Note that just as beauty has to do with sight, so Edwards here speaks of the happifying of souls that see God. This is key to Edwards's whole theology of Christian living: what do we *see?* Elsewhere in this sermon he refers to the "beatific, happifying sight of God."[18] God's beauty happifies us. It nestles us into joy. Seeing him—apprehending with the eyes of the heart his lovely holiness—we are changed. Edwards even argues in a sermon on James 1:17 that the reason no one can see God and live is not God's wrath or justice, but be-cause "God is arrayed with an infinite brightness" that "fills with excess of joy and delight," so that "the joy and pleasure in beholding would be too

[14] *WJE*, 16:799.
[15] *WJE*, 10:478.
[16] Quoted anonymously by permission.
[17] *WJE*, 17:61; cf. 2:184. Edwards uses this word "happifying" three times throughout this sermon ("The Pure in Heart Blessed"), and also elsewhere throughout his writings (e.g., *WJE*, 8:453, reproduced in a miscellany in *WJE*, 23:104).
[18] *WJE*, 17:63.

strong for a frail nature."[19] According to Edwards, it isn't God's terribleness that would incinerate us. It is the joy that would erupt within us that we cannot handle.

One further point should be made about divine beauty: God is the only place true beauty is found. There simply is nowhere else and no one else who has it. All true beauty in the universe is found either in God himself or in the direct reflection of God. "All the beauty to be found throughout the whole creation, is but the reflection of the diffused beams of that Being."[20] What a cold underground spring is to a mountain lake, God is to all real beauty in the universe. Edwards uses this very image: God is "the foundation and fountain of all being and all beauty; from whom all is perfectly derived, and on whom all is most absolutely and perfectly dependent."[21]

Beauty in Christ

Divine beauty must be given a sharper edge, however. God's beauty is specifically seen in Jesus Christ. The actual, tangible setting forth of the loveliness of God is manifested in the Son. Christ "is the brightness of God's glory." (Here as elsewhere Edwards uses *glory* and *beauty* as virtual synonyms.) That is: "He is more excellent than the angels of heaven. He is among them for amiable and divine beauty, as the sun is among the stars. In beholding his beauty, the angels do day and night entertain and feast their souls and in celebrating of it do they continually employ their praises."[22] Edwards goes on to argue that despite the ongoing enjoyment of the angels ("that blessed society") of Christ's loveliness, they can never exhaust it, nor their enjoyment of it.

Jonathan Edwards's vision of the beauty of God is not compatible with other world religions that likewise wish to speak of divine beauty but in a non-Christ-centered and non-Trinitarian way. Edwards is not here focusing on the truth that the incarnate Christ is the beauty of God in flesh and blood, though he certainly affirms that. Rather he is saying that even in his pre-incarnate state, the Son has always been the epitome of divine resplendence.[23]

---

[19] Edwards, "That God Is the Father of Lights," in *The Blessing of God: Previously Unpublished Sermons of Jonathan Edwards*, ed. M. McMullen (Nashville: Broadman & Holman, 2003), 346.
[20] *WJE*, 8:550.
[21] On divine beauty as the source of all of creation's beauty, see further James Byrd, *Jonathan Edwards for Armchair Theologians* (Louisville: Westminster John Knox, 2008), 138–39.
[22] Edwards, "The Dying Love of Christ," in McMullen, *Blessing of God*, 292. Similarly, *WJE*, 2:123, 302.
[23] We will explore at greater length Edwards's Trinitarianism later in this chapter.

In a 1752 sermon Edwards says that it is Christ, supremely in his mercy to sinners, who is the magnetic beauty to which we are drawn. It is a

> sight of the divine beauty of Christ, that bows the wills, and draws the hearts of men. A sight of the greatness of God in his attributes, may overwhelm men, and be more than they can endure; but the enmity and opposition of the heart, may remain in its full strength, and the will remain inflexible; whereas, one glimpse of the moral and spiritual glory of God, and supreme amiableness of Jesus Christ, shining into the heart, overcomes and abolishes this opposition, and inclines the soul to Christ, as it were, by an omnipotent power.[24]

Not only Christ but the gospel that is revealed in him is an object of exquisite beauty. "Herein primarily consists the glory of the gospel, that it is a holy gospel, and so bright an emanation of the holy beauty of God and Jesus Christ: herein consists the spiritual beauty of its doctrines, that they are holy doctrines." In his *Personal Narrative* Edwards again says that "the gospel has seemed to me to be the richest treasure. . . . The way of salvation by Christ, has appeared in a general way, glorious and excellent, and most pleasant and beautiful."[25] The gospel above all else is where God's beauty is beheld.[26]

The thinking Edwards gives to the role of sight in the believer's life is not limited solely to *spiritual* vision. In one miscellany that considers the glorified body of Christ, Edwards reflects on what believers' physical eyes will be like in their glorified existence in the new earth. He surmises that believers in the new heavens and the new earth will be able to see across the entire universe since Christ, not the sun, will be lighting the whole universe, and the light emitted by Christ's glorified body must be far faster than the speed of light in a solar system lit up by our sun.[27]

Beauty in Nature

Edwards's radical God-centeredness is seen in the way he speaks of the beauty of the created order. Yet we must understand that according to Edwards it is not, strictly speaking, nature itself that radiates beauty.

---

[24] *WJE*, 25:635; also, 22:289, 293.
[25] *WJE*, 16:799; also, 2:248.
[26] *WJE*, 25:542–43, 705.
[27] *WJE*, 20:169.

On the one hand, the loveliness of creation cannot be denied. Indeed, it is exquisite. "We admire at the beauty of creation, at the beautiful order of it, at the glory of the sun, moon, and stars."[28] As a boy Edwards enjoyed studying the world around him—from the way light worked, to the human eye, to the habits of spiders. Later in life he would often ride his horse out into the countryside, enjoying the world around him.

But the mature Edwards would say that in the deepest sense there is no beauty in nature itself. There is beauty only in God, and all beauty perceived in the creation is simply the reflection of God himself. Picking up the above quote about the "beauty of creation," Edwards goes on, as he always does, to raise our eyes from the loveliness of creation to the loveliness of God. We have "reason from the beauty of the sun to admire at the invisible glory of that God whose fingers have formed it."[29] Later in this sermon he says, "The beauty of trees, plants, and flowers, with which God has bespangled the face of the earth, is delightful; . . . the beauty of the highest heavens is transcendent; the excellency of angels and the saints in light is very glorious: but it is all deformity and darkness in comparison of the brighter glories and beauties of the Creator of all."[30] The loveliness of the created order exists for God's sake, not its own.

In one miscellany he makes the fascinating suggestion that just as when we see a radiant countenance on someone's face, we discern spiritual beauty within, so too when we see beauty in the created order, we discern spiritual beauty in Christ.

> When we see beautiful airs of look and gesture, we naturally think the mind that resides within is beautiful. We have all the same, and more, reason to conclude the spiritual beauty of Christ from the beauty of the world; for all the beauties of the universe do as immediately result from the efficiency of Christ, as a cast of an eye or a smile of the countenance depends on the efficiency of the human soul.

In other words, the created order is the radiant face of Christ. This creation-face tells us what Christ is really like.

---

[28] *WJE*, 10:420.
[29] Ibid.
[30] *WJE*, 10:421. Bombaro writes that "the very beauty of God not only immediately extends into the created order, but the created order itself only exists in, with, and as, a matrix of divine beauty" (Bombaro, *Edwards's Vision of Reality*, 63).

Beauty in Christians

Divine beauty is not only to be apprehended in God. It is to be reflected in us. It's why we exist.

The psalmist wrote that those who trust in idols become like them (Pss. 115:8; 135:18). The inverse of this is equally true, that those who trust in the true God become like him. "The light of the Sun of Righteousness don't [sic] only shine upon them," says Edwards of Christians, "but is so communicated to them that they shine also, and become little images of that Sun which shines upon them."[31] As George Herbert wrote a century before Edwards, in the poem "The Forerunners,"

> True beauty dwells on high: ours is a flame
> But borrow'd thence to light us thither.[32]

Divine beauty is, in its own finite way, to be reproduced. The supreme instance of divine beauty being reflected in creation is not in the sun or the Grand Canyon or a nightingale's song, but in a Christian. This is why Psalm 8 compares the glory of a human being to the glory of the galaxy (Ps. 8:3, 5). A Christian is a mini-advertisement for divine beauty. To be a Christian is to be a little, frail, finite, morally faltering picture of the beauty of God. When Edwards speaks of participating in and reflecting God's own excellency, holiness, happiness, or good, he is getting at the same reality from different angles. He is talking about God's beauty. Consider the following, from an undated sermon:

> God is with his people as they have fellowship and communion with God and as they are partakers with God in his good, possessing infinite good, and those are partakers with him in the same excellency and happiness. God communicates himself to his people. He imparts of his own beauty. They are said to be partakers of the divine nature (2 Pet 1:4). They are partakers of God's holiness (Heb 12:10).
> So God communicates to his people of his own happiness. They are partakers of that infinite fountain of joy and blessedness by which he himself is happy. God is infinitely happy in himself, and he gives his people to be happy in him. . . .

---

[31] Here and elsewhere Edwards often used the contraction *don't* where we today would say *doesn't*.

[32] George Herbert, "The Forerunners," in *George Herbert: The Country Parson, The Temple*, ed. John N. Wall Jr., Classics of Western Spirituality (Mahwah, NJ: Paulist Press, 1981), 303. I am grateful to Jerram Barrs for pointing me to this poem of Herbert's.

> That grace and holiness, that divine light and love, and that peace and joy that is in the hearts of the saints is a communication from God. Those are streams, or rather drops, from the infinite fountain of God's holiness and blessedness. 'Tis a ray from the fountain of light.[33]

Right at the heart of what Edwards contributes to historic Christianity is his insistence that Christian living is not mere mental assent, or association with a particular church, or scrupulous behavior monitoring, or anything else that is able to remain relatively external to the believer. Christian living is participation in God, in "the supreme loveliness of his nature."[34] And if what defines God supremely is his beauty or loveliness or excellency, then to participate in the triune life of God is to be swept up into, and to exude, that heavenly resplendence. A Christian is one who is being beautified. This is because Christian living is fundamentally participation in the unceasing explosion of delighted intratrinitarian joy and love.

Consider a Sunday morning. You and your wife (or husband, or roommate, or whoever) have been arguing all weekend. Your heart feels dead. As you grouchily slide into the pew, all you want is for no one to speak to you, and all you can think of is the relational strife in which you are embroiled, and perhaps what you plan to have for lunch. In due course the pastor stands up, someone you deem a very unimpressive man. Maybe you're right. He begins to speak of the heart of God for sinners from the opening verses of Ephesians 2, or maybe Titus 3, or Romans 5, or one of the psalms, or just about anywhere else in the Bible. Though you couldn't have manufactured it in a self-generated way, you feel your heart relaxing just a bit. The hardening melts. You begin to see your own contribution to the weekend strife. You mourn over your silliness. Soon you are in quiet repentance. Before long, without engineering it on your own, you find your heart—just a little bit, and with much distraction—drawn out to Christ. You're pulled toward him.

Here is how Jonathan Edwards would articulate your experience: *you have just been taken up into the Trinity.*[35]

Not metaphorically, but truly.[36] You have been swept up into the com-

---

[33] Jonathan Edwards, "It Is What May Well Make Us Willing and Desirous to God with God's People, That God Is with Them," in *The Glory and Honor of God: Volume 2 of the Previously Unpublished Sermons of Jonathan Edwards*, ed. Michael D. McMullen (Nashville: Broadman & Holman, 2004), 155.

[34] *WJE*, 2:242; cf. 22:356.

[35] See the editorial comments in *WJE*, 21:61.

[36] This is a subtheme of Jesus's extended discourse with his disciples in his upper room, concluding with Jesus's own prayer for all who would believe in him "that they may all be one, just as you, Father, are in me, and I in you, that they also may be in us" (John 17:21; cf. 14:20; 15:9; 17:6–8).

munal love and adoration that stretches back into time immemorial and the overflow of which caused the very universe to be brought into existence—so that you, on a bland Sunday morning, as a sinner, could participate in the joy of the triune God, Father delighting in Son, Son adoring Father, with the Holy Spirit being himself the very bond of love into which you are swept up. This is why the world exists. And though you will not take on new physical features when you leave church that morning, you will have been beautified, and the perceptive onlooker will note the difference in your countenance (Ps. 34:5)—a change which is a glimpse of the final state of paradise in the new heavens and the new earth.

For Edwards, this human reflection of divine beauty is particularly crucial for pastors, those given to lead and shepherd God's people. "We see in natural bodies," preached Edwards in 1744, "that when heat is raised in them to a high degree, at length they begin to shine. And a principle of true grace in the soul is like an inward heat, a holy ardor of a heavenly fire kindled in the soul." He then makes his intended application:

> This in ministers of the gospel ought to be to that degree, as to shine forth brightly in all their conversation; and there should as it were be a light about them wherever they go, exhibiting to all that behold them, the amiable, delightful image of the beauty and brightness of their glorious Master.[37]

A pastor, above all, is to provide for people a glimpse of the radiant loveliness of Christ. All their preaching, discipling, counseling, and administrating are channels through which divine luminosity is beheld. The fundamental calling of leaders of God's people is not only to be undershepherds of the chief Shepherd but also under-beautifiers of the chief Beautifier.

Beauty in Edwards's Literary Efforts

It is not only the content of Edwards's theology that is beautiful, but also the way in which he expresses himself that is beautiful.

When lifting up the delights of love, for example, in Christian living, he does so with writing that is itself lovely. How he communicates is fitting to what he is communicating. Consider this:

---

[37] *WJE*, 25:94.

He who has divine love in him has a wellspring of true happiness that he carries about in his own breast, a fountain of sweetness, a spring of the water of life. There is a pleasant calmness and serenity and brightness in the soul that accompanies the exercises of this holy affection.[38]

God in Christ allows such little, poor creatures as you are to come to him, to love communion with him, and to maintain a communication of love with him. You may go to God and tell him how you love him and open your heart and he will accept of it. . . . He is come down from heaven and has taken upon him the human nature in purpose, that he might be near to you and might be, as it were, your companion.[39]

Or this, from a letter to a woman whose only son had just died—a letter written in 1751, just after his own life had gone into meltdown with the ugly cutting short of his ministry in Northampton:

We see then, dear Madam, how rich and how adequate is the provision, which God has made for our consolation, in all our afflictions, in giving us a Redeemer of such glory and such love, especially, when it is considered, what were the ends of this great manifestation of beauty and love in his death.

He suffered that we might be delivered. His soul was exceeding sorrowful, even unto death, to take away the sting of sorrow, and to impart everlasting consolation. He was oppressed and afflicted, that we might be supported. He was overwhelmed in the darkness of death, that we might have the light of life. He was cast into the furnace of God's wrath, that we might drink of the rivers of his pleasures. His soul was overwhelmed with a flood of sorrow, that our hearts might be overwhelmed with a flood of eternal joy.

Death may deprive us of our friends here, but it cannot deprive us of our best Friend. . . . Therefore, in this we may be confident, though the earth be removed, in him we shall triumph with everlasting joy. Now, when storms and tempests arise, we may resort to him, who is a hiding-place from the storm, and a covert from the tempest. When we thirst, we may come to him, who is as rivers of water in a dry place. When we are weary, we may go to him, who is as a shadow of a great rock in a weary land.[40]

---

[38] Jonathan Edwards, "The Spirit of the True Saints Is a Spirit of Divine Love," in McMullen, *Glory and Honor of God*, 332.

[39] Ibid., 339. Other examples of beauty in Edwards's writing that I find particularly moving can be seen in *WJE*, 25:243–44; cf. 25:231.

[40] From a letter to a Mrs. Mary Pepperrell, in Michael Haykin, ed., *A Sweet Flame: Piety in the Letters of Jonathan Edwards* (Grand Rapids: Reformation Heritage, 2007), 129–30.

Beauty colors not only what Edwards says but how he says it. My point in reproducing these excerpts is to prevent anyone from getting to know Edwards mainly by reading published dissertations on him and concluding that the degree of elegance with which scholars expound Edwards's thought indicates the degree of elegance in Edwards's own writing. If all we know of Van Gogh is what we read in art history books without ever actually viewing a Van Gogh painting, we will have an impoverished appreciation of this great artist. We must go to the artistry itself.

Beauty in Edwards's Life

Finally, not only do his content and how he conveys it radiate beauty; so too does Edwards's own life. Surely it need not be said that Edwards was not perfect? I certainly would not want to convey a notion of a flawless man, and the final chapter of this book will reflect on some weaknesses in Edwards's legacy concerning the Christian life. But we are under biblical orders to consider the lives of those who have spoken the word of God to us and to imitate their faith (Heb. 13:7).

It is in that spirit that we would be wise to consider who Edwards himself was as a man. What would a conversation with him at Starbucks have been like? I contend that beauty colors not only his theology of the Christian life but also his own Christian life itself. When Edwards wrote of the sweetness of communing with the infinitely beautiful Savior, he was speaking not as a detached theoretician but out of the fullness of his own soul. This was the knowledge, to use his own image, not of one who knows what honey consists of chemically but of one who has tasted.[41] Edwards was himself a beautiful man, for he himself had had the blinds of his sinfulness pulled aside to behold the flooding sunbeams of divine beauty. "Edwards' religion was from its root," writes one modern theologian, "a sheer beholding of God's beauty."[42] Time with him would itself have been beautifying.

By all this I don't mean we would have shared many laughs and chit-chat over that cup of coffee. He was a rather somber character, from what we can gather. But is joy really measured by such things anyway? In chapter 4 we'll discuss the solemnity of true joy. Some of our most miserable

---

[41] *WJE*, 2:206–9, 260, 272.
[42] Robert W. Jenson, *America's Theologian: A Recommendation of Jonathan Edwards* (New York: Oxford University Press, 1988), 15.

moments are laugh-filled and some of our most joyful are tear-filled. Edwards would not be entertaining to sit down with. But we would leave with just a bit more solidity and calm beauty.

Perhaps the most persuasive evidence of the beauty of Edwards's life is the way others spoke of him. One thinks, for example, of how he is described by his own family. When he died in March 1758, his wife, Sarah, wrote to their daughter Lucy:

> My very dear Child,
>
> What shall I say? A holy and good God has covered us with a very dark cloud. O that we may kiss the rod, and lay our hands on our mouths! The Lord has done it. He has made me adore his goodness, that we had him so long. But my God lives; and he has my heart. O what a legacy my husband, and your father, has left us! We are all given to God; and there I am, and love to be.
>
> Your ever affectionate mother,
Sarah Edwards[43]

Even more revealing are the ways his children spoke of him. On April 3, 1758, another daughter, Susannah, wrote to her older sister Esther and reflected on her father's final sermon three months earlier there in Stockbridge before he left to take up the presidency at Princeton (then College of New Jersey). Her admiration comes through clearly.

> My father took leave of all his people and family as affectionately as if he knew he should not come again. On the Sabbath afternoon he preached from these words, "We have no continuing city, therefore let us seek one to come." The chapter that he read was Acts the 20th. O, how proper. What could he have done more?[44]

A troubled Esther wrote down in her journal more touching words yet about her father after a trip to Stockbridge to visit him.

> Last eve I had some free discourse with My Father on the great things that concern my best Interest—I opened my difficulties to him very freely and he as freely advised and directed. The conversation has removed some

---

[43] *Works of Jonathan Edwards Online*, vol. 32, *Correspondence by, to, and about Edwards and His Family* (Jonathan Edwards Center at Yale University).
[44] Haykin, *A Sweet Flame*, 161.

distressing doubts that discouraged me much in my Christian warfare—
He gave me some excellent directions to be observed in secret that tend to
keep my soul near to God, as well as others to be observed in a more public
way—What a mercy that I have such a Father! Such a Guide![45]

We also see the beauty of Edwards's own life in the events that show
what is inside a man more effectively than anything else: pain. In the series
of church meetings in 1750 at which he was rejected by his church by a
vote of 230 to 23, one eyewitness, a pastor named David Hall, remarked: "I
never saw the least symptoms of displeasure in his countenance the whole
week, but he appeared like a man of God, whose happiness was out of the
reach of his enemies, and whose treasure was not only a future but a present good, overbalancing all imaginable ills of life." Hall says this calmness
on Edwards's part was "to the astonishment of" those who opposed him.[46]
Such hostility to Edwards, as to so many faithful saints through the ages,
was not sporadic but settled and at times strident. One thinks of Bernard
Bartlett, member of Northampton Church, who in 1735 recorded that his
pastor "was as Great an Instrument as the Devil Had on this Side of Hell to
bring Souls to Hell."[47]

No saint of history is worthy of exhaustive imitation save One. But few
saints of history are worthy of greater imitation than Jonathan Edwards.
Perhaps not his study habits, perhaps not his personal temperament, and
certainly not his level of personal social engagement. But the vibrant animating center to his heart and life—the beauty of Christ, seen, enjoyed,
reflected, and contagiously transferred to those around him.

Conclusion

By nature, we are sinners in the hands of an angry God. But by grace, we
are saints in the hands of a beautiful God. This is the pulsating core of
Edwards's vision of the Christian life. "Edwards was not obsessed by the
wrath of God but by his beauty,"[48] writes John Bombaro.

A Christian is a human being beautified—decisively in the past, pro-
gressively in the present, perfectly in the future. In the rest of this book we

---

[45] Esther Edwards Burr, *The Journal of Esther Edwards Burr, 1754–57*, ed. Carol F. Karlsen and Laurie Crum-
packer (New Haven, CT: Yale University Press, 1984), 224.
[46] Quoted in Marsden, *Jonathan Edwards*, 361.
[47] Quoted in Kenneth Minkema, "Personal Writings," in *The Cambridge Companion to Jonathan Edwards*,
ed. Stephen J. Stein (Cambridge: Cambridge University Press, 2006), 39.
[48] Bombaro, *Edwards's Vision of Reality*, 14.

will consider Edwards's distinctive emphases in his theology of the Christian life. Throughout, we will never be far from his vision of divine beauty. The remaining chapters of this book do not add to but explore different manifestations of Edwards's vision of divine beauty.

The resplendent beauty of God is the sunshine in which every aspect of Christian living blossoms: love, joy, prayer, obedience, and all the rest are given brightness and life.

CHAPTER 2

NEW BIRTH

The Ignition of the Christian Life

Jonathan Edwards believed that the Christian life is of God. Having set his love on every one of his elect children before the foundation of the world,[1] God then makes this election an experienced reality in the person's life. Salvation is doubly of grace: grace planned in the past, grace activated in the present.

And the way this grace in the present is triggered is new birth, or regeneration.[2] This ignites the Christian life. "The conversion of one that is brought to believe savingly on the Lord Jesus," says Edwards in a 1739 sermon, "is like the dawning of the day, the first shining of the light of the Sun in a soul that before was filled with the greatest darkness."[3]

Becoming a Christian is not essentially the making of a decision or the praying of a prayer or the dedication of one's life or the believing of a doctrine. It is not less than such things. But in essence the beginning of the Christian life is a sovereignly granted explosion of new life, a change so radical, carrying with it such a break with the past, that it is nothing less than a second birth. In the new birth we are, for the first time, alive to beauty. This is unsettling to us, even frightening, because it rests solely in the hands of God. Yet it is refreshingly liberating too, because it affirms

---

[1] *WJE*, 8:295; 17:279–80.
[2] "God's love to his elect is the first foundation of their love to him, as it is the foundation of their regeneration" (*WJE*, 2:249).
[3] *WJE*, 22:55.

what our hearts know: true and lasting transformation cannot come from any humanly wrought strategies or efforts. We can't change ourselves. Edwards wrote to the Scottish pastor John Erskine in 1757, "There can properly be no such thing, or anything akin to what the Scripture speaks of conversion, renovation of the heart, regeneration, etc. if growing good, by a number of self-determined acts, are all that is required."[4]

This is a word in season for us. The church today needs to recover the doctrine of the new birth. It is the nonnegotiable, irreplaceable, and yet underemphasized ignition of the Christian life. It is also a central teaching of the New Testament, taught clearly by Jesus, Paul, and Peter (John 1:12–13; 3:1–15; Titus 3:5; 1 Pet. 1:3, 23).[5]

In this chapter we will consider six characteristics of new birth, make a brief critique of Edwards's theology of regeneration, and then conclude by reflecting on the need to recover this doctrine in the twenty-first-century church.

Edwards on New Birth: Six Characteristics

Edwards viewed regeneration as necessarily paired with conversion, conversion being the active side of salvation, and regeneration the passive side.[6] The clearest and most concise definition he gives is right at the start of a sermon titled, simply, "Born Again." By new birth, Edwards says, "is meant that great change that is wrought in man by the mighty power of God, at his conversion from sin to God: his being changed from a wicked to a holy man."[7] In *Religious Affections* Edwards puts it even more succinctly: regeneration "is that work of God in which grace is infused."[8] Six truths about new birth surface throughout Edwards's writings as he repeatedly returns to this doctrine during the course of his preaching and writing ministry.

New Birth Is Necessary

It is "absolutely necessary for everyone," says Edwards, "that he be regenerated, or born again."[9] Regeneration is not one way sinners are saved. It is *the* way. There is no Plan B to fall back on. Whatever one thinks of Jesus's

---

[4] *WJE*, 16:723.

[5] Edwards had little trouble finding types of regeneration in the Old Testament, too, such as in circumcision (*WJE*, 18:166–67; 25:412), or when Naaman is told to wash in the Jordan River (*WJE*, 2:360).

[6] *WJE*, 3:362.

[7] *WJE*, 17:186.

[8] *WJE*, 2:398.

[9] *WJE*, 3:361.

teaching or example, however much one gives to the church, however great one sacrifices—without new birth, all is useless. With it, nothing else is needed. All people, without exception, are born into sin, belonging to Adam. All people, without exception, must be born again by grace if they are to belong to Christ.

> What is born in the first birth of man, is nothing but man as he is of himself, without anything divine in him; depraved, debased, sinful, ruined man, utterly unfit to enter into the kingdom of God, and incapable of the spiritual divine happiness of that kingdom: but that which is born in the new birth, of the Spirit of God, is a spiritual principle, and holy and divine nature, meet for the divine and heavenly kingdom.[10]

All roads to the new earth pass through the gate of new birth.[11] For this reason religious people stand in need of new birth no less than irreligious people. The only difference is that religious people may presume they have it—in which case they are worse off, not better off, than irreligious people. "It is a truth of the utmost certainty," Edwards says, "with respect to every man, born of the race of Adam, by ordinary generation, that unless he be born again, he cannot see the kingdom of God. This is true, not only of the heathen, but of them that are born of the professing people of God, as Nicodemus, and the Jews."[12] The great distinction between sinners is not between those who need new birth and those who do not, for all need it; the great distinction is between those who *know* they need it and those who do not. Jesus told a religious man, "You must be born again" (John 3:7). The religious men and women in our lives and neighborhoods today cannot be told anything less.

New Birth Changes Us

A newborn baby is the same child as the one that has just spent nine months in the womb. Yet the child has gone through a fundamental change—now breathing, crying, nursing, seeing, and so on. The infant is in touch with the real world in a way that was only dimly possible while in the womb.[13] These differences help us understand why the biblical writers speak of sal-

---

[10] *WJE*, 3:279–80.
[11] See *WJE*, 17:184, 191.
[12] *WJE*, 3:370; similarly, 25:501.
[13] Edwards compares the new birth to natural birth at several points: e.g., *WJE*, 2:366; 8:332; 13:357; 25:501.

vation as a new birth. For in our new, supernatural birth, as in our first, natural birth, we are ushered by the will of another into an utterly new mode of existence which, while sharing certain marks of one's previous life, is fundamentally different.

The seventh sign of authentic Christianity in *Religious Affections* is that those in whom the Spirit has truly been working have a change in their very nature. Incorporating new birth into his comments, Edwards explains:

> The Scripture representations of conversion do strongly imply and signify a change of nature: such as being born again; becoming new creatures; rising from the dead; being renewed in the spirit of the mind; dying to sin, and living to righteousness; putting off the old man, and putting on the new man; a being ingrafted into a new stock; a having a divine seed implanted in the heart; a being made partakers of the divine nature, etc.[14]

He concludes that "if there be no great and remarkable, abiding change in persons, that think they have experienced a work of conversion, vain are all their imaginations and pretenses."[15]

In asking why this is so—why those who are born again are necessarily different, or else they are not born again—we come to one of Edwards's central contributions to Christian theology: the new "sense of the heart" granted to the regenerate. Edwards taught that regeneration implants within the believer a new inclination toward holiness. Wakened spiritual taste buds now find God and godliness strangely attractive.[16] He writes, "the work of the Spirit of God in regeneration is often in Scripture compared to the giving of a new sense, giving eyes to see, and ears to hear."[17]

We must be careful not to water down the radical change Edwards writes about here. New birth does not simply change us by giving us a new

---

[14] *WJE*, 2:340; see also 2:206. Cf. Bavinck: "In the Scriptures of the Old and New Testaments, while there is a difference between them in language and manner of presentation, there is essentially complete agreement. Whether rebirth is called 'the circumcision of the heart,' the giving of a new heart and a new spirit, 'efficacious calling,' a drawing by the Father, or birth from God, it is always in the strict sense a work of God by which a person is inwardly changed and renewed. It has its deepest cause in God's mercy; it is based on the resurrection of Christ and is brought about in communion with Christ, to whom the Word bears witness, and manifests itself in a holy life" (Herman Bavinck, *Reformed Dogmatics*, ed. John Bolt, trans. John Vriend, 4 vols. (Grand Rapids: Baker, 2003–2008), 4:52.

[15] As Sinclair Ferguson concisely puts it in reflecting on John Owen's theology of the Christian life, "Sanctification is the flower from the seed of regeneration" (Sinclair Ferguson, *John Owen on the Christian Life* [Edinburgh: Banner of Truth, 1987], 89).

[16] I have explored this theme of Edwards's at length in Dane Ortlund, *A New Inner Relish: Christian Motivation in the Thought of Jonathan Edwards* (Fearn, UK: Christian Focus, 2008). See also Michael J. McClymond, "Apprehension: Spiritual Perception in Jonathan Edwards," in *Encounters with God: An Approach to the Theology of Jonathan Edwards* (New York: Oxford University Press, 1998), 9–26.

[17] *WJE*, 2:206.

power to do the same things we always wanted to do. It changes us by getting down underneath even the very level of our desires and changing *what we want*. This is one of the key pillars of his carefully crafted argument in *The Freedom of the Will*. Sovereign, regenerating grace does not enable us to do what we don't want to do. More deeply, it brings us to want to do what we should want to do. Regenerating grace is grace that softens us way down deep at the core of who we are. This is taste-bud transformation. In a miracle that can never be humanly manufactured, we find ourselves, strangely, delighting to love God. We are changed. The will itself is renovated. We see things as they really are. True beauty is now seen to be beautiful.

Indeed, this theme of beauty captures well the change that takes place in regeneration. In essence, regeneration is the decisive, initial beautification of the believer. Edwards believes this is the meaning, for example, of 2 Peter 1:4, which speaks of our becoming "partakers of the divine nature." Does this mean believers become deified, as emphasized by the Eastern tradition of the church? No, says Edwards—we are not deified; we are *beautified*. "Not that the saints are made partakers of the essence of God, and so are 'Godded' with God, and 'Christed' with Christ, according to the abominable and blasphemous language and notions of some heretics." Rather, "they are made partakers of God's fullness, *that is, of God's spiritual beauty and happiness*, according to the measure and capacity of a creature."[18]

New Birth Is Completely a Work of God

As is already becoming clear, we can make ourselves come alive to the beauty of Christ no more than a rotting corpse can make itself come alive to the beauty of the meadow in which it is buried.

The editors of volume 22 in the Yale edition of Edwards's works are wrong when they define the new birth in Edwards's theology as "a dramatic spiritual moment when the individual, despairing of personal ability to effect forgiveness of sins and salvation, completely surrendered his or her soul to Christ."[19] Edwards would say that everything described here is

---

[18] *WJE*, 2:203, emphasis added. Note also Edwards's answer to an objection in a letter that in speaking of believers participating in the divine nature, he was going too far: "Light and heat may in a special manner be said to be the proper nature of the sun; and yet none will say that everything to which the sun communicates a little of its light and heat has therefore communicated to it the essence of the sun, and is sunned with the sun, or becomes the same being with the sun, or becomes equal to that immense fountain of light and heat. A diamond or crystal that is held forth in the sun's beams may properly be said to have some of the sun's brightness communicated to it; for though it hasn't the same individual brightness with that which is inherent in the sun, and be immensely less in degree, yet it is something of the same nature" (*WJE*, 8:640).

[19] *WJE*, 22:224.

necessary but is a result of new birth, not new birth itself. The editors here describe conversion, not regeneration. New birth is not self-surrender *essentially*, but divinely imported life. "The new birth is not the product of the will of man but of the will of God," Edwards says. God regenerates "with a potent irresistible energy. If any are converted and saved it is not of man that wills originally but of God that wills and works according to his will."[20] Theologians call this a *unilateral* (as opposed to bilateral) or *monergistic* (as opposed to synergistic) work of God. Both terms communicate that salvation is not a cooperative agreement. New birth is the sovereign softening of a hard heart that cannot soften itself.

This does not mean sinners should passively wait for God to regenerate them, for God uses means in saving sinners. Human seeking does not replace, but is the manifestation of, God's transforming grace. "'Tis God's manner to give his Spirit in a way of earnest striving."[21] And yet looking back upon such striving, even this, the Christian knows, is wholly due to God's grace.

This feels destabilizing at first, but it is in fact our only true stability. For new birth is something we are wholly given. It works on us from the inside, but comes to us from the outside. It changes us internally but is provided externally. The sheer grace of new birth is therefore mysterious. Solely intellectual categories fail us; we cannot understand it exhaustively. Edwards wrestles with this in a handwritten note jotted down in his *Blank Bible* next to John 3:8: "This question, How is a man born again? may be asked out of a vain curiosity, and with a conceit of men's own wisdom and ability to trace the footsteps of the Spirit of God in this work."[22] On the other hand, a conviction of sovereignly wrought regeneration is sanity restoring. For the utter gratuity of new birth wonderfully drains our law-marinated hearts of our inveterate quest to save ourselves. We are hardwired to resist the utter gratuity of divine grace and to introduce some modest contribution into our salvation. The doctrine of new birth as taught by Edwards confounds this moralizing tendency.

In September 2008 *The New York Times* ran a story entitled "For a Fee, a Thai Temple Offers a Head Start on Rebirth."[23] Reporter Seth Mydans ex-

[20] *Works of Jonathan Edwards Online*, vol. 28, *Minor Controversial Writings* (Jonathan Edwards Center at Yale University).
[21] *WJE*, 13:33.
[22] *WJE*, 24:928.
[23] Seth Mydans, "For a Fee, a Thai Temple Offers a Head Start on Rebirth," *New York Times*, accessed January 26, 2013, www.nytimes.com/2008/09/27/world/asia/27thailand.html?partner=rssuserland&emc=rss&

plained that a Buddhist temple in Thailand was providing, "for a small fee, an opportunity to die, rise up again newborn and make a fresh start on life." Fallen human beings know intuitively that we need new birth. This notion is not restricted to Christianity but transcends cultural context. We tacitly know that we are broken and need fixing, healing so profound that it grants us a completely new start. But it cannot be bought. It cannot be manipulated through anything we bring to the table. The only way in is through the supernatural gift of new birth of which Jesus tells Nicodemus in John 3.

God saves us. God alone. Christians are those "who were born, not of blood nor of the will of the flesh nor of the will of man, but of God" (John 1:13). This is liberating security. For just as a child can never go back into his mother's womb (as Nicodemus astutely observed in John 3:4), a sinner who has been given new birth can never revert back into a state of being unregenerate. We are now alive. We have been wakened. God has swept us irreversibly into life. He will never hit rewind on our regeneration. It was God and God alone who gave us new life, and it is God and God alone who will sustain us in that new life. Those who have been given new birth "are a soil in which this heavenly seed has been sown and in which it abides."[24]

New Birth Does Not Perfect Us

The fact that new birth secures and changes us does not mean that no trace of the old man remains in the regenerate. New birth grants a new direction, not a new perfection. Edwards was not naïve; he knew that "the godly, after they have grace in their hearts, many times do gradually sink down into very ill frames through their unwatchfulness: they insensibly get into carnal frames."[25] In another place he again acknowledges that while, on the one hand, "a man is brought, when converted, wholly to renounce all his sins," yet, on the other hand, "that don't argue that he is wholly freed from all remains of sin."[26] In *Charity and Its Fruits* Edwards remarks that "when the Scripture speaks of holiness of life in Christians, this is not the meaning of it, that it should be a perfect life." Rather, the truly Christian life "is of that kind which has a *tendency* to practice."[27] Edwards goes on to explain

pagewanted=all&_r=0. Edwards too speaks of the new birth being sold for money, not by Buddhists but by the Roman Catholic Church (*WJE*, 15:314).

[24] *WJE*, 8:388.

[25] *WJE*, 22:189.

[26] *WJE*, 22:257. See also George Marsden, who connects this Edwardsian realism to Edwards's own moral struggles, in *Jonathan Edwards: A Life* (New Haven, CT: Yale University Press, 2003), 137.

[27] *WJE*, 8:309–10, emphasis added.

that it is not the *absence* of sin that is the key mark of regeneration but the *hatred* of it.[28] Sin dwells, but no longer reigns, in believers.[29]

In *The Voyage of the Dawn Treader* C. S. Lewis captures an Edwardsian view of regeneration in his depiction of the change wrought in the previously obnoxious Eustace: "It would be nice, and fairly nearly true, to say that 'from that time forth Eustace was a different boy.' To be strictly accurate, he began to be a different boy. He had relapses. There were still many days when he could be very tiresome. But most of those I shall not notice. The cure had begun."[30]

In the new birth the cure has begun. Like Eustace, the dragons that we all naturally are by birth have been decisively peeled off in the new birth. Old tendencies remain, but the fundamental change has secured us once and for all as new creatures.

New Birth Is the Source of Real Joy

Regeneration fundamentally changes us by granting not only an inclination toward holiness but also a fresh and true capacity for happiness. Indeed, for Edwards, holiness and happiness rise and fall together. In a world that tells us we must choose between the two, Edwards insists that holiness is the source, not a substitute, for happiness. Holiness fans, not douses, the flames of real joy.

A Christian's new birth brings a "change made in the views of his mind, and relish of his heart," Edwards says in *Religious Affections*, so that the regenerate person "seeks his interest and happiness in God."[31] In concluding the final sermon in *Charity and Its Fruits*, Edwards speaks of

> all ye who are out of Christ, who were never born again, and never had
> any blessed renovation of your hearts implanting a spirit of divine love
> there, leading you to choose that happiness which consists in holy love

---

[28] I have dealt with this tension at greater length in *New Inner Relish*, 122–35.

[29] Calvin makes strikingly similar observations about the moral struggle of the regenerate: "The children of God are freed through regeneration from bondage to sin. Yet they do not obtain full possession of freedom so as to feel no more annoyance from their flesh, but there still remains in them a continuing occasion for struggle whereby they may be exercised; and not only be exercised, but also better learn their own weakness. . . . There remains in a regenerate man a smoldering cinder of evil, from which desires continually leap forth to allure and spur him to commit sin." In regeneration, Calvin goes on to say, "the sway of sin is abolished in them. For the Spirit dispenses a power whereby they may gain the upper hand and become victors in the struggle. But sin ceases only to reign; it does not also cease to dwell in them" (John Calvin, *Institutes of the Christian Religion*, ed. John T. McNeill, trans. Ford Lewis Battles, 2 vols. [Louisville: Westminster John Knox, 1960], 3.3.10–11).

[30] C. S. Lewis, *The Voyage of the Dawn Treader* (1952; repr., New York: HarperCollins, 1994), 119–20.

[31] *WJE*, 2:241.

as your best and sweetest good, and to spend your life in struggling after happiness.[32]

Here new birth and joy are clearly connected as root to fruit. Those who have been born again are not those who have successfully cleaned up their lives. They are those who finally see and enjoy true beauty.

The Doctrines of Justification and New Birth Do Not Compete with but Complement One Another

Few have thought so penetratingly about the doctrine of justification as Edwards, as ongoing articles and dissertations attest.[33] He himself said that it was his extended sermon series on justification by faith that God used to spark the 1734–1735 revival in Northampton. Yet even more pervasive in his writing and preaching ministry was the "divine and supernatural light" decisively wrought in the new birth. Edwards viewed justification, the decisive verdict *over* us, and regeneration, the decisive change *in* us, as mutually reinforcing. In *Original Sin* he pairs together justification and regeneration as forming in part "the very ground of the Christian life."[34] William Cooper's preface to *Distinguishing Marks of a Work of the Spirit of God* rightly centralizes regeneration and justification as Cooper speaks of Edwards and other faithful preachers of the day:

> The doctrines they insist on, are the doctrines of the Reformation. . . . The points on which their preaching mainly turns, are those important ones of man's guilt, corruption, and impotence; supernatural regeneration by the Spirit of God, and free justification by faith in the righteousness of Christ; and the marks of the new birth.[35]

This dual upholding of both the work of God *for* us by the Son and the work of God *in* us by the Spirit is a word in season to the church today.

---

[32] *WJE*, 8:392.

[33] E.g., Samuel T. Logan, "The Doctrine of Justification in the Theology of Jonathan Edwards," *Westminster Theological Journal* 46 (1984): 26–52; George Hunsinger, "Dispositional Soteriology: Jonathan Edwards on Justification by Faith Alone," *Westminster Theological Journal* 66 (2004): 107–20; Jeffrey C. Waddington, "Jonathan Edwards's 'Ambiguous and Somewhat Precarious' Doctrine of Justification?," *Westminster Theological Journal* 66 (2004): 357–72; Gerald R. McDermott, "Jonathan Edwards on Justification: Closer to Luther or Aquinas?," *Reformation & Revival Journal* 14, no. 1 (2005): 119–38; Josh Moody, ed., *Jonathan Edwards and Justification* (Wheaton, IL: Crossway, 2012); Hyun-Jin Cho, *Jonathan Edwards on Justification: Reform Development of the Doctrine in Eighteenth-Century New England* (Lanham, MD: University Press of America, 2012).

[34] *WJE*, 3:185.

[35] *WJE*, 4:218. Note Paul Ramsey's comparison between Calvin's framework of a *duplex gratia*, a double grace, through which we receive both regeneration (by which Calvin at times meant repentance, not a new inclination, as Edwards often did) and justification (*WJE*, 8:745–50).

Discussions continue to proliferate, especially online, that wrestle with how we put the two together: the objective and the subjective, the externally granted and the internally worked, grace as pardon and grace as power, the legal and the mystical, God declaring us righteous and God making us righteous. The two must be held together. Emphasizing regeneration to the neglect of justification makes us introspective, worried, and lacking in assurance. Emphasizing justification to the neglect of regeneration makes us cold, apathetic, and pessimistic about truly growing.

A Passing Critique

Even a modest familiarity with Edwards's doctrine of new birth makes clear that he views new birth as introducing a radical discontinuity between what one was and what one now is.[36] As he puts it in "A Divine and Supernatural Light"—a sermon that may capture Edwards's theology of the Christian life as well as any—the true Christian is so rebuilt that "he is become quite another man than he was before."[37] In regeneration "he is a new creature, he is just as if he was not the same, but were born again, created over a second time."[38] Or as he puts it in *Religious Affections*, "The gracious influences which the saints are subjects of . . . are entirely above nature, altogether of a different kind from anything that men find within themselves by nature."[39]

Conrad Cherry is therefore correct to remark that Edwards's view of conversion "is grounded in the conviction that an immense chasm exists between nature and grace."[40] We will return to a handful of criticisms of

---

[36] The question of whether Edwards's theology of the "new sense of the heart" is essentially continuous or discontinuous with one's pre-regenerate state has been heavily debated among Edwards scholars since Perry Miller's "Jonathan Edwards on the Sense of the Heart," *The Harvard Theological Review* 41 (1948): 123–45. I do side with those, such as Paul Helm and David Lyttle, who see Edwards as emphasizing discontinuity; see McClymond, *Encounters with God*, 9–10. Yet I cannot enter the debate at length here. More importantly, among interpreters of Edwards who share his supernaturalistic convictions and basic theology of original sin and regeneration, there is general consensus that something more is going on in conversion and the new sense that accompanies it than simply a non-transcendental "perception" or "apprehension," as Miller put it.

[37] *WJE*, 14:81.

[38] Ibid.

[39] *WJE*, 2:205.

[40] Conrad Cherry, *The Theology of Jonathan Edwards: A Reappraisal*, rev. ed. (Bloomington, IN: Indiana University Press, 1990), 58; see also 30, 32, 37–38, 56–70. For more secondary literature exploring Edwards's insight into and emphasis on the new birth and the discontinuity it introduces into the convert's life, see Clyde A. Holbrook, *The Ethics of Jonathan Edwards: Morality and Aesthetics* (Ann Arbor, MI: University of Michigan Press, 1973), esp. 23; Robert W. Jenson, *Jonathan Edwards: America's Theologian* (Oxford: Oxford University Press, 1988), 66–73; Marsden, *Jonathan Edwards*, 157–58, 286; Stephen J. Nichols, *An Absolute Sort of Certainty: The Holy Spirit and the Apologetics of Jonathan Edwards* (Phillipsburg, NJ: P&R,

Edwards in the final chapter, but given all we have just said in this chapter, a brief word is appropriate here. The critique I wish to make is that in centralizing regeneration, Edwards rightly drives home the radical discontinuity between pre- and post-regenerate moral life, yet he fails to complement this truth with the equally biblical emphasis on salvation as *restorative*.

One almost gets the impression that in regeneration a human sinner becomes another species altogether. This is perhaps unfair, since one can find, if enough of Edwards is read, tempering statements that retain some semblance of continuity between pre- and post-regeneration life.[41] Yet the weight of what Edwards hammers home time and again is one-sided. He neglects the truth that the unregenerate are made in God's image and therefore have, as Calvin taught, a *sensus divinitatis* (a tacit knowledge of God), which regeneration restores and fills out. In new birth we become human again; we become what we were intended to be. Salvation not only introduces something utterly foreign as God grants new spiritual inclinations, but also restores our true self. Doug Wilson captures this by saying, "When we are born again, a dramatic miracle happens. When we are born again, *we are turned into people.*"[42]

A theologian in the Reformed tradition who brings precisely the emphasis Edwards lacked is the Dutch thinker Herman Bavinck. No fewer than three major monographs on Bavinck argue that "grace restoring nature" is the center of Bavinck's thought.[43] That is, the grace of God in the gospel saves a fallen race and a fallen cosmos not by starting over but by restoring them to their true design and purpose. While Cherry speaks of the "immense chasm between nature and grace" in Edwards's theology, Bavinck brings these two closely together. Here is a representative statement by Bavinck, from his discussion of calling/regeneration in his *Reformed Dogmatics*:

2003), esp. 47–75; William J. Danaher, *The Trinitarian Ethics of Jonathan Edwards* (Louisville: Westminster John Knox, 2004), 124–28.

[41] E.g., *WJE*, 2:206.

[42] Douglas Wilson, "Regular Wine That Got Here Remarkably," *Blog and Mablog: Furious Scribblings from Douglas Wilson*, September 13, 2010, www.dougwils.com/Life-in-the-Regeneration/regular-wine-that -got-here-remarkably.html. Emphasis original.

[43] Ronald N. Gleason, "The Centrality of the *unio mystica* in the Theology of Herman Bavinck" (PhD diss., Westminster Theological Seminary, 2001). The three works to which Gleason refers are E. P. Heideman, *The Relation of Revelation and Reason in E. Brunner and H. Bavinck* (Assen: Van Gorcum & Comp., 1959); Jan Veenhof, *Revelatie en inspiratie: De openbarings-en schriftbeschouwing van Herman Bavinck in vergelijking met die der ethische theologie* (Amsterdam: Buijten & Schipperheijn, 1968); John Bolt, "The Imitation of Christ Theme in the Cultural-Ethical Ideal of Herman Bavinck" (PhD diss., Toronto School of Theology, 1982).

The purpose of regeneration is to make us spiritual people, those who live and walk by the Spirit. This life is a life of intimate communion with God in Christ. Though believers are made new creatures in Christ, this does not mean that their created nature is qualitatively transformed. Believers remain fully human, fully created image-bearers of God as in the beginning. As in creation itself, no new substance enters into the world with redemption; the creature is liberated from sin's futility and bondage. Sin is not of the essence of creation but its deformity; Christ is not a second Creator but creation's Redeemer. Salvation is the restoration of creation and the reformation of life.[44]

Similar statements could be proliferated. "Grace serves, not to take up humans into a supernatural order, but to free them from sin. Grace is opposed not to nature, only to sin. . . . Grace restores nature and takes it to its highest pinnacle, but it does not add to it any new and heterogeneous constituents."[45] This theme in Bavinck is the heart of Jan Veenhof's little book *Nature and Grace in Herman Bavinck*.[46] For Bavinck, regenerating grace is restoring grace. We return to our true home; we become human again. We experience what Jewel the unicorn does at the end of all things in Narnia: "I have come home at last! This is my real country! I belong here. This is the land I have been looking for all my life, though I never knew it till now."[47]

It would be artificial to pit Edwards and Bavinck against one another in categorical, black-and-white terms. Surely part of the reason for their distinct emphases is their different historical contexts. And we do find in Edwards the occasional statement of grace as restorative, as we also find in Bavinck a rich sense of the newness of regeneration. Yet Bavinck provides a needed balance to Edwards's theology of regeneration. Bavinck's focus on continuity complements Edwards's focus on discontinuity. Edwards's own contribution ought not to be diluted by overreacting to what he says. And yet a healthy injection of Bavinck's macro-theme of "grace restoring nature" would go a long way toward bringing fullness to Edwards's theology of new birth.[48]

---

[44] Bavinck, *Reformed Dogmatics*, 4:32–33.
[45] Ibid., 3:577; see also 2:545, 573–76; 4:92–94.
[46] Jan Veenhof, *Nature and Grace in Herman Bavinck*, trans. Albert M. Wolters (Sioux Center, IA: Dordt College Press, 2006), 17. This book is an excerpt from Veenhof's doctoral research on Bavinck.
[47] C. S. Lewis, *The Last Battle* (1956; repr., New York: HarperCollins, 2005), 213.
[48] I explore this difference between Edwards and Bavinck, and wrestle with how to integrate the two, at greater length in Dane C. Ortlund, "'Created Over a Second Time' or 'Grace Restoring Nature'? Edwards and Bavinck on the Heart of Salvation," *The Bavinck Review* 3 (2012): 9–29.

Regeneration: Present Neglect

All this is a mild critique and ought not to cool our appreciation and reception of what Edwards clarifies for us. We need Edwards today on regeneration. Salvation is not, in essence, what many seem to think. It is not *essentially* a gradual process of moral improvement, or rational assent, or ecclesial association, or doctrinal rightness—important as all these are. Salvation is new birth.

In *The Forgotten Spurgeon*, Iain Murray observes:

> The brief doctrinal articles of modern evangelicalism—as distinct from the Reformed confessions of the 16th and 17th centuries—have nothing to say on these issues [of the order of regeneration and faith, and other Calvinistic tenets], presumably because it is no longer thought to be necessary. The prevalent attitude has been to frown on distinct and definite propositions of truth and to contend for obscurity and indefiniteness as though the latter were more spiritual and biblical, and more preservative of unity.[49]

Edwards was clear on new birth. So must we be. Indeed, it is striking to consider Edwards's pervasive emphasis on regeneration in light of current doctrinal emphases in the church.

John Wesley and George Whitefield both said that the transatlantic revival of the 1740s was fueled by the recovery of two great doctrines: justification by faith and the new birth. This is a striking observation in light of the present evangelical scene. In recent years books and blog posts, conferences and colloquiums have sprung up like mushrooms (some nourishing, some poisonous) to deal with the doctrine of justification. We hear far less, however, about regeneration, as J. I. Packer indicated in a 2008 interview.[50] The flood of teaching on regeneration in the past has slowed to a trickle.[51]

The solution to the present neglect of the new birth is not abject hand-wringing that a golden age of the past has slipped through our fingers. Even

---

[49] Iain H. Murray, *The Forgotten Spurgeon* (London: Banner of Truth, 1966), 63.

[50] J. I. Packer, interview by Mark Driscoll, *Resurgence*, http://theresurgence.com/2008/07/30/j-i-packer -on-young-christian-leaders.

[51] Past treatments of regeneration include not only Whitefield's and Wesley's sermons on the subject but also whole books (or similar extended treatments) given to the subject by Richard Sibbes, Richard Baxter, John Owen, Francis Turretin, Stephen Charnock, John Howe, Peter Van Mastricht (whom Edwards said had a profound influence on him), Joseph Alleine, Henry Scougal, Archibald Alexander, George Duffield, William Anderson, J. C. Ryle, and A. W. Pink. In a more recent generation we heard of the new birth from Billy Graham, John Stott, and J. I. Packer. Robust treatments shine forth also in the great confessions of the past, such as the Canons of Dordt, the Scots Confession of 1560, the Belgic Confession, and the Second Helvetic Confession.

if we could, we would not *want* to reestablish the past. God has a fresh purpose of grace for the church in our generation. But we do want to learn from those who have gone before us. And as we become familiar with the saints of the past who saw revival up close and whose ministries had a hand, under God, in fostering it, one doctrine crops up time and again— new birth. We must allow ourselves to be instructed here. A sage guide is Jonathan Edwards. Who else knew God and Scripture so well, planted himself in the ministry of a local church, saw authentic revival up close, wisely received and promoted what was real while exposing and rejecting what wasn't—and, through it all, returned time and again to the doctrine of regeneration?

Collin Hansen and John Woodbridge's recent book recounts past outpourings of grace and looks in hope toward the future.[52] One way we can prepare for such flood-like blessing in our own day is a renewed lifting up of the doctrine of the new birth. There is no formula to conjure up revival,[53] but there is still much that we can do to prepare for the outpouring of the Spirit.[54]

This will require renewed doctrinal clarity. We live in a day rife with sermonic exhortations to "get born again!" by walking down an aisle, raising a hand, or praying a prayer. George Barna and others have further muddied the water by designating as "born again" any who align themselves with basic Christian belief, however nominally. It would therefore be easy to allow deficient teaching on the new birth to sour us to the doctrine itself. But the answer to a deficiently explained doctrine is not to ignore the doctrine altogether, any more than the answer to a deficiently advertised cure for cancer is to ignore the cure altogether.

One also thinks of those today who, in the name of gospel liberty, are careless in how they live. Yet Edwards speaks of those who "flatter themselves with the gospel and make use of the glorious and joyful tidings it brings of God's infinite mercy and readiness to pardon as a pillow on which they may indulge their sloth and quiet their consciences in ways of sin."[55] Such a life is no true Christian life, because it forsakes the reality of new birth.

---

[52] Collin Hansen and John Woodbridge, *A God-Sized Vision: Revival Stories That Stretch and Stir* (Grand Rapids: Zondervan, 2010).

[53] See Iain H. Murray, *Revival and Revivalism: The Making and Marring of American Evangelicalism 1750– 1858* (Edinburgh: Banner of Truth, 1994).

[54] See Raymond C. Ortlund Jr., *When God Comes to Church: A Biblical Model for Revival Today* (Grand Rapids: Baker, 2000), 145–92.

[55] *WJE*, 22:58.

Let us therefore receive what Jonathan Edwards has to teach us about the new birth. Let us do so discerningly, incorporating truths that Edwards may have underemphasized given his own context. But he has much to say to help us learn afresh of the fundamental and all-important reality of regeneration.

Edwards was buried near Princeton Theological Seminary, which today houses a center devoted to the study of Edwards. While the school is a different place today than it was in its early years, its first professor, Archibald Alexander (1772–1851), taught regeneration as his theological forefather Jonathan Edwards did. He provides a fitting, and Edwardsian, word of conclusion:

> There is no more important event, which occurs in our world, than the new birth of an immortal soul. Heirs to titles and estates, to kingdoms and empires, are frequently born, and such events are blazoned with imposing pomp, and celebrated by poets and orators; but what are all these honors and possessions but the gewgaws of children, when compared with the inheritance and glory to which every child of God is born an heir!
>
> The implantation of spiritual life in a soul dead in sin, is an event, the consequences of which will never end. When you plant an acorn, and it grows, you expect not to see the maturity, much less the end of the majestic oak, which will expand its boughs and strike deeply into the earth its roots. The fierce blast of centuries of winters may beat upon it and agitate it; but it resists them all. Yet finally this majestic oak, and all its towering branches, must fall. Trees die with old age, as well as men. But the plants of grace shall ever live. They shall flourish in everlasting verdure.[56]

---

[56] Archibald Alexander, *Thoughts on Religious Experience* (Philadelphia: Presbyterian Board of Publication, 1844), 35–36.

CHAPTER 3

LOVE

The Essence of the Christian Life

Augustine has been called "the theologian of love,"[1] and rightly so. But Jonathan Edwards could equally lay claim to that title. One scholar called Edwards the "theologian of the Great Commandment."[2] If there is one mark of the Christian life to which Edwards returns more than any other, it is love.

Love, Edwards says, is "the life and soul of all religion."[3] It is definitive, not merely descriptive, of authentic Christianity. What is the essence of the Christian life? Tunneling down, drilling in, to the very heart and pulsating core of what it means to be a follower of Christ, what do we find? Edwards answers: love.

In this chapter we consider Edwards's vision of love. We begin by reflecting on what he believed is the fountain of all true love—God's own love among the persons of the Trinity. We then turn to our love, love that expresses itself both vertically (for God) and horizontally (for others). Because the focus of this book is Edwards's view of the Christian life, we will spend the bulk of this chapter reflecting on love as exercised by the

---

[1] E.g., Heiko Oberman, *The Reformation: Roots and Ramifications*, trans. Andrew Colin Gow (London: T&T Clark, 2004), 82; Thomas Jay Oord, *The Nature of Love: A Theology* (St. Louis: Chalice, 2010), 56.
[2] Joseph G. Haroutunian, "Jonathan Edwards: Theologian of the Great Commandment," *Theology Today* 1 (1944): 361–77. See also Conrad Cherry's remarks on Edwards's greater emphasis on love than Calvin and Luther (Conrad Cherry, *The Theology of Jonathan Edwards: A Reappraisal* [Bloomington, IN: Indiana University Press, 1990], 77). George Marsden writes that the sermons of *Charity and Its Fruits*, "simple and practical as they were, stood close to the heart of Edwards' theological enterprise" (George M. Marsden, *Jonathan Edwards: A Life* [New Haven, CT: Yale University Press, 2004], 191).
[3] *WJE*, 8:131.

believer, identifying seven elements of special importance to Edwards as he describes Christian love.

Divine Love in the Godhead: Love in Heaven

For Jonathan Edwards, the fountain for all Christian loving is the love of God himself. This love has existed within the Godhead from all eternity, ultimately spilling out in the divine act of creation, an act that filled no need on God's part but was simply the natural overflow of God's own joyous intratrinitarian refulgence.

The mutual rejoicing that takes place within the Godhead is expressed most clearly by Edwards in his famous essay on the Trinity. He opens by asserting that the tri-unity of God is not unbelievable but rather a sensible and even necessary conclusion if we are to take seriously the fact that God loves. Reflecting on the two places in 1 John where we are told that "God is love" (1 John 4:8, 16), Edwards argues that this assertion "shows that there are more persons than one in the Deity: for it shows love to be essential and necessary to the Deity, so that his nature consists in it."[4] Love is who God *is*. For God to love is for God to be God. "The very nature of God is love. If it should be enquired what God is, it might be answered that he is an infinite and incomprehensible fountain of love."[5]

In his famous *Discourse on the Trinity*, Edwards describes the Trinity precisely in terms of intratrinitarian love. Christ, the second person of the Trinity, is "God's idea of himself"[6]—the form, image, representation of the Father. Between these two, Father and Son, "there proceeds a most pure act, and an infinitely holy and sweet energy arises between the Father and Son: for their love and joy is mutual, in mutually loving and delighting in each other."[7] Edwards then makes the striking claim that this holy energy of love between Father and Son *is* the Holy Spirit. Drawing on 1 John 4, he suggests that if God dwelling in believers produces love in them (1 John 4:12), and God dwells in believers by his Spirit (1 John 4:13), then this divine love in them must, quite simply, be the Holy Spirit. The Spirit "is God's infinite love to

---

[4] *WJE*, 21:113–14; similarly, in a miscellany written when he was twenty years old, see *WJE*, 13:262, and the comments on this miscellany of Amy Plantinga Pauw, *The Supreme Harmony of All: The Trinitarian Theology of Jonathan Edwards* (Grand Rapids: Eerdmans, 2002), 4–5.

[5] Jonathan Edwards, "The Spirit of the True Saints Is a Spirit of Divine Love," in *The Glory and Honor of God: Volume 2 of the Previously Unpublished Sermons of Jonathan Edwards*, ed. Michael D. McMullen (Nashville: Broadman & Holman, 2004), 305.

[6] *WJE*, 21:120.

[7] *WJE*, 21:121.

himself and happiness in himself."[8] Edwards returns to this point repeatedly throughout this essay, speaking of the Trinity in terms of love in an effort to correct a perceived neglect of the Spirit in Trinitarian thought.[9] For Edwards, "the very essence of God" is "divine love." And this divine love is "the Holy Spirit, the spirit of divine love, in whom the very essence of God, as it were, all flows out or is breathed forth in love."[10] This close identification of love with the Holy Spirit is the reason this book does not have a separate chapter on the Holy Spirit. A treatment of divine love is a treatment of the Spirit.

To say that "God is love," then, for Edwards, is not a doctrinally anemic reduction of the full character of God, who, the Bible teaches, is not only "a God merciful and gracious, slow to anger" but also one "who will by no means clear the guilty" (Ex. 34:6–7). Wrath and justice belong to the character of this full, biblical God no less than love. After all, the Bible tells us not only that "God is love" but also that "God is light" (1 John 1:5)—holy light; that is, light as opposed to (moral) darkness. Yet God's love is more astonishing and wonderful, not less, when set against the full backdrop of the panorama of God's diverse attributes.

When Edwards teaches what it means to say that "God is love," then, he has in mind a doctrinally robust and non-reductionistic view of divine love. He has in mind the holy energy of mutual delight exercised within the Godhead himself: the Father and the Son rejoicing in and spotlighting one another, with a delight the energy of which is the Holy Spirit. This is the love of God.

And this love, for Edwards, impelled the creation of the world. The very nature of God's intratrinitarian love means it must spill forth in outward expression. It resists being contained. In this sense God's love is the most unstoppable force in the universe. For love by its very nature seeks the good of the other, rejoices in the other. Static love is self-contradictory. "The creation of the world," says Edwards, "is to gratify divine love."[11]

Divine Love in His People: Love on Earth

As we transition from love in God to love in believers, the one who loves changes but the nature of love itself does not. For the love that dwells in the

---

[8] *WJE*, 21:138.
[9] "If we suppose no more than used to be supposed about the Holy Ghost, the concern of the Holy Ghost in the work of redemption is not equal with the Father's and the Son's, nor is there an equal part of the glory of this work [that] belongs to him" (*WJE*, 21:137).
[10] *WJE*, 8:370.
[11] *WJE*, 21:142.

heart of believers is, according to Edwards, divine love. Christian love is the implantation of the very love of God. The creature is, as Lewis put it, caught up in the great dance.[12] The new birth incorporates a human creature into the mutually flowing, and overflowing, intratrinitarian love of God. When Edwards speaks of "divine love," therefore, he is often referring not to God's love as exercised by God but to God's love as inhabiting and exercised by believers.

Before moving to divine love in Edwards's theology of the Christian life, we should make two further clarifications.

First, Edwards speaks of love in terms of benevolence and also in terms of complacence. These were commonly used categories of eighteenth-century discussions of morality, though we don't use the terms today. By love of *benevolence* he means delighting in the welfare of another. By love of *complacence* he means simply delighting in another.[13] Benevolence wishes for good to be enjoyed *by* the beloved; complacence wishes to enjoy good *in* the beloved.[14] And it is complacence, says Edwards, that is the more fundamental element in divine love and which he is describing in *Charity and Its Fruits*. Complacence will therefore be our focus as we discuss Edwards's vision of love in the Christian life.

Second, Edwards is uncomfortable with any strong disjunction between Christian love for God and Christian love for others. The two can be distinguished but not separated. We see this in Edwards's identification of divine love with the Holy Spirit. When God saves a human being and pours his Holy Spirit into that person, God is, to say the same thing a different way, pouring his love into that person. Edwards notes in a miscellany that this is exactly what one would expect from a close reading of the New Testament, which speaks not only of God "pouring out" his Holy Spirit into believers (Acts 2:17–18; Titus 3:6) but also of God "pouring out" his love into believers (Rom. 5:5).[15] "Christian love to both God and men," says Edwards, "is wrought in the heart by the same work of the Spirit. There are not two works of the Spirit of God, one to infuse a spirit of love to God and another a spirit of love to men." Instead, "in doing one he doth the other."[16] The Holy Spirit establishes within God's children a new outward-oriented impulse

---

[12] C. S. Lewis, *Mere Christianity* (1952; repr., San Francisco: Harper, 2001), 175; cf. Lewis, *Perelandra* (1944; repr., New York: Simon & Schuster, 1996), 183–87.
[13] *WJE*, 8:212–13.
[14] See the editorial remarks in *WJE*, 8:73–74; cf. 8:143.
[15] Miscellany no. 336, in *WJE*, 13:412.
[16] *WJE*, 8:133.

that, while finding expression both vertically and horizontally, is a single impulse nonetheless. True love to God will always be accompanied by love to people; true love to people will always be accompanied by love to God. "The Spirit of God in the work of conversion renews the heart by giving it a divine temper. . . . And it is the same divine temper which is wrought in the heart that flows out in love both to God and men."[17]

We move, then, to considering seven core axioms that draw out Edwards's magnificent vision of love in the Christian life.

Love Sums Up the Entire Christian Life

In the first of these seven characteristics of love, we arrive at the heart of this chapter and, perhaps, the heart of this book on Jonathan Edwards's teaching on the Christian life. The Christian life, if nothing else, is a life of love. Believers delight in the well-being and joy of others. It is who they are.

Love, says Edwards, is "the greatest and most essential thing, and indeed the sum of all that is essential, distinguishing and saving in Christianity, and . . . the very life and soul of all religion."[18] To be a Christian is to love. Love is neither optional nor peripheral. It is not required of only certain personality types. A Christian is one who has been welcomed into the great dance of mutual delight within the triune Godhead, having had the very love of this Godhead implanted in his own soul.

The supremacy of love in Christian living is especially clear in Edwards's opening sermon of *Charity and Its Fruits*. The whole fifteen-sermon series is based on 1 Corinthians 13, and this first sermon has in mind the first three verses in particular, which read:

> If I speak in the tongues of men and of angels, but have not love, I am a noisy gong or a clanging cymbal. And if I have prophetic powers, and understand all mysteries and all knowledge, and if I have all faith, so as to remove mountains, but have not love, I am nothing. If I give away all I have, and if I deliver up my body to be burned, but have not love, I gain nothing. (1 Cor. 13:1–3)

Edwards observes that the Christian realities with which love is compared here—angelic tongues, prophetic powers, vast knowledge, mountain-

---

[17] Ibid.

[18] *WJE*, 8:185; see also 4:298–99; 25:91, 527. On love as the sum of the Christian life in Edwards's theology, see Michael J. McClymond and Gerald R. McDermott, *The Theology of Jonathan Edwards* (New York: Oxford University Press, 2012), 537–41.

moving faith—could not be higher or more lofty. Yet they are all rendered utterly worthless without love. "Let a man have what he will, and let him do what he will, it signifies nothing without charity."[19] For love "is the life and soul of all religion, without which other things . . . are empty and vain."[20]

While Paul can at times speak of love as one virtue among others (Gal. 5:22–23), Edwards would say that even when love appears in a list alongside other virtues, these others are all subsumed within, or are diverse manifestations of, love. Love is "a comprehension of all virtues."[21] This is why "divine love is the sum of all holiness."[22]

For a Christian, moreover, love is not a bonus to sound doctrine—a nice extra or add-on for some believers. No, love is the very point of sound doctrine. Sound doctrine without love is itself deeply self-contradictory— "a cold and hard-hearted Christian is the greatest absurdity and contradiction. It is as if one should speak of dark brightness, or a false truth!"[23] Accumulation of doctrinal knowledge nets out as loss, not gain, if such theological growth fails to foster benevolent, heartfelt goodwill toward others.

> Doubtless there are many nowadays greatly to be reproved for this, that although they have been so long in the school of Christ, and under the teachings of the gospel, they yet remain, in a great measure, ignorant what kind of spirit a truly Christian spirit is, what spirit is proper for the followers of Christ and for the gospel dispensation under which we live.[24]

Accumulated doctrinal knowledge does not offset the need for love. On the contrary, the greater one's doctrinal sophistication, the greater the obligation to leverage such knowledge into love.

In centralizing love, Edwards stands in good company. He is simply echoing the teaching of Paul, who declared to a mightily gifted church that "the greatest of these is love" (1 Cor. 13:13); of John, who pronounced that "anyone who does not love does not know God" (1 John 4:8); of James, who equated love with fulfilling the whole law (James 2:8); of Peter, who ex-

---

[19] WJE, 8:131. It should be clarified that when Edwards speaks of "charity," he has in mind not acts of monetary generosity to the needy but, more broadly, "love"—as Edwards himself explains in the opening pages to this first sermon of Charity and Its Fruits (WJE, 8:129–30).
[20] WJE, 8:131.
[21] WJE, 8:136.
[22] WJE, 8:360.
[23] WJE, 8:147.
[24] WJE, 8:143.

horted his readers that they "above all, keep loving one another earnestly" (1 Pet. 4:8); and of Jesus himself, who proclaimed that the greatest commandment of all is that of love (Mark 12:28–31).

Christian Love Lies beneath Every Other Virtue

Divinely implanted love is not only the sum of all Christian living but also the "root and spring" of all Christian living.[25] Not only does love fulfill all that a Christian is called to do. It is also true that any given virtue is, when considered carefully, a specific manifestation of love. Love is "that from which all good dispositions and behavior do arise, the stock on which all good fruit grows, and the fountain in which all that is good is contained and from whence it flows."[26]

This becomes clear in reading through the middle sermons of *Charity and Its Fruits*, which expound Paul's multifaceted description of love in 1 Corinthians 13 (remember that by "charity" Edwards simply refers to love). As Edwards begins in the fourth sermon to preach on the characteristics of love identified in verses 4–7, he speaks of these characteristics of love as "fruits" of charity.[27]

Long-suffering, therefore, which Paul mentions in 1 Corinthians 13:4, is simply a very specific manifestation of love. Edwards shows this in two ways—vertically and horizontally. Vertically, love to God breeds long-suffering through the gratitude evoked by considering God's long-suffering shown *us*.[28] Love to God also cultivates long-suffering by putting believers out of reach from the ill will of others. "None can hurt those who are true lovers of God," says Edwards. "The more men love God, the more they will place all their happiness in God; they will look on God as their all, and this happiness and portion is what men cannot touch."[29] Supreme love to God gives Christians a kind of quiet invincibility, for no earthly pain can threaten their greatest love, which is God himself. Love, then, is itself the source of long-suffering. Put differently, long-suffering is what love does when under duress. Long-suffering is love afflicted. In this and subsequent sermons in *Charity and Its Fruits* Edwards goes on to make similar arguments about love lying beneath all the various virtues listed in 1 Corinthi-

---

[25] *WJE*, 8:136.
[26] *WJE*, 8:351; see also 2:106.
[27] *WJE*, 8:185.
[28] *WJE*, 8:194.
[29] *WJE*, 8:195.

ans 13:4–7. Love lies beneath kindness (sermon 4), not envying (sermon 5), not boasting (sermon 6), not being selfish (sermon 7), not being easily provoked (sermon 8), not being judgmental (sermon 9), rejoicing in the truth (sermon 10), and suffering for Christ (sermon 11).

The way all these are simply manifestations of love is further reinforced in sermon 12, in which Edwards proposes that all these virtues are, to use his word, "concatenated"—that is, "the graces of Christianity are all linked together or united one to another and within one another, as the links of a chain."[30] And the fundamental link in this chain is love. After all, all the graces of Christianity are the fruit of the Holy Spirit, yet Edwards, we have seen, equates the Holy Spirit with the love that is planted in believers. As a result, "however many names we may give the different ways and manners of the exercise of grace; yet if we strictly examine them, they are all related to one."[31] That one, he says, is love.

Every particular evidence of grace emanating from a true believer, according to Edwards, is the fruit of love.[32]

Love Is More "Excellent" than the Extraordinary Gifts

This is the point of the second sermon in *Charity and Its Fruits*. As the thesis statement of that sermon puts it, "The ordinary influence of God's Spirit, working saving grace in the heart, is a more excellent blessing than any of the extraordinary gifts of the Spirit."[33] By "excellent" Edwards means having spiritual harmony and beauty.

The question of Edwards's cessationism need not come into play here, for Edwards's point is rooted in what was true of the first century, when the supernatural gifts were, by any account, in action. By "extraordinary gifts" we have in mind here, as Edwards did, tongues, prophecy, knowledge, and faith.[34]

Edwards was aware of how believers tend to exaggerate the spiritual significance of the more flashy signs of the Spirit while underplaying the spiritual significance of the quieter, less fantastic signs of the Spirit. Yet such prioritizing is backward. The (ordinary) fruit of the Spirit takes spiri-

---

[30] *WJE*, 8:327.
[31] *WJE*, 8:333.
[32] See also Stephen A. Wilson, *Virtue Reformed: Rereading Jonathan Edwards's Ethics*, Brill's Studies in Intellectual History 132 (Leiden: Brill, 2005), 117.
[33] *WJE*, 8:152.
[34] By the latter two, Edwards has in mind supernatural or special gifts of knowledge and faith, not the universal growth in knowledge and everyday exercise of faith that are to be displayed in all believers.

tual precedence over the (extraordinary) gifts. And the fruit of the Spirit is summed up, at its core, in love.[35]

In all this Edwards does not want to let the pendulum swing too far in the other direction, trading in an unhealthy obsessing with the extraordinary for an unhealthy sidelining of the extraordinary. He spends a good portion of his sermon defending the great privilege of the extraordinary gifts of the Spirit as described in the New Testament.[36]

> When God endows anyone with a spirit of prophecy and favors him with immediate inspiration, or when he gives any a power of working miracles, healing the sick, casting out devils, and the like, these are great privileges which God bestows on men; they are the highest kind of privileges which he bestows on men next to saving grace.[37]

Edwards avoids being reactionary, then. In his eagerness to lift up the pre-eminence of love he does not treat the extraordinary gifts with unhealthy disdain or suspicion. Yet, as great a privilege as the extraordinary gifts are, "the ordinary influences of the Spirit of God working grace in the heart is a far greater privilege."[38]

What is so striking about this sermon, in particular, is the *penetration* Edwards applies to the relationship between the ordinary and extraordinary gifts. Consider how he reasons in this extended quote, noting especially how he connects the ordinary gifts with the very "nature" of a man:

> This blessing of the saving grace of God is a quality inherent in the nature of him who is the subject of it. This gift of the Spirit of God, working a saving Christian temper and exciting gracious exercises, confers a blessing which has its seat in the heart; a blessing which makes a man's heart and nature excellent. Yea, the very excellency of the nature consists in it. Now it is not so with respect to those extraordinary gifts of the Spirit. They are excellent things, but not properly the excellency of a man's nature; for they are not things which are inherent in the nature. . . . Extraordinary gifts are nothing properly inherent in the man. . . . Extraordinary gifts of the Spirit are, as it were, precious jewels, which a man carries about him. But true grace in the heart is, as it were, the preciousness of the heart,

---

[35] *WJE*, 8:169.
[36] *WJE*, 8:154–57.
[37] *WJE*, 8:154.
[38] *WJE*, 8:157.

by which it becomes precious or excellent; by which the very soul itself becomes a precious jewel.[39]

The ordinary exercise of grace in the heart, in other words, supremely manifested in love, expresses who the believer *is*. Love is native to the believer. The extraordinary gifts are, so to speak, foreign to the believer. They are temporary expressions that do not emanate from the believer's very heart in the same way that love does. Edwards drives his point home with the poignant observation that the extraordinary gifts are not reserved for those closest to God, but have been manifested in the downright godless— Balaam, King Saul, Judas, and the followers of Christ who prophesied and cast out demons yet are rejected on the final day (Matt. 7:22–23).[40]

Extraordinary grace is great grace. Ordinary grace, expressed supremely in Christian love, is the greatest grace.

Christian Love Cannot Sit Still

The main point of the tenth sermon in *Charity and Its Fruits* is that "all true Christian grace tends to [i.e., leads to] holy practice." By "holy practice" Edwards means concrete godliness in daily living. Just as God's love had to spill out in creation, Christian love has to spill out in concrete action.

The need for godliness to work itself out in light of what God has done in the new birth is a recurrent theme throughout Edwards's writings. In *Religious Affections*, for example, the twelfth and final sign of authentic godliness that Edwards lists is this very thing. True godly affections *act*.[41] Edwards gives this sign more space (about 80 pages) than any of the other eleven signs. We will return to the importance of "practice," fruit-bearing obedience in Christian living, in chapter 7.

Here, specifically, we note the way Edwards roots Christian practice in love. Reflecting on Paul's words in 1 Corinthians 13:6 that love does not rejoice at wrongdoing but rejoices in the truth, Edwards interprets "wrongdoing" (or "iniquity" as his KJV put it) as "everything which is sinful in life and practice," and "truth" as "everything which is good in life."[42] In short, then, Paul is teaching here that love rejoices in what is morally right and

---

[39] *WJE*, 8:157–58.
[40] *WJE*, 8:159–61.
[41] *WJE*, 2:383–461.
[42] *WJE*, 8:293.

acts accordingly. Love thus spurs us toward "walking in holy practice, or well-doing."[43]

Such well-doing, says Edwards, is not merely *descriptive* but *definitive* of love. Love *loves*. Love that sits still is not real love. "A principle of love is a principle whence flow acts of love."[44] One cannot choose between divine love residing in the heart and a life of love toward others. It is both or neither. To lack one is to prove that one lacks the other. Though Edwards does not draw attention to this fact, every descriptor of love in 1 Corinthians 13:4–7 is in verbal form. Thus "love is patient" is the Greek noun *love* with the Greek verb for "be patient." "Love is kind" is the noun for love with the verb for "act kindly." It is difficult to express such verbs in English, and our best option makes it look as if Paul is using adjectives. But such is not the case, reinforcing Edwards's penetrating point about the necessary movement of true divine love in the heart of the Christian.

True Christian love, then, cannot sit still. This is not to say, however, that a life of love is robotic or effortless. "Labor to live a life of love," he exhorts.[45] Nor is it to say that by "practice" Edwards has in mind only external, visible actions. That would be a reductionistic misunderstanding of Edwards at this point. By "practice" he has in mind not only observable acts of goodwill but also actions such as "desires after God," "delighting in God and taking contentment in him."[46] This too is love-induced Christian "practice," even if such practice is invisible to the eyes of others. Indeed, Edwards knew well from observing revival up close that such invisibility was a safeguard against the incorrigible human proclivity to parade virtue, however subtly, for others to see.

And yet, on the flipside, Edwards's theology of love was not ethereal and abstract. Time and again, for example, he preached on the Christian's bound duty to assist the poor in tangible ways.[47] Edwards's preaching ministry, taken as a whole, resists the disjunction one often sees today between caring for the soul and caring for the body.

Powerfully defending his assertion that love necessarily exercises itself, Edwards draws attention to the universally verifiable truth that we always act on what we truly love. Indeed, we cannot help but act out our true

---

[43] *WJE*, 8:294. Cf. John E. Smith, *Jonathan Edwards: Puritan, Preacher, Philosopher* (Notre Dame, IN: University of Notre Dame Press, 1992), 110–11.
[44] *WJE*, 8:298.
[45] Edwards, "Spirit of the True Saints," 333.
[46] *WJE*, 8:303.
[47] E.g., *WJE*, 2:430; 8:174–75; 17:369–404.

loves. The professing Christian who says he loves Christ above all as he consistently bends the truth in an effort to cultivate a certain reputation does not love Christ's name above all, but loves his own name. "A man's actions are the most proper trial and evidence of his love."[48] Our actions show who, and what, we really love. Speaking of our idols as "creature objects," Edwards observes: "Love to creature objects, we see, does powerfully influence men in their actions and practice. Yea, what is it which chiefly keeps the world of mankind in action from day to day, and from year to year, but love of some kind or other."[49] He then gives examples of what he means:

> He who loves money is influenced by his love of that enjoyment in his practice, and kept in continual pursuit of it. And he who loves honor is governed in his practice by that. His actions through the course of his life are regulated by such a principle. And so lovers of carnal pleasures; how they pursue after them in their practice! And so also he who truly loves God is influenced by that in his practice; he earnestly seeks God in the course of his life, seeks his favor and acceptance, and seeks his glory.[50]

True love to God is restless. Like the kicking legs of an infant, the vitality that resides in love insists on expressing itself.[51]

Real Christian Love Is Always Linked with Truth

Here we connect love with another pervasive theme in Edwards—the union of light and heat, mind and heart, thinking and feeling. "The peculiarity of Edwards' theological work," wrote B. B. Warfield, "is due to the union in it of the richest religious sentiment with the highest intellectual powers."[52] Here I wish only to point out, however, the way Edwards applies this wedding of thought and affection to Christian love.

Divine love in the soul of a Christian, for Edwards, can be exercised with spiritual health no further than such love is built on the solid foundation of truth. Truth kindles love. "When the truth of the glorious doctrines

---

[48] WJE, 8:302.
[49] Ibid.
[50] WJE, 8:302–3.
[51] Note Gerald R. McDermott's comments along these lines in his delineation of love as a public virtue in One Holy and Happy Society: The Public Theology of Jonathan Edwards (University Park, PA: The Pennsylvania State University Press, 1992), 108–9.
[52] B. B. Warfield, "Edwards and the New England Theology," in Biblical and Theological Studies, ed. Samuel G. Craig (Philadelphia: Presbyterian & Reformed, 1952), 527–28.

and promises of the gospel is seen, those doctrines and those promises are like so many bands, which take hold of the heart to draw it in love to God and Christ."[53] Edwards says that love is "the life and soul of a practical faith. A truly practical and saving faith is light and heat together, or light and love. That which is only speculative, is only light without heat."[54] Such a life is no different from the devils, Edwards goes on to say. Truth without love describes Satan himself. He is the best theologian in the universe. As Edwards puts it in a 1752 sermon, "The devil is orthodox in his faith; he believes the true scheme of doctrine; he is no Deist, Socinian, Arian, Pelagian, or antinomian; the articles of his faith are all sound."[55] The Devil's orthodoxy is not linked with *love*.

Truth is not only the kindling for love but also its test. Truth not only precedes love, fueling it, but also follows love, circumscribing it. When we think we are acting in love, we can test such experience with doctrinal truth as found in the Bible. If professing believers

> seem to have an affectionate love towards God and Christ, they should inquire whether this be accompanied with a real conviction of the soul of the reality of Christ, of the truth of the gospel which reveals him, with a conviction that he is the Son of God, that he is the only Savior, the glorious and all-sufficient Savior. Herein is one great difference between false affections and true affections: false affections and a delusory saving love to God and Christ are not accompanied with this conviction; they do not withal see the truth and reality of divine things.[56]

This statement, which comes in the course of Edwards's twelfth sermon in *Charity and Its Fruits*, was reiterated a few years later in the fifth of his twelve signs of authentic spirituality in *Religious Affections*: "Truly gracious affections are attended with a reasonable and spiritual conviction of the judgment, of the reality and certainty of divine things."[57] Authentic feeling and doctrinal fidelity rise and fall together. It is not surprising, then, that in Edwards's delineation in *Distinguishing Marks* of the five positive signs that identify a work of the Spirit of God, the fourth is the

---

[53] *WJE*, 8:146.

[54] *WJE*, 8:139; see also 8:296–97.

[55] Edward Hickman, ed., *The Works of Jonathan Edwards*, 2 vols. (London, 1834; repr., Edinburgh: Banner of Truth, 1974), 2:43.

[56] *WJE*, 8:336.

[57] *WJE*, 2:291. As John E. Smith puts it in an editorial comment, Edwards "did not, in his insistence that the seat of true virtue or of divine love was in the heart, so bifurcate men that the new sense of heart was without conviction concerning the truth" (*WJE*, 8:336n3).

upholding of truth, and the fifth is genuine love.[58] In all this we see that the emphasis on love in Edwards's theology of the Christian life does not find faithful descendants in the theologies of Schleiermacher and his heirs, who extract the subjective (experienced love) to the neglect of the objective (revealed truth).

Love without truth is rootless. Truth without love is lifeless. Neither is true Christianity. True divine love is never divorced from, but always founded on, God-revealed truth.

Divine Love Is the Sweetest Earthly Joy

The first two virtues listed by Paul in Galatians 5 as the "fruit of the Spirit" are love and joy. For Edwards, as for the apostle, the two belong naturally together. Though we will deal with Edwards's theology of joy more fully in the next chapter, here we briefly comment on joy's relationship to love.

Divine love in the heart of a Christian is the sweetest joy that can be experienced in this world. Genuine happiness is not something to be sought alongside love but something to be enjoyed in divine love. A life of love is the only life of solid joy. And in the case of both love and joy, the regenerate are experiencing the very life of the Trinity. The believer's joy is a vital participation in the joy that the persons of the triune God have been mutually enjoying in one another from eternity, and the believer's love is a vital participation in the love that the persons of the triune God have been mutually expressing in one another.

The connection between joy and love comes through especially clearly in a sermon on 1 John 4:16 entitled "The Spirit of the True Saints Is a Spirit of Divine Love."[59] In some ways this sermon may sum up the heart of Edwards's theology of the Christian life more than any other single extant sermon. Several distinctly Edwardsian emphases are here: the beauty of God, the new birth, satisfaction in God as our supreme happiness, the nature of hell and Satan, Christ as the supreme manifestation of God's mercy, humility, the Holy Spirit as the divine energy of delight between the Father and the Son, the labor involved in Christian living—and, of course, love.

What is especially noteworthy for our purposes is the way Edwards consistently intertwines joy and love in the Christian life. "They who love

---

[58] *WJE*, 4:254–59. See also Edwards, "Spirit of the True Saints," 312.
[59] Edwards, "Spirit of the True Saints," 297–344.

God set their hearts on the secret of happiness which will never fail them, and they will be happy to all eternity in spite of death and hell."[60] How is it, though, that divine love can never fail us? "He who has divine love in him has a wellspring of true happiness that he carries about in his own breast, a fountain of sweetness, a spring of the water of life. There is a pleasant calmness and serenity and brightness in the soul that accompanies the exercises of this holy affection."[61] Whatever circumstances befall the Christian, nothing can steal such love as long as the believer delights in God above all.

The happiness that pervades lovers of God is so great, says Edwards, that it cannot be fully articulated.

> The joy that a saint has in God and in a Redeemer is unspeakable. The unspeakableness of it seems to be a special property that belongs to it. There are no words to express that kind of sweetness or humble exultation that arises from the sensible presence of God to the soul that is filled with divine love.[62]

The language of "sweetness" is deeply Edwardsian and expresses the exquisite pleasantness of divine love in the heart. "What more pleasant life can there be than a life of love?" he asks.[63]

Other sermons reiterate the correlation between joy and love. The joy of heaven, says Edwards in the final sermon of *Charity and Its Fruits*, is the presence of divine love that will be perfectly enjoyed there. Believers "will live and . . . they will reign in love, and in that godlike joy which is the blessed fruit of it."[64] In an earlier sermon in this series Edwards spoke of the way love produces joy on earth, too, when he called on believers "earnestly to seek the spirit of Christian love, that excellent spirit of divine charity which will lead us always to rejoice in the welfare of others and which will fill our own hearts with happiness."[65]

Divine love, flowing out to God and to men, is the sweetest, most pleasant earthly joy that can be experienced.

---

[60] Ibid., 328.
[61] Ibid., 332.
[62] Ibid., 304.
[63] Ibid., 310–11.
[64] *WJE*, 8:386.
[65] *WJE*, 8:231. See the comments of George M. Marsden, "Challenging the Presumptions of the Age: The Two Dissertations," in *The Legacy of Jonathan Edwards: American Religion and the Evangelical Tradition*, ed. D. G. Hart, Sean Michael Lucas, and Stephen J. Nichols (Grand Rapids: Baker, 2003), 112.

Christian Love Is Humble Love

With this seventh and final key mark of divine love we come to what is perhaps the most uniquely Edwardsian contribution to the historic church's understanding of what Christian love is. If there is only one characteristic of love to be identified in Edwards's theology of the Christian life, this is it. Real love is humble love. "He who has true divine love desires to be emptied of himself that God may fill him. He loves to renounce his own honor that God may have honor. . . . He loves to be low that God may be high."[66]

This is the point of the sixth sermon of *Charity and Its Fruits.* "True divine love," says Edwards, "is an humble love. It is essential to true love that it be so that love that is not an humble love is not true divine love."[67] When a believer truly loves others, this love does not parade itself for the sake of being noticed. Such self-vaunting proves that it is not in fact love that is at work. Self-promoting acts of service may mimic the form but lack the essence of genuine love.

We should pause before moving on to be clear about what Edwards means by humility. Does he have in mind smarmy self-loathing? The groveling, misanthropic, psychological self-flagellation of those who refuse to think they might contribute anything valuable to the world? No—

> True Christian humility of heart tends to make persons resigned to the will of God, patient and submissive to his holy hand under afflictions, full of awful reverence towards the Deity, ready to treat divine things with great respect, and of a meek behavior towards men, condescending to inferiors and respectful towards superiors, gentle, easy to be entreated, not self-willed, not envious, but contented with his own condition, of a peaceable and quiet spirit, not disposed bitterly to resent injuries, but apt to forgive.[68]

Humility is not thinking poorly of oneself. It is rather thinking of oneself in harmonious proportion and appropriate relation to God.

If this is Edwards's description of humility, why is humility definitive of love? Edwards gives two answers.

First, when believers are born again, they are given a sense of the infinite loveliness of God as compared with us. Humility is generated not

---

[66] Edwards, "Spirit of the True Saints," 325.
[67] WJE, 8:243.
[68] WJE, 8:304–5. By "awful" Edwards means "awe-full."

simply in the new awareness that God is infinitely above us in greatness but also in the new awareness that he is infinitely above us in beauty. If all that were needed to generate humility were a sense of God's greatness, the demons would be the most humble beings in the universe, for they perceive God's infinitude more clearly than anyone else.[69]

Second, the *gospel* results in humble love—"such kind of exercises of love as the gospel tends to draw forth do in a special manner tend to and imply humility." The reason for this is the humility God in Christ demonstrated in the provision of rescue and redemption for guilty sinners. "The gospel teaches how God . . . stooped so low as to take an infinitely gracious notice of poor vile worms of the dust, and to concern himself for their salvation, so as to send his only begotten Son to die for them that they might be honored and brought into eternal fellowship with him."[70] The gospel affects us not only with the astonishing condescension of God in the incarnation but also with the humility of Christ in his earthly life. "The gospel leads us to love Christ, as an humble person."[71] And not only in his incarnation and life but also in his suffering and death we are led to humble love. "If we therefore behave ourselves as the followers of a crucified Jesus we shall walk humbly before God and men all the days of our lives."[72] And finally, not only in his incarnation, life, and death, but also in his death *for our sins* we are brought to "humble exercises of love."[73]

The unspeakable loveliness of God, then, and the humble sacrifice of Christ, unite to teach us that the love at the center of the Christian life is humble love. In short, that "divine love which is the sum of the Christian temper implies and tends to humility."[74]

Before leaving this subject, consider once more the penetration that Edwards applies to the humility of divine love. When insisting that Christian love be flavored with humility, Edwards will not let his readers slip into a pattern of thinking well of their own humility—a thought pattern that is self-indicting, like a husband shouting at his wife, "I never shout at you!" or a former basketball star telling reporters, "I never like to mention the fact that I scored 42 points in my final game." As Conrad Cherry explains,

---

[69] *WJE*, 8:243–45. In *Religious Affections* Edwards unpacks his sixth sign of authentic Christianity (the one on humility) by speaking of no longer admiring one's own moral beauty but God's (*WJE*, 2:322–23).
[70] *WJE*, 8:247.
[71] Ibid.
[72] *WJE*, 8:248.
[73] *WJE*, 8:249.
[74] *WJE*, 8:246.

"Genuine humility refuses to acknowledge as righteous *any* human experience, including humility itself. Humility is not a self-contained possession; it is not something one 'has' to which he can point. It is a relation."[75]

We see Edwards making this point most clearly in *Religious Affections* as he concludes his discussion of humility under the sixth sign of authentic affections. "Let not the reader lightly pass over these things in application to himself," he says.

> If you once have taken it in, that it is a bad sign for a person to be apt to think himself a better saint than others, there will arise a blinding prejudice in your own favor; and there will probably be need of a great strictness of self-examination, in order to determine whether it be so with you. If on the proposal of the question, you answer, "No, it seems to me, none are so bad as I." Don't let the matter pass off so; but examine again, whether or no you don't think yourself better than others on this very account, because you imagine you think so meanly of yourself. Haven't you an high opinion of this humility? And if you answer again, "No; I have not an high opinion of my humility; it seems to me I am as proud as the devil"; yet examine again, whether self-conceit don't rise up under this cover; whether on this very account, that you think yourself as proud as the devil, you don't think yourself to be very humble.[76]

The very admission of pride, if given sustained self-reflection, naturally introduces pride. Looking at ourselves, even in sober acknowledgment of pride, tends toward pride, keeping true love beyond our reach. The only way out is to look at Christ. To look at our humility is to make it vanish; to look at the infinitely lovely God, supremely manifest in Christ, is to bring humility in the back door of the heart.

If anything distinguishes authentic love, it is humility. This is its surest test.[77] Love that lacks humility indicts itself, for love that is paraded for others to see is not divine love, from the Spirit, but self-love, from the flesh.

Conclusion

George Marsden insightfully observes that Benjamin Franklin's *Autobiography* stands in stark contrast to another book of the same time, Jonathan

---

[75] Cherry, *Theology of Jonathan Edwards*, 81.
[76] *WJE*, 1:336.
[77] *WJE*, 4:257.

Edwards's *Life of David Brainerd*—Franklin portraying "the self-made man" and Brainerd "the self-renouncing man."[78] Brainerd, the young missionary whom Edwards befriended, epitomized Edwards's theology of humble love.

In his poem "The Clod and the Pebble," William Blake writes:

> Love seeketh not itself to please,
> Nor for itself hath any care,
> But for another gives its ease,
> And builds a heaven in hell's despair.[79]

This is Edwards's vision of the Christian life. The beautiful life is the life of love, of others-directed service and affection. With love, even circumstantial hell can be transformed into a taste of heaven.

A loveless Christian is not, for Jonathan Edwards, merely an unfortunate incompletion; it is a profound contradiction. A Christian, by definition, is not someone who has taken up a new strategy for life, one element of which is love. A Christian—a true Christian—is someone whose inborn selfish tendencies have been decisively uprooted by the all-conquering love of God, love felt and made real through the Holy Spirit. Such a life has taken on an entirely new flavor. Sinful desires remain. The old man, though dying, is not yet dead. But a new impulse of tender goodwill now sits on the throne of the believer's heart. Selfishness still exists; but selfishness no longer reigns. As the final verse of Ephesians puts it, believers are those "who love our Lord Jesus Christ *with love incorruptible*" (Eph. 6:24).

At the end of the fourteenth sermon in *Charity and Its Fruits*, Edwards reflects on the eternal nature of divine love. His closing exhortation there leaves us with a poignant word on which to conclude this chapter.

> This is the most excellent fruit of the Spirit. . . . Let us therefore earnestly seek this blessed fruit of the Spirit; and let us seek that it may abound in our hearts, that the love of God may more and more be shed abroad in our hearts, that we may love the Lord Jesus Christ in sincerity, and love one another as Christ hath loved us.[80]

---

[78] Marsden, *Jonathan Edwards*, 333.
[79] William Blake, "The Clod and the Pebble," in *Blake's Poetry and Designs*, ed. Mary Lynn Johnson and John E. Grant (New York: Norton, 1979), 42.
[80] *WJE*, 8:365.

CHAPTER 4

JOY

The Fuel of the Christian Life

The difference between a Christian life with or without joy is the difference between a boat being driven along by a tired oarsman or by a sail full of wind. Without the winds of joy we may make progress, at least on calm days—but it will be slow, painful, and exhausting. And on a day when the waves of circumstances are against us, we can only be driven backward, no matter how resolved the will.

For Jonathan Edwards, joy is not the add-on to Christian living it seems to be for many believers. To be sure, a selective reading of the New Testament might lead one to think that what really matters in living the Christian life is determined bending of the will to God. One might ask: Isn't the confession of the Christian, "I am an unworthy servant; I have only done my duty"? (cf. Luke 17:10). Joy is considered nice, but a bonus. It is, after all, just one among many manifestations of the fruit of the Spirit—"love, *joy*, peace, patience," and so on (Gal. 5:22). The way forward in the Christian life, it might seem, is simply not gratifying the desires of the flesh but rather crucifying them (Gal. 5:17, 24). The Christian is a soldier, battling his way, jaw set, through this fallen world (Luke 14:31; Rom. 7:23; 1 Pet. 2:11). Why stop to ask if we're happy? We need to keep our head down and our eyes fixed on the goal, not worry about whether we're smiling or not.

Whether joy is necessarily connected with smiles is a question in itself that will be dealt with below. But for Edwards, nothing could be further from the truth than the notion that joy is the extra credit of the Christian life. He saw that joy is not an optional addition to godliness but rather its driving force. It is central, not peripheral. Joy is the fuel of, not a bonus to, Christian living.

What Is Joy?

Edwards himself makes a definite and unique contribution to the church's understanding of joy. When we first picture joy, we might think of loud shouts of praise, exuberant exclamations, expressive displays of exultation— the sort of response you'd expect from someone who has just won the lottery. Edwards's theology of joy goes in a different direction. He speaks of the quiet *sweetness* of true joy. The calm, exquisite contentedness—what he and others of his time called "complacency"—of resting satisfied in God, in his beauty and love. Edwards teaches us the nondramatic, discreet happiness of a heart filled with the love of heaven. Authentic joy is not ostentatious. It does not draw attention to itself. It need not; it has all it needs in God.

Though we know tacitly what joy is, it isn't easy to define it. Edwards resists prosaic definitions of joy, describing it instead (as does the Bible itself) largely through metaphor and analogy. He wanted his hearers and readers to *feel* the reality of joy. Before moving to a few of the metaphors Edwards uses in describing it, we should answer the question of where joy comes from. Edwards is crystal clear that there is no true joy that does not come from the triune God. The universe itself is the overflow of God's own intratrinitarian delight—the Father delighting in the Son, the Son delighting in the Father, and the Spirit being the joyous love that is expressed between the two.[1]

To be born again is to be welcomed into the fountain-like heavenly delight of intratrinitarian love. We are swept up into this divine love—receiving it, absorbing it, and reflecting it. As we have seen, in a sermon on 1 John 4:16 Edwards says that "he who has divine love in him has a wellspring of true happiness that he carries about in his own breast, a fountain of sweetness, a spring of the water of life. There is a pleasant calmness and serenity and brightness in the soul that accompanies the exercises of this holy affection."[2]

And as with all that we are drawing from Edwards in this book, joy

---

[1] See Edwards's *Discourse on the Trinity* in *WJE*, 21:113–44 (also touched upon in the previous chapter).
[2] Jonathan Edwards, "The Spirit of the True Saints Is a Spirit of Divine Love," in *The Glory and Honor of God: Volume 2 of the Previously Unpublished Sermons of Jonathan Edwards*, ed. Michael D. McMullen (Nashville: Broadman & Holman, 2004), 332.

exists in relation to divine beauty. Specifically, joy enters the individual believer's heart when, through regeneration, God sovereignly through the Spirit opens a sinner's eyes to *see* God—and specifically, the beauty of Christ. It is when one is made alive to beauty that joy ignites. The "spring of all their delights, and the cream of all their pleasures," and "the joy of their joy," says Edwards of true believers, is "the view of the beautiful and delightful nature of divine things."[3] The good things of this world—the tastes, the sights, the smells, the accomplishments, the relationships— are all echoes of the true Joy, the joy of which every earthly pleasure is a shadow. Edwards would agree with the way modern thinker Cornelius Plantinga puts it: "Ultimate joy comes not *from* a lover or a landscape or a home, but *through* them. . . . They point to what is 'higher up' and 'further back.'"[4] The Christian life is not an ascetic life, but a life in which every received pleasure draws the mind up to supreme Pleasure, Christ himself, in his resplendent beauty. Joy is fundamentally a vision of God.[5]

Edwards therefore saw what many writers and preachers today do not: that the way to cultivate joy in God's people was not to talk about joy but to talk about God. If a New York park guide wants to help his band of tourists feel awe at the Niagara Falls, he doesn't give a lecture on awe. He shows them the falls. If a Christian leader wants believers to feel joy in Christ, he doesn't mainly tell them about joy. He shows them Christ. Joy sneaks unbidden in the back door.

Edwards teaches us, then, of the God-centeredness of all joy in this fallen world. He reminds us that the formula to joy is not God *and* _____ so much as God *in* _____. Christ is not one more element to fit into an already packed schedule—one more item on a growing list of priorities. Knowing Christ means seeing all of life in a new way, with new glasses. Jesus Christ gives meaning to *all* priorities, not only heading the list but coloring every one with new and exciting meaning. To become a Christian is to make all of life sacramental. "From him and through him and to him are all things"

---

[3] *WJE*, 2:250.

[4] Cornelius Plantinga, *Engaging God's World: A Christian Vision of Faith, Learning, and Living* (Grand Rapids: Eerdmans, 2002), 6; emphasis original. Plantinga is drawing on Augustine, Calvin, Lewis, and Tolkien when he makes this statement.

[5] This picks up a theme for which Thomas Aquinas is famous, not only the "Beatific Vision" of heaven but the beginning of that vision here and now. Says Thomas: "Final and perfect happiness can consist in nothing else than the vision of the Divine Essence. . . . The very sight of God causes delight. Consequently, he who sees God cannot need delight" (*Summa Theologica*, IaIIae, q. 3, art. 8; IaIIae, q. 4, art. 1, ad. 2). The reader is referred to the whole of Aquinas's discussion of happiness and the human will in IaIIae, qq. 2–33 of his *Summa*. Relying heavily both on Scripture and Augustine, Aquinas anticipates much of what Edwards would say on these two subjects half a millennium later.

(Rom. 11:36). True joy derives not from God *and* job, family, sex, friends, food, rest, driving, buying a home, reading a book, drinking coffee—but from God *in* these things.

> The glorious excellencies and beauty of God will be what will forever entertain the minds of the saints. . . . The redeemed will indeed enjoy other things: they will enjoy the angels, and will enjoy one another; but that which they shall enjoy in the angels, or each other, or in anything else whatsoever, that will yield them delight and happiness, will be what will be seen of God in them.[6]

Every taste of beauty in this world, from the roar of waterfalls to the chatter of birds to the richness of true friendship to the ecstasy of sexual experience, is a drop from the ocean of divine beauty. Every pleasure is an arrow pointing back to him. Joy is from, and only finally in, God.

Joy and Light

The most frequent metaphor through which Edwards portrays joy is light or brightness. In *Religious Affections*, for example, he reflects on 1 Peter 1:8, the key text on which the entire book is based. Peter speaks of a joy that is "inexpressible and filled with glory," and Edwards comments:

> In rejoicing with this joy, their minds were filled, as it were, with a glorious brightness, and their natures exalted and perfected: it was a most worthy, noble rejoicing, that did not corrupt and debase the mind, as many carnal joys do; but did greatly beautify and dignify it . . . it filled their minds with the light of God's glory, and made 'em themselves to shine with some communication of that glory.[7]

Note the connection between light and joy here, which is repeated throughout the Edwards corpus.[8] In this Edwards is simply following the lead of Scripture, which likewise speaks of joy in terms of light, such as Psalm 97:11:

> Light is sown for the righteous,
> and joy for the upright in heart.[9]

---

[6] *WJE*, 17:208; similarly, 13:167.
[7] *WJE*, 2:95.
[8] E.g., *WJE*, 2:113, 179; 4:125, 189, 332;
[9] Cf. also Est. 8:16; Isa. 26:19; John 5:35.

Edwards himself observed that "light is very often in Scripture put for comfort, joy, happiness and for good in general."[10]

What does this mean? In casting Christian joy in terms of light and brightness Edwards is helping us feel the weight of joy as a reality that, when present, is all-enveloping, ever-flowing, life-giving, and beautiful. What the sun does to a valley as night gives way to day is what joy does to the Christian as the heart is filled with joy.

Indeed, joy is often literally and directly connected to light. Those who live in cloudy parts of the world are well familiar with seasonal affective disorder (making the appropriate acronym, SAD). One study linked cognitive ability to varying amounts of sunlight, with greater sunlight tending toward greater cognitive functionality.[11]

In Edwards's thinking, however, true joy comes not from the sun but from the triune God—though in a miscellany Edwards uses the sun as a way of explaining the joy that God brings. The Father is the sun itself, the Son is the brightness of the sun, and the Spirit is the warmth of the sun.[12]

Yet the sun is not simply a convenient analogy for explaining Christian joy. To Edwards's mind, this would be to put the matter backward. God gave us the sun to point to himself. "The whole outward creation, which is but the shadows of beings, is so made as to represent spiritual things."[13] Edwards would therefore go on to say that the very reason the sun exists at all is ultimately to portray spiritual realities, preeminently *God*, and in a unique way the Son of God. Edwards felt compelled by texts such as Revelation 21:23[14] to call Christ "the infinite fountain of all light . . . the Sun of Righteousness, in comparison of whose brightness the sun is but darkness."[15]

A green valley bathed in morning sunlight is a picture of Christian joy.

Joy and Desire

On first thought it would seem that joy and desire are mutually exclusive—if one desires something, one does not have it, and therefore cannot experience the joy of having it. For Edwards, however, joy and desire are bound up with one another. They rise and fall together.

---

[10] *WJE*, 8:521.
[11] The study can be accessed on Biomed Central's website, www.biomedcentral.com.
[12] *WJE*, 13:434.
[13] Ibid.
[14] "And the city has no need of sun or moon to shine on it, for the glory of God gives it light, and its lamp is the Lamb."
[15] *WJE*, 15:130.

In *Religious Affections* Edwards describes David as a man of "earnest desires, thirstings and pantings of soul after God, delight and joy in God."[16] Notice again the metaphors Edwards uses to portray the joy of desire—*thirstings* and *pantings*. Throughout his writings he sees holy desire and holy joy not as competing but as mutually reinforcing.[17] The more one sees of the beauty of God, the more one longs for it—yet the seeing and the longing are themselves joy-generating. Indeed, such longings not only generate joy; they themselves are a joy. The wanting is the having. To long for God is to enjoy him. Misery is, from one perspective, simply the absence of longing. No desire, no joy. Edwards opens his treatment of the tenth sign of authentic Christianity in *Religious Affections* with this sentence: "Another great and very distinguishing difference between gracious affections and others is, that gracious affections, the higher they are raised, the more is a spiritual appetite and longing of soul after spiritual attainments, increased."[18] As Samuel Rutherford wrote to a friend a century before Edwards, "Hunger on, for there is food in hunger for Christ."[19] The desiring is the possessing.

We see this in a deeply personal way in Edwards's account of his own awakening to true joy. In the opening pages of his *Personal Narrative* he refers to his time of awakening as consisting of both "delights which I now felt in things of religion" that were of a "pure, soul-animating and refreshing nature" *and* "vehement longings of soul after God and Christ, and after more holiness; wherewith my heart seemed to be full, and ready to break."[20] Though he would not develop this connection between joy and desire to the same degree, Edwards would agree with the way C. S. Lewis described joy with the German word *Sehnsucht*, a term difficult to translate that denotes a yearning or longing shot through with joyful nostalgia. It is a pervasive theme in *The Pilgrim's Regress*, in which Lewis comments that "this hunger is better than all fullness; this poverty better than all other wealth."[21] More personally, Lewis could say in his autobiography that "the central story" of his own life is "that of an unsatisfied desire which is itself more desirable than any other satisfaction. I call it Joy."[22]

---

[16] *WJE*, 2:108.

[17] Cf., e.g., *WJE*, 2:104–5, 266; 4:338; 13:442–43.

[18] *WJE*, 2:376.

[19] Samuel Rutherford, writing to James Bautie in 1637, in *The Letters of Samuel Rutherford* (Edinburgh, 1891), 492.

[20] *WJE*, 16:794.

[21] C. S. Lewis, *The Pilgrim's Regress* (1933; repr., Grand Rapids: Eerdmans, 1958), 202.

[22] C. S. Lewis, *Surprised by Joy* (Orlando: Harcourt, 1955), 17–18. Cf. Stephen Logan, "Literary Theorist," in *The Cambridge Companion to C. S. Lewis*, ed. Robert MacSwain and Michael Ward (Cambridge: Cambridge University Press, 2010), 37.

Lewis and Edwards believed that joy in this world is experienced largely as yearnings. True joy is almost painful, because it is a glimpse of something we deeply long for but are not yet united with. Here and now we get only tantalizing whiffs of it. One thinks too of Tolkien's notion of *eucatastrophe*, "the sudden happy turn in a story which pierces you with a joy that brings tears."[23] In a 1944 letter to his son Christopher, Tolkien described eucatastrophe as "qualitatively so like sorrow, because it comes from those places where Joy and Sorrow are at one."[24]

There is a paradox here. For while Edwards can describe joy as "thirstings and pantings," he also says that the joy that Christ pours into the hearts of his people is perfectly satisfying. Nothing more is longed for. "The pleasure and joy that is in Christ Jesus . . . is of such a nature that those that receive it desire no other kind of joy."[25] To see Christ in his beauty is to long for more of such a sight; and yet the sight itself drives out all need for anything to supplement it. Paradoxically, a sense of the beauty of Christ brings deep longing and utter contentment *together*. Neither squeezes out the other. The longing is itself a satisfaction of longing.

Joy and Solemnity

Another paradox emerges when we consider Edwardsian joy from another angle. For Edwards, a person may be enjoying true joy yet without *looking* joyful in terms of the way the world tends to define joy. True joy is not frothy. It does not equate with laughing or joking. Edwards would even say that to the degree that our joy is not purely divine and heavenly, it will have more such "levity":

> It is because the joy of some Christians is thus mixed with what is carnal, that their joy is attended with something of levity; and when they talk of their experiences, they do it with something of lightness, with too much of an air of a light sort of mirth, which shows that their joy is not all divine, but there is a mixture of something carnal in it.[26]

---

[23] Humphrey Carpenter, ed., *The Letters of J. R. R. Tolkien* (New York: Houghton Mifflin, 2000), 100. The classic place in which Tolkien unpacks this notion of eucatastrophe is his essay "On Fairy-Stories," the text of which can be read in Verlyn Flieger and Douglas A. Anderson, eds., *Tolkien on Fairy-Stories* (New York: HarperCollins, 2008).

[24] Carpenter, *Letters of J. R. R. Tolkien*, 101.

[25] *WJE*, 17:136.

[26] *Works of Jonathan Edwards Online*, vol. 73, *Sermons, Series II, 1756–1758, Undated, and Fragments* (Jonathan Edwards Center at Yale University).

Rather, "The purest and best joy is a *solid* joy."[27] Edwards understood that "even in laughter the heart may ache" (Prov. 14:13), while at the same time "by sadness of face the heart is made glad" (Eccles. 7:3). He knew that when others might be most tempted to ask, "Why so somber, Jonathan?" those were sometimes his most joy-filled moments. Edwards reminds us that there is a frothiness that laughs and jokes and jeers which is utterly devoid of real joy. And there is a quiet sobriety that fights back tears, the joy is so intense. One is external joy hiding internal misery. The other is external seriousness hiding internal delight. Edwards would reprove many of us for medicating our inner emptiness with *Saturday Night Live* and the inane banter that mutes our emptiness in the moment but in the long run only exacerbates it. True joy is solemn joy.

After the local Northampton revival of 1734–1735 came the Great Awakening in 1740–1742. Note Edwards's fascinating observation about a difference between the two revivals in his *Distinguishing Marks of a Work of the Spirit of God*, a more mature and seasoned reflection on revival than the earlier *Narrative of Surprising Conversions*.

> There has been a remarkable difference in this respect, that whereas many before, in their comforts and rejoicings, did too much forget their distance from God, and were ready in their conversation together of the things of God and of their own experiences, to talk with too much of an air of lightness, and something of laughter; now they seem to have no dis-position to it, but rejoice with a more solemn, reverential, humble joy. . . .
>
> 'Tis not because the joy is not as great, and in many of them much greater. . . . Their rejoicing operates in another manner: it only abases and solemnizes them; breaks their hearts, and brings them into the dust: now when they speak of their joys, it is not with laughter, but a flood of tears. Thus those that laughed before, weep now; and yet, by their united testimony, their joy is vastly purer and sweeter than that which before did more raise their animal spirits.[28]

The local revival produced valid joy, but the Great Awakening brought joy that was both more intense *and* more solemn. Joy and solemnity grew together, not in competition with one another.

Edwards's words here land with particular force on twenty-first-century Western Christians because we are generally uncomfortable with

---

[27] Ibid., emphasis added.
[28] *WJE*, 4:270.

any conversation that seeks to penetrate more deeply than sprightly frivolity, even on Sunday mornings. We quickly cover our miserable insecurities with jokes and surfacy chatter that leaves the heart undisturbed and unhelped. Edwards recalibrates us to the serious business of joy.

He is not alone in doing so. One thinks of Spurgeon's comment in *Lectures to My Students*: "Cheerfulness is one thing, and frivolity is another; he is a wise man who by a serious happiness of conversation steers between the dark rocks of moroseness, and the quicksands of levity."[29] And as with so much of what Edwards says concerning this "serious happiness," Lewis once more echoes Edwards's emphasis on serious joy in the poignant comment in *The Last Battle*, "There is a kind of happiness and wonder that makes you serious. It is too good to waste on jokes."[30]

Edwards was not an advocate for misanthropic somberness. In his quest for joy he simply wanted the real thing, not a flashy counterfeit. If anyone should know what uproarious laughter is, Christians should. We are involved in the greatest comedy (in the classic sense of that word) the world has ever known. We know it will all turn out well in the end. The world wins now to lose then; we lose now to win then. We know God is going to one day hit rewind on these decaying bodies and restore the world to normal, Eden 2.0, with Jesus at the center, and, as Edwards draws out beautifully in the sermon "Heaven Is a World of Love," perfect love and joy experienced by everyone whom God has united to him.

We have more reason for joy than anyone else. But Edwards steers us away from the frothy frivolity that we tend to substitute for the real thing. True joy does not compete with seriousness. True joy solemnizes.

Joy and Humility

One of Edwards's distinct contributions to a Christian theology of joy is the connection he frequently makes between humility and joy. We have touched on this just above in discussing joy and solemnity, but the point merits its own brief reflection.

It is the Christian's great delight to be low before God. We first see this in Edwards in his own experience, which he recounts in his *Personal Narrative*. Shortly after going to his first pastorate in New York City, Edwards recounts, he discovered that his truest delights were in being "low and

---

[29] C. H. Spurgeon, *Lectures to My Students* (Grand Rapids: Zondervan, 1954), 310.
[30] C. S. Lewis, *The Last Battle* (1956; repr., San Francisco: HarperCollins, 2009), 212.

humble on the ground," which he likened to a spring flower delighting to be low and drink in the glory of the sun.[31] "There was no part of creature-holiness, that I then, and at other times, had so great a sense of the loveliness of, as humility, brokenness of heart and poverty of spirit: and there was nothing that I had such a spirit to long for."[32]

Edwards makes humility a programmatic element of joy in *Religious Affections*. His discussion of the sixth sign of authentic affections must surely rank among the classic treatments of humility in all of Christian literature.[33] He argues that a tender-hearted humility ought to flavor every virtue, not least joy. In a statement foundational to Edwards's vision of the Christian life he says: "All gracious affections, that are a sweet odor to Christ, and that fill the soul of a Christian with a heavenly sweetness and fragrancy, are brokenhearted affections." After speaking of love, desires, and hope as each to be clothed in humility, Edwards turns to joy. Christian "joy, even when it is 'unspeakable, and full of glory,' is a humble, brokenhearted joy, and leaves the Christian more poor in spirit, and more like a little child."[34] Christian joy is not flamboyant or showy but rather delights to say, with John the Baptist, "He must increase, but I must decrease" (John 3:30). Mature believers know that to parade one's spiritual experiences before others has a way of immediately eviscerating the joy itself. There is a sacredness to the richness of authentic communion with God. It must not be spoiled by self-spotlighting advertising of our spiritual experiences.

Edwards teaches us that a joy that is shot through with tenderness, humility, and brokenheartedness is not the kind that will manifest itself in a certain slice of the Myers-Briggs personality profile. Tender-hearted joy is not optional. It is for Christians: all Christians.[35] As the apostle Peter said, "Finally, *all* of you, have unity of mind, sympathy, brotherly love, a *tender* heart, and a *humble* mind" (1 Pet. 3:8).

The point here is not that we should pursue joy along with humility. The point is that the two pursuits are one. It is in a contented lowliness and an increasingly cultivated Other-exalting reflex that the richest happiness blossoms. The best joys, says Edwards, cast the soul "down low and in the dust in humility and poverty of spirit. Though it be a much sweeter joy than that which so elevates the soul, yet it is attended with too solemn a sense of

---

[31] *WJE*, 16:796.
[32] Ibid.
[33] *WJE*, 2:311–40.
[34] *WJE*, 2:339–40.
[35] *WJE*, 2:364.

the infinite greatness of divine things, the awful excellency of Christ, and majesty of God, and its own nothingness." And yet it is in this very lostness in the greatness of God and the nothingness of self that "the soul is filled with joy."[36] In short, as Edwards puts it in a November 1735 sermon, "There is such a thing as praising God in a humble, brokenhearted manner, and yet in a very joyful manner at the same time."[37]

Joy and Heaven

We will devote a whole chapter to the role the hope of heaven plays in Christian living here and now. But we cannot close this chapter before drawing attention to Edwards's rich and full and exquisite vision of heaven as joy consummated. The joy that begins decisively in this life is brought to unhindered, flooding fulfillment in the next. "The love and joy of the saints on earth, is the beginning and dawning of the light, life, and blessedness of heaven."[38] Heaven *is* joy, because in heaven we are with Christ, loving him without filter and expressing love to him without filter.

Heaven is joy consummated.

Conclusion

In the wake of spiritual revival among Edwards's church in 1742, a member of the congregation grew frustrated with his pastor. This parishioner, according to Samuel Hopkins, had a "warm temperament" and tended to be "carried away by feelings." Finally the man approached Edwards and expressed dismay at the preacher's "moderation and quiet. I fear that some of your people will continue to sleep till they fall into hell, and I can scarcely refrain, at times, from rising in the midst of your service, and calling on them to awake." Edwards promptly responded, "If you should, sir, I shall request the tithing-man to take you by the hand and lead you out of the house."[39] This from the man who considered it a matter of homiletical faithfulness to seek to "raise the affections of my hearers as high as I possibly can."[40]

There is no real tension here. Edwards wanted his people to have real

---

[36] *WJE Online*, vol. 73, *Sermons, Series II, 1756–1758, Undated, and Fragments.*
[37] *WJE*, 19:470.
[38] *WJE*, 2:113.
[39] William Patten, *Reminiscences of the Late Rev. Samuel Hopkins* (Boston, 1743), 26–27; as recounted by the editors in the introduction to the sermon "Keeping the Presence of God," in *WJE*, 22:519. A "tithing-man" in early New England context was responsible for enforcing Sabbath rules and preventing disorderly conduct.
[40] *WJE*, 4:387.

joy, not a counterfeit. He wanted to raise affections the way the apostle Paul did—not with humanly manufactured or manipulated emotionalism, but by a "demonstration of the Spirit and of power" (1 Cor. 2:4). True joy comes, Edwards believed, through a calm, beautiful, reasoned, and inescapably truthful exultation in the manifold beauty of God. Edwards the preacher, in Packer's inimitable words, "bore down on his listeners' consciences with the plain old truths of sin and salvation, and the calm majesty of his inexorable analysis was no less used of God to make men feel the force of truth than was the rhapsodic vehemence of George Whitefield."[41] This was Edwards's method for seeking to cultivate joy in his people, and the method fit his theology of joy more broadly: joy is solemn and humble as much as it is bright and sweet.

A fitting excerpt from Edwards to close this chapter comes from a sermon preached on September 19, 1746, at the ordination service of Samuel Buell, the dear friend of David Brainerd. Here Edwards brings together many of the dimensions of his theology of joy in reflecting on the dawning of the new heavens and the new earth, once more casting joy in terms of beauty apprehended:

> In that resurrection morning, when the Sun of Righteousness shall appear in the heavens, shining in all his brightness and glory, he will come forth as a bridegroom; he shall come in the glory of his Father, with all his holy angels.
>
> And at that glorious appearing of the great God, and our Savior Jesus Christ, shall the whole elect church, complete as to every individual member and each member with the whole man, both body and soul, and both in perfect glory, ascend up to meet the Lord in the air, to be thenceforth forever with the Lord. That will be a joyful meeting of this glorious bridegroom and bride indeed. Then the bridegroom will appear in all his glory without any veil: and then the saints shall shine forth as the sun in the kingdom of their Father, and at the right hand of their Redeemer.[42]

Edwards continues by filling out the marital image between Christ and believers. In doing so, he implicitly seems to draw on the conjugal union of husband and wife on their wedding night to speak of the final and consummate uniting of Christ with his bride. This is one example of what we will

---

[41] J. I. Packer, *A Quest for Godliness: The Puritan Vision of the Christian Life* (Wheaton, IL: Crossway, 1990), 314.
[42] *WJE*, 25:183.

see below in chapter 10, that all of human life and nature gives us images of spiritual reality.

What we notice for our purposes in this chapter on joy is that Edwards appears to use sex as a faint picture of the rapturous pleasures of being finally united to Christ. Both he and his age were too modest to be explicit in public discourse about sex. But when we read between the lines of the excerpt below, this appears to be Edwards's point. The connection certainly has biblical precedent, such as in 1 Corinthians 6, where Paul appeals to one's union with Christ as a reason not to be united with a prostitute (1 Cor. 6:16–17).

Perhaps we could put it like this, then. For us today, the most exquisite physical pleasure conceivable is sexual union. My five-year-old, whose highest physical pleasure is ice cream, cannot conceive of how this experience his parents have could transcend ice cream. But an adult explaining sex to a five-year-old whose highest pleasure is ice cream is like a glorified saint explaining heaven to a human adult whose highest physical pleasure is an orgasm. We cannot imagine enjoying heaven perfectly without sexual pleasure; neither can the five-year-old imagine enjoying sex without ice cream in the bed. Yet one is not thinking of ice cream. And on "that resurrection morning," we will not be thinking of sex. That to which all physical pleasure and marriage itself point will have arrived (Rev. 21:2). We will trade in the matchbox cars for NASCAR, shadow for reality. Here is what Edwards says, and on this note we conclude this chapter:

> Then will come the time, when Christ will sweetly invite his spouse to enter in with him into the palace of his glory, which he had been preparing for her from the foundation of the world, and shall as it were take her by the hand, and lead her in with him: and this glorious bridegroom and bride shall with all their shining ornaments, ascend up together into the heaven of heaven; the whole multitude of glorious angels waiting upon them: and this Son and daughter of God shall, in their united glory and joy, present themselves together before the Father; when Christ shall say, "Here am I, and the children which thou hast given me": and they both shall in that relation and union, together receive the Father's blessing; and shall thenceforward rejoice together, in consummate, uninterrupted, immutable, and everlasting glory, in the love and embraces of each other, and joint enjoyment of the love of the Father.[43]

---

[43] *WJE*, 25:183–84. In a miscellany in *WJE*, 13:351, Edwards again seems to draw on sexual sensation to describe the superior pleasures of heaven.

CHAPTER 5

GENTLENESS

The Aroma of the Christian Life

It may seem odd to include a chapter on gentleness in a book on Jonathan Edwards's view of the Christian life. Are there not more central, more significant virtues to focus on?

Edwards didn't think so. He wrote that "a lamblike, dovelike spirit and temper" is "*the* true, and distinguishing disposition of the hearts of Christians."[1] And he has something to teach us. We give a chapter to gentleness here because it is a neglected virtue both in what others have unearthed in Edwards's writings and more generally in the Christian church today. Not many have identified gentleness as a major theme in Edwards (more common are titles such as *Jonathan Edwards: The Fiery Puritan*);[2] and not many identify gentleness as a major need in the church right now. And yet gentleness is perhaps the most neglected virtue among Christians today. Edwards wrote in his diary on February 16, 1725: "A virtue, which I need in a higher degree, to give a beauty and luster to my behavior, is gentleness. If I had more of an air of gentleness, I should be much mended."[3] True for him then. True for us today.

Some may hesitate to agree. Indeed, it may seem to many that the urgent need in the twenty-first-century church is not gentleness but its

---

[1] *WJE*, 2:344–45, emphasis added.
[2] Henry B. Parkes, *Jonathan Edwards: The Fiery Puritan* (New York: Menton, Balch & Co., 1930).
[3] *WJE*, 16:787.

opposite: steely, grim-faced, jaw-set, warrior-like championing of sound doctrine, moral living, and strategic social agendas. Will the kingdom of God truly advance through *gentleness?* Being gentle is nice. But will it really change anything?

Yes. The most steely, warrior-like theologian of church history, Martin Luther, wrote in 1528 to Duke John Frederick: "God has promised great mercy to those who seek peace and endure guile when he says: 'Blessed are the meek, for they shall inherit the earth.' War does not gain much, but loses much and risks everything. Gentleness, however, loses nothing, risks little, and gains everything."[4]

Jonathan Edwards would agree. And unlike Luther, Edwards returns again and again to this theme of gentleness in exploring the Christian life.[5] In this chapter we first unearth what Edwards means by "gentle." We will then consider, through his eyes, how gentleness is compatible with three equally biblical calls—warring, zeal, and manliness.

In this angry world, gentleness sticks out. Jonathan Edwards guides us into such a life.

What Is Gentleness?

But what precisely is it? Though we know gentleness tacitly when we see it, it is difficult to define. Looking to Edwards, we discover six points.

First, we begin to get the flavor of what Edwards means by gentleness simply by noting what other words he tends to string together with it. Edwards returns to the same synonyms time and again when speaking of gentleness: calmness, long-suffering, forbearance, quietness, patience, kindness, a "lamb-like" or "dove-like" spirit, and—especially—meekness.[6] Gentleness makes us "like little children."[7] In one 1750 sermon he brings much of this together when he speaks of divine grace generating "those sweet, calming, and quieting principles of humility, meekness, resignation, patience, gentleness, forgiveness, and sweet reliance on God."[8]

---

[4] Martin Luther, *Luther's Works*, vol. 49, *Letters II*, ed. Gottfried G. Krodel (Philadelphia: Fortress, 1972), 196. Another window into Luther's ability to be truly tender and gentle is his moving word to a friend upon the death of Luther's one-year-old daughter (ibid., 203).
[5] A quick search at the *Works of Jonathan Edwards Online* provided by Yale University lists 349 independent instances of "gentle"/"gentleness." See edwards.yale.edu.
[6] On the overlapping relationship between gentleness and meekness in Edwards, see Paul Ramsey's editorial note in *WJE*, 8:189n4.
[7] *WJE*, 14:259.
[8] *WJE*, 25:544.

A second way to get at what Edwards means by gentleness is to see how he defines what it isn't. In *Charity and Its Fruits*, Edwards explains what Paul means when the apostle calls love "patient and kind" in 1 Corinthians 13:4 (or as Edwards's KJV had it, "Charity suffereth long"). Edwards suggests that to be long-suffering includes within it being gentle, and he cites James 3:17 (on the gentleness of the wisdom from above) and Galatians 5:22 (on gentleness as a fruit of the Spirit).[9] Edwards then identifies the photo negative of gentleness: "In him who exercises the Christian spirit as he ought there will be no passionate, rash and hasty expression; there will not be a bitter exasperated countenance, or air of behavior, no violence in talk or carriage, but on the contrary, those words and that behavior which savor of peaceableness and calmness."[10]

Third, gentleness is essential to Christian living. It is not an add-on. It is, for Edwards, one of the few indisputable evidences of the Holy Spirit alive and well within someone. Gentleness is not just for some Christians, those wired a certain way. It cannot merely be an inherent character trait, a result of personality or genetic predisposition, because it is listed as part of the fruit of the Spirit in Galatians 5. Looked at another way, nowhere in the New Testament's lists of spiritual gifts is gentleness identified as one such gift. It is not a *gift* of the Spirit for a few. It is the *fruit* of the Spirit for all. To be gentle is to become who we were meant to be; that is, to return to who we once were, in Eden.[11]

Fourth, gentleness is not only for all Christians but also for all times. It is not a "mode" into which a believer shifts on occasion. In this way gentleness is different from many other Christian virtues. Courage, for example, or chastity, is summoned forth by specific concrete circumstances. Gentleness is not summoned from time to time; it is what we are. It is not a virtue that is triggered but air that is exhaled. Edwards speaks of gentleness as a "spirit" that is "breathed."[12] It is an aroma. Those who are alive to beauty have a certain fragrance about them that hangs over all they do, sweetening their words, their actions, and their countenance. "The eminently humble Christian is as it were clothed with lowliness, mildness, meekness, gentle-

---

[9] These are the two New Testament texts to which Edwards returns time and again when speaking of gentleness.

[10] *WJE*, 8:189–90.

[11] In a 1945 letter to his son, J. R. R. Tolkien connected Eden and gentleness: "Certainly there was an Eden on this very unhappy earth. We all long for it, and we are constantly glimpsing it: our whole nature at its best and least corrupted, its gentlest and most humane, is still soaked with the sense of 'exile'" (Humphrey Carpenter, ed., *The Letters of J. R. R. Tolkien* [New York: Houghton Mifflin, 2000], 110).

[12] *WJE*, 3:91.

ness of spirit and behavior, and with a soft, sweet, condescending, winning air and deportment; these things are just like garments to him; he is
clothed all over with them."[13]

Fifth, a high view of God's sovereignty fuels Christian gentleness.
The theological tradition and system to which Edwards belonged, which
is often stereotyped as cold and harsh, in truth produces its opposite.
When Edwards's own eyes were opened to God's beauty, he saw two
things above all else: God's "majesty and meekness joined together." On
the one hand was God's utter sovereignty, which appeared to him as "an
exceedingly pleasant" and "bright" doctrine, and on the other hand was
God's condescending meekness, which was "sweet and gentle." Putting
them together, Edwards saw God as possessing "a high, and great, and
holy gentleness."[14] The sovereignty of God and the meekness of his children are mutually reinforcing. The English hymn writer John Newton
captures this connection in a letter to a Calvinistic pastor who wrote him
describing his intentions to rebuke the doctrinal errors of another pastor.
Newton responds:

> Of all people who engage in controversy, we, who are called Calvinists,
> are most expressly bound by our own principles to the exercise of gentle-
> ness and moderation. If, indeed, they who differ from us have a power of
> changing themselves, if they can open their own eyes, and soften their
> own hearts, then we might with less inconsistency be offended at their
> obstinacy: but if we believe the very contrary to this, our part is, not to
> strive, but in meekness to instruct those who oppose.[15]

Sixth, reflecting the consistent pattern of biblical ethics, the vertical
fuels the horizontal. Befriended by the gentleness of God in Jesus, we reflect that divine tenderness toward others. "Nothing," said Edwards, "has a
greater tendency to promote those amiable dispositions of mercy, forbearance, long-suffering, gentleness and forgiveness, than a sense of our own

---

[13] *WJE*, 4:422.
[14] *WJE*, 16:792–93.
[15] See the full letter online at http://www.opc.org/nh.html?article_id=217; accessed January 23, 2013.
Calvin himself, as much as anyone in his train, understood that his own theology generated rather than
snuffed out gentleness and humility. As Bavinck said: "For Calvin the passive virtues of submission, humility, patience, self-denial, cross-bearing stand in the foreground. Like St. Augustine, Calvin is mortally
afraid of pride, whereby man exalts himself above God. His strong insistence upon the inability of man
and the bondage of the will is not for the purpose of plunging man into despair, but in order to raise him
from his lethargy and to awaken in him the longing for what he lacks, to make him renounce all self-
glorying and self-reliance and put all his confidence in God alone" (Herman Bavinck, *Calvin and Common
Grace*, trans. Geerhardus Vos [New York: Westminster, 1996], 23).

extreme unworthiness and misery, and the infinite need we have of the divine pity, forbearance and forgiveness."[16] There is one place only in all four Gospels where Jesus tells us about his heart. In the one place where he opens to us who he is at his radiating core, Jesus says he is "gentle and lowly in heart" (Matt. 11:29). When we come to speak of gentleness in the Christian life, we are talking about embodying *who Jesus is*. To be Christlike is to be, if nothing else, gentle. Edwards himself feels the weight of what Spurgeon would later observe when he says of Jesus's words in Matthew 11:

> Meekness is a great part of the Christian spirit. Christ in that great call and invitation which we have in the close of the eleventh chapter of Matthew, where he calls all that labor and are heavy laden to come unto him, particularly mentions this as that in which he calls upon them who come to him to imitate him. "Learn of me, for I am meek and lowly in heart."[17]

We turn now to consider what gentleness looks like in the Christian life in light of other Christian obligations that seem at odds with it.

Gentleness and War

Reflecting on what it means to be gentle introduces a tension for those who read their Bibles carefully. For all over the New Testament believers are called to do what appears to be precisely the opposite of gentleness—fight, wage war, do battle.

In Matthew's Gospel Jesus says that the violent take the kingdom of heaven by force (Matt. 11:12), and in Luke's Gospel he tells his disciples to count the cost, likening the demands of discipleship to the demands of war (Luke 14:25–33). Paul called Timothy a "soldier" (2 Tim. 2:3–4) and told him to "wage the good warfare" (1 Tim. 1:18) and "fight the good fight" (1 Tim. 6:12). Paul told the Ephesians they are in a battle and they need to strap on their armor (Eph. 6:10–17). How does gentleness fit with such fierce, even violent, imagery?

This is a tension not only in Scripture but in Edwards too. For all his exhortations to gentleness, he could also preach:

---

[16] *WJE*, 3:424. Elsewhere Edwards makes the same point: "Christians that are but fellow worms ought at least to treat one another with as much humility and gentleness as Christ that is infinitely above them treats them" (*WJE*, 4:420).

[17] *WJE*, 8:186. "Christ when upon earth was wont to treat his disciples with wonderful tenderness and true gentleness" (*WJE*, 25:720).

The work that a Christian is called to is the work of a soldier; 'tis a warfare. He is not called to sleep but to conflict. . . . He is called to take heaven by violence and to obtain the prize by conquest. . . . The Scripture tells us of no other way of getting to heaven but by running, and fighting, and obtaining of it as it were by conquest.[18]

Evidently Edwards did not view the Bible's calls to be gentle and to be a soldier as mutually exclusive.

Edwards wrestled with the tension head-on in *Religious Affections*. Discussing the sixth sign of authentic spiritual affections—that true godly experience results in meekness, gentleness, and lowliness of spirit—he raises the objection: "But here some may be ready to say, Is there no such thing as Christian fortitude, and boldness for Christ, being good soldiers in the Christian warfare, and coming out bold against the enemies of Christ and his people?" He responds: "There doubtless is such a thing. The whole Christian life is compared to a warfare, and fitly so. And the most eminent Christians are the best soldiers, endowed with the greatest degrees of Christian fortitude."

The problem, says Edwards, and the reason gentleness and soldier-like boldness or fortitude seem to be in tension, is how we define Christian boldness and fortitude. It is not "a brutal fierceness." Rather:

True Christian fortitude consists in strength of mind, through grace, exerted in two things; in ruling and suppressing the *evil*, and unruly passions and affections of the mind; and in steadfastly and freely exerting, and following *good* affections and dispositions, without being hindered by sinful fear, or the opposition of enemies. . . .

Though Christian fortitude appears, in withstanding and counteracting the enemies that are without us; yet it much more appears, in resisting and suppressing the enemies that are within us; because they are our worst and strongest enemies, and have greatest advantage against us. The strength of the good soldier of Jesus Christ, appears in nothing more, than in steadfastly maintaining the holy calm, meekness, sweetness, and benevolence of his mind, amidst all the storms, injuries, strange behavior, and surprising acts and events of this evil and unreasonable world.[19]

---

[18] *WJE*, 22:147.
[19] *WJE*, 2:350; cf. 2:351: "If therefore we see any of the followers of Christ, in the midst of the most violent, unreasonable and wicked opposition, of God's and his own enemies, maintaining under all this temptation, the humility, quietness, and gentleness of a lamb, and the harmlessness, and love, and sweetness of a dove, we may well judge that here is a good soldier of Jesus Christ."

The Christian life is a life of war—against sin. But the sin we know best is our own. The Christian's warring is against something inside him, not outside. We might say that we war against our impulse to make war. We fight the very instinct to fight. And what such fighting looks like is generally the precise opposite of war as we think of it. For triumph over sin involves not "a brutal fierceness," says Edwards, but "holy calm" and "sweetness." Such things shake the gates of hell. Gentleness—authentic, gospel-fueled, Spirit-wrought, gentleness—is a mighty weapon wielded against the kingdom of darkness.

A major way Christians wage war is by being gentle. We do not leave gentleness behind when we take up arms against the Devil. Gentleness is itself a way we take up arms against the Devil. The film version of Tolkien's *The Hobbit* captures this when Gandalf, the wise wizard, tells Bilbo that another wizard, Saruman, "believes that it is only great power that can hold evil in check; but," Gandalf continues, "that is not what I've found. I've found it is the small things, everyday deeds of ordinary folk, that keeps the darkness at bay. Simple acts of kindness and love."[20]

Gentleness and Zeal

What then of zeal? Does not the New Testament call us to be "zealous for good works" (Titus 2:14; cf. 1 Pet. 3:13; Rev. 3:19)? And yet here too a tension arises, for gentleness and zeal seem to coexist in believers in inverse proportion.

Consider the young seminarian whose zeal for doctrinal truth outstrips his communication of that truth in love and gentleness. Or the well-meaning Christian activist whose zeal for various valid social causes is communicated in a harsh tone that undercuts her otherwise noble intentions. Or the zeal of the inexperienced preacher who exhorts his people to live a life of full surrender to Christ, yet does so without the compassion of one who knows the complexity of life in a fallen world. In all such cases, otherwise admirable zeal lacks gentleness and is consequently emptied of persuasive power. This is not the kind of zeal to which we are called.

How then do we put these things together? How can Christians appropriately be both radically zealous and beautifully gentle?

---

[20] This quote is from the 2012 film production of *The Hobbit: The Unexpected Journey*. It is not found in the book, though it gathers together various disparate remarks of Gandalf's and is true to what the wizard would say.

Edwards helps us. On the one hand, he was one of Christian history's great champions of zeal. For he knew that Christianity that is never felt, that never exercises us, is no Christianity at all. "The holy Scriptures," he said, "do everywhere place religion very much in the affections; such as fear, hope, love, hatred, desire, joy, sorrow, gratitude, compassion, and zeal."[21] Edwards preached an entire sermon on the necessity of zeal.[22]

Spiritual zeal is laudable. It is the nonnegotiable calling of all Christians. "Be zealous" (Rev. 3:19). Jesus himself was zealous (John 2:17), as Edwards reminds us.[23]

Yet for all that Edwards said on the goodness and even necessity of zeal, he said even more about its danger. "There is nothing that belongs to Christian experience that is more liable to a corrupt mixture than zeal,"[24] he remarked. In a 1743 letter to Thomas Prince in Boston, he put it this way: "The degree of grace is by no means to be judged of by . . . the degree of zeal."[25] Again: "The devil scatters the flock of Christ, and sets 'em one against another, and that with great heat of spirit, under a notion of zeal for God."[26]

Edwards had seen in the revivals how elusive godly zeal is. For unlike those sins which manifest themselves in ugliness, misdirected zeal easily disguises itself as uprightness.[27] The same heart of pride can manifest itself in meanness in one person or in zeal in another, looking like vice in the one case and virtue in the other—yet the rotten heart being no different on the inside.

In 1954 a woman wrote to C. S. Lewis asking, "Why has sex become man's chief stumbling block?" Lewis responded:

> But has it? Or is it only the most *recognisable* of the stumbling blocks? I mean, we can mistake pride for a good conscience, and cruelty for zeal, and idleness for the peace of God, etc. But when lust is upon us, then, owing to the obvious physical symptoms, we can't pretend it is anything else. Is it perhaps only the least *disguisable* of our dangers?[28]

Sin is often disguised as zeal.

---

[21] *WJE*, 2:102.
[22] "Zeal an Essential Virtue of a Christian," in *WJE*, 22:136–55.
[23] *WJE*, 2:112.
[24] *WJE*, 4:460.
[25] *WJE*, 4:556.
[26] *WJE*, 2:88.
[27] This way in which sin can disguise itself as zealous morality is a recurrent theme in Robert Jenson, *Jonathan Edwards: A Recommendation* (New York: Oxford University Press, 1988).
[28] Walter Hooper, ed., *The Collected Letters of C. S. Lewis*, vol. 3, *Narnia, Cambridge, and Joy* (San Francisco: HarperCollins, 2007), 510, emphasis original.

The fallen human heart, even the fallen human heart that has been redeemed, is strange. When we take up the cause for what we believe to be (and what likely *is*) right, personal moral zeal easily, quietly, hardens the heart. Love evaporates. We do not self-consciously send love away. But our earnestness to see truth vindicated muffles other considerations—such as *how* such earnestness is communicated. Harsh assertions, even assertions of truth, are self-contradictory and counterproductive. In a sense, truth communicated in self-righteous zeal is untrue.

To put it another way: we quickly confuse our passion for the truth and our passion to be seen as right. Though the two often look identical on the outside, one cares about God's honor, the other about mine. How easy it is to act on that sense of truth violation we perceive in others when it wells up within us, yet the intense emotion of that moment may simply be a desire that we be proved right. It is alarmingly natural to pass off cantankerous or scoffing speech as concern for truth when really it is just a form of self-vindication. A healthy self-suspicion ought to accompany all moral zeal. And when gentleness is absent, that is a sign that our zeal is not of the Spirit but of the flesh. David Brainerd, whose diary Edwards edited and published, understood this: "Oh, the pride, selfishness, hypocrisy, ignorance, bitterness, party zeal, and the want [lack] of love, candor, meekness, and gentleness, that have attended my attempts to promote religion, and virtue."[29]

In his *Distinguishing Marks of a Work of the Spirit of God*, Edwards brings together both the necessity and the danger of zeal. "Lukewarmness in religion is abominable," he says, "and zeal an excellent grace; yet above all other Christian virtues, it needs to be strictly watched and searched; for 'tis that with which corruption, and particularly pride and human passion, is exceeding apt to mix unobserved."[30] Outward passion and zeal is just as easily the Devil's influence as that of the Holy Spirit (cf. Rom. 10:2). What is unmistakably from God is gentleness, broken-heartedness, non-showy humility. Hell can imitate zeal far better than it can imitate gentleness.[31]

In speaking of the danger of zeal more often than its necessity, Edwards echoes the rhythm of the New Testament. For while indeed believers are called to be zealous for good (e.g., 2 Cor. 7:11; 9:2; Titus 2:14; 1 Pet. 3:13; Rev. 3:19), more often the New Testament speaks of zeal as something

---

[29] *WJE*, 7:206.
[30] *WJE*, 4:243.
[31] Cf. *WJE*, 4:419.

either morally neutral or downright dangerous (e.g., Rom. 10:2; 13:3; 1 Cor. 3:3; 13:4; Gal. 1:14; Phil. 3:6; James 3:14, 16; 4:2). Indeed, it is among the works of the flesh—and not, with gentleness, the fruit of the Spirit—that Paul lists zeal (Gal. 5:20).[32]

How then are we to exercise true Christian zeal without sacrificing gentleness? How do Christians keep in step with the Spirit such that they obey both Titus 2:14 (be zealous) and Galatians 5:22 (be gentle) at the same time?

Edwards answers this in *Religious Affections*. His answer, in a word, goes back to the third chapter of this book: love. "As some are much mistaken concerning the nature of true *boldness* for Christ, so they are concerning Christian *zeal*. 'Tis indeed a flame, but a sweet one." How so? Edwards explains:

> For the flame of which it is the heat, is no other than that of divine love, or Christian charity; which is the sweetest and most benevolent thing that is, or can be, in the heart of man or angel. Zeal is the fervor of this flame, as it ardently and vigorously goes out towards the good that is its object, in desires of it, and pursuit after it: and so consequentially, in opposition to the evil that is contrary to it, and impedes it. There is indeed opposition, and vigorous opposition, that is a part of it, or rather is an attendant of it; but it is against *things*, and not *persons*. Bitterness against the *persons* of men is no part of it, but is very contrary to it; insomuch that so much the warmer true zeal is, and the higher it is raised, so much the further are persons from such bitterness, and so much fuller of love.[33]

And so Edwards concludes by bringing together both zeal *and* gentleness: "Therefore there is nothing in a true Christian zeal, that is contrary to that spirit of meekness, gentleness and love, that spirit of a little child, a lamb and dove."[34] On the contrary, Edwards goes on to say, true zeal fuels, rather than competes with, gentleness. Even in his sermon "Zeal an Essential Virtue of a Christian," Edwards defines zeal, intriguingly, in

---

[32] Most English translations have not "zeal" but "jealousy," but it is the Greek word *zēlos*, from which we get our English word *zeal*, and which in many other New Testament texts is translated "zeal."

[33] *WJE*, 2:352–53. On gentleness as subsumed within love, see also the first sermon in *Charity and Its Fruits*: "Love will dispose men to meekness and gentleness in their carriage towards their neighbors, and not to treat them with passion or violence, but with moderation and calmness. Love checks and restrains a bitter spirit. For love has no bitterness in it. It is altogether a sweet disposition and affection of the soul" (*WJE*, 8:136). See also *WJE*, 25:527.

[34] *WJE*, 2:353.

terms of love. The "affection that is principal in this virtue is love. Zeal is an inward heat or fervency of spirit, and love is the flame whence that heat comes."[35]

For many Christians today, zealous holiness is most immediately associated with outward fervency, vehemence, ardor, passion. A more truly Edwardsian vision of zealous holiness would instead be associated with the words "sweet, pleasant, charming, serene, calm"—as the following bit from his *Personal Narrative* testifies:

> Holiness, as I then wrote down some of my contemplations on it, appeared to me to be of a sweet, pleasant, charming, serene, calm nature, which brought an inexpressible purity, brightness, peacefulness and ravishment to the soul. In other words . . . it made the soul like a field or garden of God, with all manner of pleasant flowers; all pleasant, delightful, and undisturbed; enjoying a sweet calm. . . .
>
> The soul of a true Christian, as I then wrote my meditations, appeared like such a little white flower as we see in the spring of the years; low and humble on the ground, opening its bosom to receive the pleasant beams of the sun's glory, rejoicing as it were in a calm rapture; diffusing around a sweet fragrance; standing peacefully and lovingly, in the midst of other flowers round about; all in like manner opening their bosoms, to drink in the light of the sun.[36]

Gentleness and Manliness

Finally, some—I have in mind here my brothers—resist gentleness because they associate it with being effeminate. Strength and gentleness, courage and meekness, are viewed as mutually exclusive. As we picture what it means to man up and be a leader in the home and in the church, gentleness is not, for many of us, part of that picture.

Once more, the way forward is not by choosing gentleness over against manliness, but by rightly defining manliness. Is the Hulk the epitome of masculinity? According to Hollywood, perhaps, but not according to Jesus Christ. After all, if anyone was ever a man, a true man, he was. And yet while he could drive the money changers from the temple, he also delighted to gather up into his arms the little children whom his disciples tried to send away (Matt. 19:13–15). He dealt gently with outsiders. He wept

---

[35] *WJE*, 22:141.
[36] *WJE*, 16:796.

over the death of a friend (John 11:35). He welcomed healthy, manly physical affection with his dear disciples. The apostle John, for example, was (to translate the text literally) "reclining . . . at Jesus's bosom" (John 13:23—the very relationship said to exist between Jesus and the Father earlier in John, at 1:18).

The supreme display of Jesus's manhood, however, was in his sacrificial laying down of his life on behalf of his bride, the church. When the apostle Paul defines what it means to be a husband, he can speak simultaneously of the husband's headship and the husband's sacrificial, Christ-imitating laying down of his life on behalf of his bride (Eph. 5:25–33). Such sacrifice is not unmanly: it is the supreme display of masculinity. Any immature man can be a forceful, unheeding, unloving "leader." Only a true man can be gentle.

Men who long to be the leaders God is calling them to be must see that the glory of Christ, into whose image they are being formed, is the uniting together of awesome majesty and tender gentleness. In the sermon preached at David Brainerd's funeral, Edwards speaks of what saints in heaven will look upon when they see Christ:

> The nature of this glory of Christ that they shall see, will be such as will draw and encourage them, for they will not only see infinite majesty and greatness; but infinite grace, condescension and mildness, and gentleness and sweetness, equal to his majesty . . . so that the sight of Christ's great kingly majesty will be no terror to them; but will only serve the more to heighten their pleasure and surprise.[37]

True manhood, to Jonathan Edwards, is not a hard, tough exterior with a soft, spineless interior, but just the opposite—a steely, rock-solid interior mediated through an exterior emanating with the beauty of gentleness. Manliness is not machismo. Masculinity is not inadequacy-mitigating posturing and chest-puffing. On the other hand, gentleness is not cowardice. Both non-gentle masculinity and non-manly gentleness are to be avoided. What we are not after in the Christian life is cowardice clothed as gentleness. We are after a life that is both courageous and contrite, both tough and tender, both manly and gentle. Francis Schaeffer observed that it is relatively easy to show either one or the other of these two poles—either

---

[37] WJE, 25:233.

toughness or gentleness. But only in the power of the Holy Spirit can we be both at the same time.[38]

In God himself, as Edwards reminds us, these two poles are "admirably tempered together in the revelation of the Gospel: there is a proportionable manifestation of justice and mercy, holiness and grace, majesty and gentleness."[39] Thus the same man who wrote Galatians 3:1 ("O foolish Galatians!") and the searing tone of 2 Corinthians 10–13 also told the young pastor Timothy to engage his opponents "with gentleness" (2 Tim. 2:23–25). Paul said, "Be watchful, stand firm in the faith, act like men" (1 Cor. 16:13), *and* he said repeatedly to do all things with gentleness (Gal. 5:23; Eph. 4:2). How could this be? Edwards's answer is: whether he was sharply attacking or gently comforting, Paul was doing all in love. Paul was being a man.

A mature oak tree is immovable when the storms rage against it, but it is also beautiful, and provides shelter for others. This is the vision of Christian manhood painted for us by Jonathan Edwards.

Conclusion

The Princeton theologian B. B. Warfield embodied Edwards's vision of gentleness in the Christian life. Warfield's personal acquaintance F. T. McGill wrote, in a letter to a certain John Meeter:

> But if Dr Warfield was great in intellectuality, he was just as great in goodness. Over a long period of years this man stands out in my mind as the most Christ-like man that I have ever known. In spite of his brilliance of mind, there was no spirit of superciliousness, no purpose to offend the dullest pupil, no haughtiness of heart. . . . Rather there was always the spirit of humility and meekness and the spirit of kindness and gentleness toward others.[40]

This is what Edwards was after in his vision of gentleness. By the gentle life Edwards had in mind not cowardice or a lack of conviction but the calm and quiet strength of one who has been made alive to true beauty.

The turning point of Ephesians drives home Jonathan Edwards's insistence on the importance of gentleness in the Christian life. Taking a breath

---

[38] On this observation by Schaeffer see Dick Keyes, *Chameleon Christianity: Moving beyond Safety and Conformity* (Grand Rapids: Baker, 1999), 22.

[39] *WJE*, 4:463; see also 10:275; 16:416.

[40] Cited in Fred Zaspel, *The Theology of B. B. Warfield: A Systematic Summary* (Wheaton, IL: Crossway, 2010), 32–33.

after three exultant chapters that remind his readers of what God in Christ has done, Paul turns in Ephesians 4 to remind them what this means for their personal conduct: "I therefore, a prisoner for the Lord, urge you to walk in a manner worthy of the calling to which you have been called, with all . . ." (Eph. 4:1–2).

How would you expect Paul to finish that sentence? Having exulted in the truths of the gospel for three chapters, Paul now turns his attention to his Ephesian readers; he is not so much looking at Christ in light of the Ephesians but looking at the Ephesians in light of Christ.

We might expect something like "with all sacrifice," "with all zeal," "with all boldness," "with all fortitude." Paul says, "with all humility and gentleness." That is where the first three chapters of Ephesians take us. Jonathan Edwards understood this. The lofty theological discourse of Ephesians 1–3 funnels down, above all else, into an aroma of gentleness exuded by ordinary Christians in their ordinary lives. Yet such an aroma is not ordinary. It is extraordinary, supernatural. It is where the Spirit takes us.

CHAPTER 6

SCRIPTURE

The Treasure of the Christian Life

Communicating the role of the Bible in Edwards's life and theology is something like capturing the role of food in a chef's life. Scripture was in him. He ate it; and when he spoke, his words were filled with it. But not only that, Edwards's lifelong calling was to feed others with it. The Bible was both his own life source and his vocation.

When we immerse ourselves in Edwards's writings, we do not find him speaking *of* Scripture so much as speaking *from* it. The Bible was not only what he looked at but also what he looked with. It is thus a bit elusive to construct Edwards's theology of Scripture. Nevertheless, certain convictions about the Bible clearly emerge from the Edwards corpus. In this chapter we will identify several of them.

In short, Scripture—every word—is that through which God speaks of his own beauty. Scripture is God's tool of human beautification.[1] It is that through which God comforts and changes us. It is therefore the treasure of the Christian life.

Scripture Is a Treasure

I am calling Scripture "the treasure of the Christian life" here because this is precisely what Edwards calls the Bible. "What a precious treasure God

---

[1] For more on Edwards's view of Scripture, see Douglas A. Sweeney, *Jonathan Edwards and the Ministry of the Word: A Model of Faith and Thought* (Downers Grove, IL: InterVarsity, 2009), esp. 83–106.

has committed into our hands in that he has given us the Bible," says Edwards in his *History of the Work of Redemption*. "How little do most persons consider how much they enjoy in that they have the possession of that holy book the Bible which they have in their hearts and may converse with as they please. What an excellent book is this, and how far exceeding all human writings."[2] If Edwards had one metaphor to use for the Bible, this would be it: it is a treasure. Jonathan Edwards was the best kind of prosperity preacher. He believed vast riches were at believers' fingertips—not in what was in their bank accounts but in what was on their shelves: the Holy Bible. Ponder the power of a typically Edwardsian illustration:

> If there were a great treasure of gold and pearls hid in the earth but should accidentally be found, and should be opened among us with such circumstances that all might have as much as they could gather of it; would not every one think it worth his while to make a business of gathering it while it should last? But that treasure of divine knowledge, which is contained in the Scriptures, and is provided for everyone to gather to himself as much of it as he can, is a far more rich treasure than any one of gold and pearls.[3]

One of the great tragedies of a Christian life, to Edwards, is to own but neglect the Bible. This is akin to a sick man neglecting his medicine or a poverty-stricken man neglecting the inheritance that has just come to him. The Bible is to be plundered, not yawned over.

Kent Hughes tells a story of Mrs. Bertha Adams, who died alone of malnutrition in Florida in 1976. Her neighbors testified to her begging for food at their doors, and her clothes came from the Salvation Army. When her home was investigated, however, two keys were discovered to safety deposit boxes that contained stocks, bonds, securities, and cash totaling over one million dollars.[4] This is a picture of how Edwards viewed Christians who neglected the Bible. They are living in abject poverty of soul when the great remedy, the great treasure, awaits, needing simply to be accessed. "Whatever treasures the Scriptures contain," says Edwards, "we shall be never the better for them if we don't observe what is there. He that has a Bible, and don't observe what is contained in it, is like a man that has a box

---

[2] *WJE*, 9:290.
[3] *WJE*, 22:92; again, 22:95, 97–98, 101.
[4] R. Kent Hughes, *The Sermon on the Mount*, Preaching the Word (Wheaton, IL: Crossway, 2001), 205.

full of silver and gold, and don't know it, don't observe that it is anything more than a vessel filled with common stones."[5]

Why is Scripture a treasure? Two reasons—what the Bible recounts, and what the Bible is. First, we have in the Bible a record of what has happened in history for our sake—that is, we see what God has done, supremely in Jesus, for hopeless sinners. "Shall we prize a history," says Edwards, "that gives us a clear account of some great earthly prince or mighty warrior, as of Alexander the Great or Julius Caesar, or the duke of Marlborough, and shall we not prize the history that God has given us of the glorious kingdom of his son, Jesus Christ, the prince and savior of the world?"[6]

Second, more broadly, we have in the Bible the very words of God. This brings us to our next point.

Scripture Is the Word of God

It is a truism to call the Bible God's Word. But before moving too quickly past this conviction of Edwards's, consider what this meant to him. Edwards believed that *God speaks today.* Cessationist though he was, he believed that the age of God speaking clearly and directly to individual believers is not over. For this is precisely what God does in the Bible.

Every word of Scripture is God himself speaking. "Scripture is the Word of God, and has nothing in it which is wrong, but is pure and perfect."[7] Edwards did not believe God speaks only at times through the Scripture. He believed that every word of Scripture is, whatever happens subjectively in the reader's experience, itself the very word of God. And because God himself is utterly perfect in every way, so too are the words that proceed from his mouth and come to us in the Bible. Therefore, to the degree that we depend solely upon the Bible, Edwards argued, we depend upon God.[8]

God speaks. He has revealed himself to us. Knowledge of God is the one kind of human knowledge that requires more than the cumulative wisdom of human learning across the ages; knowledge of God requires that he deign to reveal himself to us.[9] He has done this in Scripture, his own word to us.

---

[5] *WJE*, 9:291; similarly, 22:97–98.
[6] *WJE*, 9:291.
[7] *WJE*, 2:143.
[8] *WJE*, 18:80.
[9] *WJE*, 22:86, 93.

Scripture Is Food

The food-and-chef metaphor with which this chapter began would reso-
nate with Edwards, because he himself calls the Bible our food. Reflecting
on the "pure spiritual milk" that the apostle Peter exhorts believers to long
for (1 Pet. 2:2), Edwards writes: "We may observe what the Word of God is
here called, viz. sincere milk. 'Tis compared to milk, for as the mother's
milk is the proper nourishment of one lately born, so is the Word of God
the proper food and nourishment of the soul that is new born."[10] Just as
we regularly take in food to nourish the body, so we must regularly take
in Scripture to nourish the soul. Neglect of the Bible is self-starvation. Re-
counting his own awakening in his younger years, Edwards spoke of the
Bible as "a refreshing ravishing food."[11]

This is not to say that the Bible itself has any inherent power, crassly
conceived. While every word of Scripture is God himself speaking, it is
possible for his words to land on deaf ears. The Holy Spirit must unstop
our ears and give us ears to hear the voice of God. Or to return to the food
metaphor, the Spirit must awaken our taste buds to enjoy the Word of God.

In the 1739 sermon "The Importance and Advantage of a Thorough
Knowledge of Divine Truth," Edwards distinguishes between two different
kinds of knowledge of Scripture. One "remains only in the head," while the
other "rests not entirely in the head or in the speculative ideas of things; but
the heart is concerned in it." Consequently, Edwards suggests, this latter
kind of knowledge "may not only be called seeing, but feeling or tasting."[12]
The crucial question is not whether we can explain what is in the Bible, but
whether we can enjoy it. Like a chef who has mastered an elaborate recipe
yet does not enjoy eating it, Christians can master what is in the Bible yet
not taste the succulence of it. This is not to say we should shun knowing
what is in the Bible.[13] We must know the recipe if we are to enjoy the dish.
"Such is the nature of man, that nothing can come at the heart but through
the door of the understanding."[14] But the dish is not made to be dissected
and scrutinized. It is made to be eaten.

In short, God must give us eyes to see the beauty of God that is before us

---

[10] WJE, 11:139; similarly, 24:40, 619, 1045.
[11] WJE, 16:797.
[12] WJE, 22:87.
[13] Cf. ibid.: "A spiritual and practical knowledge of divinity, is of the greatest importance; for a speculative
knowledge of it, without a spiritual knowledge, is in vain and to no purpose, but to make our condemnation the greater. Yet a speculative knowledge is also of infinite importance in this respect, that without
it we can have no spiritual or practical knowledge."
[14] WJE, 22:88.

in Scripture. Edwards thus stands in a great and ancient tradition that keeps together Word and Spirit, the objective and the subjective.[15] The Word without the Spirit produces doctrinaire hardness; the Spirit without the Word produces unpredictable flights of fancy. Edwards saw both in his day.

In order for Scripture to feed us, God the Spirit must soften our hearts and illumine our minds to receive it.

Scripture Is Supreme

As a late Puritan, Edwards inherited the unfettered devotion to the Bible that his forebears had passed down to him. Sunday mornings were not to be cluttered with stained windows, artwork on the church walls, ornate crosses, or anything frivolous built on human tradition instead of the Bible. Church buildings themselves were simple and straightforward, providing an atmosphere to suit a simple and straightforward overarching emphasis: the Word of God. All of life, and especially all of church life, was to be governed by the sole authority of Scripture.[16]

One implication of this is that when Scripture and one's own personal experience clash, we must defer to Scripture every time. "Experiences of Christians are to be brought to the touchstone of the infallible bar," said Edwards, "and to stand or fall by it; the Bible is not to be brought to their test and judged of by them."[17] Edwards's conviction was precisely that of German Bible scholar Adolf Schlatter when he was being considered for a teaching appointment in Berlin a century ago. Asked whether he "stands on the Bible," Schlatter responded, "No, I stand under the Bible!"[18] It is deeply counter-instinctual to doubt the validity of our own experience. But one reason God has given us the Bible is to correct what we would otherwise deem to be infallible human experience.

Scripture and Preaching

The Second Helvetic Confession audaciously asserts, "The preaching of the Word of God is the word of God." Such a claim makes us nervous. Are

---

[15] This point is made most strongly by Edwards in *Religious Affections*. See *WJE*, 2:55, 212, 230, 237, 462; see also 4:153, 216, 241.

[16] Cf. Sweeney, *Edwards and the Ministry of the Word*, 25–26, 58; Michael J. McClymond and Gerald R. McDermott, *The Theology of Jonathan Edwards* (New York: Oxford University Press, 2012), 495.

[17] *WJE*, 2:497.

[18] Quoted in Andreas Köstenberger, Scott Kellum, and Charles Quarles, *The Cradle, the Cross, and the Crown: An Introduction to the New Testament* (Nashville: B&H, 2009), 52. Schlatter received the appointment, as the university wanted a conservative scholar to be in place opposite the liberal Bible scholar Adolf von Harnack.

we losing the unique authority of the inscripturated Word in elevating the preaching of the Word? But understood rightly—namely, that when the Bible is responsibly preached, it is God speaking—Edwards would agree with the sentiment.[19] "That word that is preached is the word of God," preached Edwards in the summer of 1741. "And when it is preached according to his institution, you ought to look upon it as the sounding of the trump of God to give men warning and to call them to himself."[20]

Edwards believed that when he stood up to preach, he was himself the voice of God to his people. Receiving the words of a preacher, whether of Jonathan Edwards or the unknown but faithful preacher down the road from your own house today, a congregation receives the words of God. Rejecting the preacher's words is to reject God's words and thus God himself. The preached word is "the voice of the great God."[21]

What is preaching meant to do? How does the Word get from the page of Scripture to the heart of the listener in the pew? How is a preacher to handle the Bible? Let's consider, first, Edwards's hermeneutical lens (interpretation), and then his homiletical strategy (preaching).

Jonathan Edwards stands in a long line of Christian leaders who handled the Bible out of the conviction that the entire Scripture testifies to Christ. The Bible, while rich in diversity, is fundamentally, for Edwards, a message of salvation. He believes that to read the Bible without seeing the saving person of Christ throughout is not merely to omit an important portrait from the hallway of saints, but to fail to turn on the light that illumines the entire hallway. Christ is the key that unlocks Scripture. Without him, Scripture remains a disparate collection of mini-stories, pithy sayings, and moral exhortations, all empty of power.[22]

Beyond a generally agreeable conviction about the Christ-centeredness of the Bible, however, Edwards would make many evangelicals squirm with his insistently creative connections between earlier and later events and persons in the Bible—what Bible scholars call "typology." Using the word "typical" to mean "typological" (not "to be expected"), Edwards said that

---

[19] This confession goes on to explain what it means: "Wherefore when this Word of God is now preached in the church by preachers lawfully called, we believe that the very Word of God is proclaimed, and received by the faithful; and that neither any other Word of God is to be invented nor is to be expected from heaven: and that now the Word itself which is preached is to be regarded, not the minister that preaches; for even if he be evil and a sinner, nevertheless the Word of God remains still true and good." The Second Helvetic Confession was written in the 1560s by Heinrich Bullinger in Switzerland.
[20] *WJE*, 22:444.
[21] Ibid.
[22] Cf. McClymond and McDermott, *Theology of Jonathan Edwards*, 173–74; Stephen R. C. Nichols, *Jonathan Edwards's Bible: The Relationship of the Old and New Testaments* (Eugene, OR: Pickwick, 2013), passim.

almost everything that was said or done that we have recorded in Scripture from Adam to Christ, was typical of Gospel things: persons were typical persons, their actions were typical actions, the cities were typical cities, the nation of the Jews and other nations were typical nations, the land was a typical land, God's providences towards them were typical providences, their worship was typical worship, their houses were typical houses, their magistrates typical magistrates, their clothes typical clothes, and indeed the world was a typical world. And this is God's manner, to make inferior things shadows of the superior and most excellent, outward things shadows of spiritual, and all other things shadows of those things that are the end of all things and the crown of all things.[23]

Whether Edwards went too far and was overly creative in his typology is open for debate.[24] For now, all I am pointing out is that Edwards saw the sixty-six books of the Bible as a rich, interconnected tapestry of God's sovereign grace working out in the lives of his people across history.

God's supreme purpose in the pulpit, then, is "that salvation should be offered to sinners through the preaching of the gospel."[25] Edwards is famous for scaring people out of hell with divine wrath, but he labored far more to woo people into heaven with divine love. McClymond and McDermott point out that Edwards preached almost all of his hellfire sermons in the middle period of his life and ministry; by the early 1740s he no longer preached such sermons.[26] This was not due to a change in his theology, but rather more likely a maturing of his convictions about what the preacher is called to do and what the sermon is meant to do.[27]

Yet while the hellfire sermons died out, the sermons on the joys and comforts of heaven and the beauty of the gospel never left Edwards's preaching. The "principal means" (as he often called it) of saving sinners was preaching. He lifted up what he called "evangelical preaching" (preaching of the gospel) as the preacher's goal rather than "legal preaching" (bald preaching of the law). The sermons that would eventually become the treatise *A History of the Work of Redemption*, for example, are essentially reflections on the repeated and various ways God has deigned to show grace

---

[23] *WJE*, 11:51.
[24] We will return to this question in the final chapter.
[25] *WJE*, 1:286.
[26] McClymond and McDermott, *Theology of Jonathan Edwards*, 498–99.
[27] Later in life Edwards reflected back on his earlier preaching and noted that hellfire sermons had been apparently largely ineffective (*WJE*, 25:220; and see editor's comments on this reflection of Edwards's in 25:19, 209).

to those who deserve wrath, and how all of human history finds its true significance in Christ. This theology of preaching fits naturally with Edwards's broader theology of the meaning of the universe, as he believed the very reason for the existence of the universe is the overflow of the intratrinitarian love of God.

Scripture Is Beautiful

Finally, the Bible is the treasure of the Christian life because it is the word of a beautiful God. "By this is seen the excellency of the Word of God: take away all the moral beauty and sweetness in the Word, and the Bible is left wholly a dead letter, a dry, lifeless, tasteless thing."[28] And how does the Bible acquire such beauty? By speaking of Christ from start to finish. As the first sentence of an early sermon puts it, "There is scarcely anything that is excellent, beautiful, pleasant, or profitable but what is used in the Scripture as an emblem of Christ."[29]

The Bible is therefore the single most crucial means through which the Holy Spirit beautifies sinners.[30] A Christian's devotion to the Bible and a Christian's personal loveliness rise and fall together. The world today, and often believers, tends to view the Bible as arid, stuffy, old-fashioned, obtuse. Our hyper-pragmatism approaches the Bible for quick fixes and handy tips for life. We view reading the Bible like entering a mine: we might stumble onto occasional nuggets of helpful inspiration, but only amid foreboding and impenetrable darkness.

Edwards recalibrates us. This book is a book of beauty. A four-year-old may get quickly bored with a Rembrandt, but if he grows up to be a healthy human being, he will learn to appreciate its beauty. We who get bored quickly with Scripture need to grow up. There is rich and inexhaustible beauty here for those who have eyes to see. For this is God to us, until we see him face to face. "The Bible is a book, as it were, sent down from heaven."[31]

Conclusion

A dozen good things will clamor for your attention as you slide into consciousness tomorrow morning. More sleep, checking the weather forecast,

---

[28] WJE, 2:274.
[29] WJE, 10:535.
[30] WJE, 25:285.
[31] WJE, 17:303.

dishes from the night before, nervousness about some upcoming event at work, anxieties arising from broken relationships, worry about a new bodily pain, fretting over finances, e-mail and a million interesting websites. Some will have children to attend to. Such is life.

Into the frenetic bustle of normal everyday life, Jonathan Edwards invites us to join him in the Bible, that permanent eye of the storm amid life's chaos.

Our instincts tell us that the pace of our circumstances outside us must dictate the pace of our hearts inside us. It simply is not true. When read slowly and thoughtfully, the Bible does for the human heart what an inhaler does for a third-grader with asthma. It calms us down. Franticness is soothed. We become a little more human. We are given *God*.

Edwards told the Indians in a sermon preached a few months before he died, "God gave his word for the sake of men, for their happiness."[32] This is why you own a Bible. You don't own it mainly to win theology debates at Starbucks, or to supply a guidebook for decisions, or to extract four principles for a better marriage, or to amass handy tips for life, or to demonstrate to other believers how smart you are, or to provide a measuring stick by which you can show God what a dutiful Christian you are. You own a Bible to get happy through life-giving, soul-calming communion with God. To get a taste of what Eden was like, and a taste of what our final future will be like. "Show me the condition of your Bible," wrote A. W. Tozer, "and I will accurately predict the condition of your soul."[33] Edwards would agree.

Many Christians today relate experiences in which they believe God "spoke to" them. I don't doubt that God may have spoken to them, but why go to the slipperiness of subjective experience to hear God speak? You can hear his voice any time you want. Just flop open to any passage, Genesis to Revelation. A clear, objective word.

As my dad wrote in the first Bible he gave me, a Bible is the greatest earthly treasure one could possess. Take heed from Jonathan Edwards and make the Bible your food; let it be supreme; delight in its beauty. What Moses said to the people of God about the spoken word of God is as true for us today about the written Word of God: "It is no empty word for you, but your very life" (Deut. 32:47).

---

[32] *WJE*, 25:713.
[33] A. W. Tozer, *The Crucified Life: How to Live Out of a Deeper Christian Experience* (Ventura, CA: Regal, 2011), 20.

CHAPTER 7

PRAYER

The Communion of the
Christian Life

We would be hard-pressed to find a thinker across twenty centuries of church history with a higher view of the sovereignty of God than Jonathan Edwards. A new conviction of absolute divine rule over all things was the catalyst for Edwards's own conversion as he read 1 Timothy 1:17, and the doctrine of God's sovereignty suddenly "became exceedingly pleasant, bright, and sweet."[1] And it was a consistent theme throughout the rest of Edwards's life and ministry. He even identified divine sovereignty not only as a key doctrine to awakening sinners[2] but also as a common denominator to his most fruitful sermons.[3]

Yet for all his emphasis on God's utter right to rule over every event, Edwards did not fall into the caricature of Calvinistic theology that divine sovereignty undermines the necessity of prayer. On the contrary, few theologians—of any doctrinal persuasion—have held high the importance of prayer with more frequency and urgency than Edwards.[4]

We will organize this chapter by first focusing on what *God* does in

---

[1] *WJE*, 16:792–93.
[2] *WJE*, 4:175.
[3] *WJE*, 4:168.
[4] Prayer is not a highlighted theme in much recent Edwards scholarship; it is largely ignored in Michael J. McClymond and Gerald R. McDermott, *The Theology of Jonathan Edwards* (New York: Oxford University Press, 2012); and Stephen Stein, ed., *The Cambridge Companion to Jonathan Edwards* (Cambridge: Cambridge University Press, 2007). Doug Sweeney has a substantial and helpful footnote on Edwards's theol-

113

prayer, and then what *we* do in prayer. This follows the basic rhythm of how Edwards understood prayer—God promises, and we respond. To hear Edwards teach on prayer is not to hear mainly how we are to go about it, but who God is, in all his shining beauty, drawing us to pray from a heart freshly moved.

What God Does

Edwards's radical God-centeredness means that for him, from one perspective, God does everything in prayer—he makes promises to those who will pray, he prompts them to pray, he hears the prayer, and he answers in his own good way. As Edwards put it when writing about "efficacious grace" in conversion (i.e., grace that is not merely offered to but itself transforms the will), "God does all and we do all. God produces all and we act all. For that is what he produces, our own acts. God is the only proper author and fountain."[5]

In addressing Edwards on prayer, then, as in every aspect of Christian living, we bump up against the mystery of how divine sovereignty and human responsibility cohere. Both truths are clearly taught in the Bible, but how are they compatible? If God sovereignly rules over all things and has decreed every event, why pray? Isn't prayer, given God's sovereignty, like sending an e-mail to a nation's president requesting the termination of a bill that has already been signed irrevocably into effect?

Edwards cuts through much of the mental wheel spinning we might pursue by pointing out that what God does and what we do are not two portions of one pie, one decreasing as the other increases. Rather, what God does is a circle on which what we do is overlaid. The two do not squeeze one another out. They overlap. Our prayers are not outside the bubble of God's sovereignty, feebly but impossibly trying to dent it. Our prayers are inside that bubble. From the perspective of divine sovereignty, our prayers do not change sovereignly governed reality so much as they are themselves built into sovereignly governed reality.

Indeed, it is belief in a sovereign God that encourages prayer. If my next-door neighbors are not Christians and God is not sovereign, why would I pray for them? My only hope is to speak directly *to* them—not to

---

ogy of prayer in Douglas A. Sweeney, *Jonathan Edwards and the Ministry of the Word* (Downers Grove, IL: InterVarsity, 2009), 113–14n13.

[5] *WJE*, 21:251.

speak to God *about* them. What can God really do, anyway? But if he is sovereign—if he is the one finally responsible for the softening of my neighbors' hearts—prayer for them is not only sensible but crucial. God does all; and we do all.

Edwards's greatest contribution to the church's understanding of prayer in the Christian life is not, however, the more philosophical issue of how divine sovereignty coheres with our responsibility. His enduring legacy with regard to prayer is his lifting up of the beauty of God, drawing us to pray indirectly, with a special focus on God's unfettered delight in showering his people with gifts—the greatest of which is himself.

Ponder the main point of a 1740 sermon based on Luke 11:13 ("How much more will the heavenly Father give the Holy Spirit to those who ask him!"): "Of the more excellent nature any blessing is that we stand in need of, the more ready God is to bestow it in answer to prayer."[6] Edwards unfolds this beautifully in typically irrefutable Edwardsian precision. (As Packer once inimitably put it, Edwards "uncoils a length of reasoning with a slow, smooth exactness that is almost hypnotic in its power to rivet attention on the successive folds of truth sliding out into view.")[7] Edwards points out, first, that God delights to hear our prayers; second, that not all blessings God might give are equal in value ("excellence"); third, that the more valuable the blessing to the soul, the more eagerly poised to bestow that blessing God is, for this is *who God is*; fourth, that the supremely valuable blessing is God himself in the Holy Spirit, for he is the one "by which we are actually possessed of true holiness and happiness."[8]

So, concludes Edwards, the better the blessing, the readier God is to bestow it. Hear again the central sentence of that sermon: "Of the more excellent nature any blessing is that we stand in need of, the more ready God is to bestow it in answer to prayer."

This brings us up short as it sinks in. Our intuitions tell us: the greater the blessing, the harder to receive it. Surely God must be most reluctant, most parsimonious, in handing out the most valuable blessings? Edwards refutes this with Jesus's straightforward words in Luke 11. If evil people like us delight to give gifts to our children, how much more will the Father give the greatest gift, the Holy Spirit, to his children? Following Jesus's

---

[6] *WJE*, 22:215.
[7] J. I. Packer, *A Quest for Godliness: The Puritan Vision of the Christian Life* (Wheaton, IL: Crossway, 1990), 314.
[8] *WJE*, 22:214.

logic, Edwards concludes that to the degree a gift will shower down on a
believer joyous delight from heaven, God is eager to give it. He is not who
we think he is. Our natural suspicion of divine stinginess is a projection
onto God of the way we ourselves function and the way everyone around
us tends to function. With a generosity that defies our categories, we are
perplexed. So abundant a goodness silences us. It takes getting used to,
though in truth we never do.

The realities of our sinfulness and God's justice do not threaten this
goodness that God wants to shower down upon us, because Christ has satisfied God's justice by bearing the punishment for our sinfulness in our
place. Christ has cleared the way for divine blessings to pour down from
heaven's throne room. "Christ died principally to purchase blessings of the
most excellent kind. . . . God the Father is most forward to do that which
will most gratify and answer his Son's intercession."[9] God comes to us in
Christ, who "stands at the door with his blessing in his hand ready to bestow it upon us, waiting to see whether we will have it or no."[10] We do not
need to clean ourselves up first. We do not need to pray a certain length of
time or with a certain degree of intensity before God's ears are unstopped
to us. All we need to do is ask. "If you will open your mouths wide, he will
fill them."[11] He himself will come.

And what do we receive when we ask for the Holy Spirit, that greatest
gift that God is eager to shower down on us?

Edwards cannot be lumped in with those who neglect the Holy Spirit,
a common critique of the Protestant churches. Both personal experience
and the Bible brought him to give much attention to the Spirit in his writing and preaching. Edwards would go so far as to say that the Spirit is "the
thing purchased" in salvation.[12] While Christ made the purchase, the Spirit
is the gift bought. What we are given in regeneration is the third person of
the Trinity. We could answer the question What does God give us in the
gospel? any number of ways: salvation, forgiveness, hope, freedom, joy.
None of these, to Edwards, is the best one-word answer. In the gospel God
gives us the Spirit. That is what we actually, literally, receive.

Consider what Edwards is contributing to our understanding of what
it means to pray. Prayer is not simply an added task once one becomes a

---

[9] *WJE*, 22:216.
[10] *WJE*, 22:220.
[11] Ibid.
[12] *WJE*, 21:136.

Christian, an opportunity to bring our laundry list of requests to God for health and travel mercies, or something to feel guilty about for not doing. Prayer is God the Holy Spirit bringing us to commune with God the Father through God the Son. Far from arid drudgery, prayer is opening the door to "an infinite fountain of divine glory and sweetness."[13] We make prayer boring; God doesn't. You wouldn't blame the Sistine Chapel when the three-year-old begs to go home twenty minutes into the tour. It is the human's lack of capacity, not the object's lack of worthiness, that causes boredom.

Who God is, and what he promises to those who simply ask, brings us to our knees in fresh awareness of the unspeakably precious avenue of communion God has opened up in prayer.

What We Do

To sum up what we've said so far: God is sovereign over all things, including our prayers, and God invites us to pray with irresistible promises of what he will do as we pray.

Our job, simply, is to pray.

Much contemporary evangelical exhortation to pray fails to land on us with power because it holds out before believers the urgency of the task and how practically to go about it more than the beauty of the One with whom we are communing and the greatness of what he promises. But the way to motivate praying is not to focus on praying but to focus on God. You do not need to pull out *The Dummy's Guide to Verbal Admiration* when you stand before Victoria Falls in southern Africa. Beauty arrests us. The words of awe tumble out on their own.

This is what Edwards does. He paints a portrait of a God so lovely, so delightful, so eager to commune with us and beautify us through the Holy Spirit, that we are drawn up into prayer almost before we realize what is happening. In prayer, we are fundamentally pulled (by divine beauty), not pushed (by exhortation). Drawn, not coerced. Seeing who God is, through the coaching of Jonathan Edwards, we enter in to the joyous dance of heaven enjoyed by Father, Son, and Spirit from all eternity.

And yet after all his lifting up of the beauty of God to draw us into prayer indirectly, Edwards does have some concrete fatherly instruction for us. Having focused on God himself in the first part of this chapter,

---

[13] *WJE*, 16:801.

consider three tangible words of counsel Edwards leaves with us regarding prayer.

Soul-Concerned Prayer

First, we do not pray mainly for circumstances. Prayers of this kind are so common in evangelicalism today that this way of praying has come to feel, for many of us, normal. Consider your most recent experience of exchanging prayer requests in a group setting. What was shared? A biopsy coming back from the doctor, perhaps. A lost job. Upcoming travel. Political events. A brother's friend's father-in-law's niece's sickness. And even when we share requests about our own lives, we stick to the circumstantial. Our external, not internal, well-being. Our houses, bank accounts, and bodies—not our hearts.

To be sure, Edwards was always ready to exult in God's loving care for the details of our lives, "the compassion and kindness of a father" for his children's well-being.[14] But Edwards saw the vastly greater significance of what is happening to us on the inside versus what is happening to us on the outside, and the strange way we tend to treat the two in inverse proportion to their eternal significance when we pray.

Indeed, it is adversity on the outside that is often the catalyst for regained fellowship with God on the inside (Ps. 119:67). In 1745 Boston pastor Benjamin Colman's daughter died, following the death of another daughter, the debilitating illness of his wife, and the death of his associate pastor. Edwards wrote a moving letter to Colman with a desire that

> when you are thus deprived of the company of your temporal friends, you may have sweet communion with the Lord Jesus Christ more abundantly, and that as God has gradually been darkening this world to you, putting out one of its lights after another, so he would cause the light of his eternal glory more and more to dawn within you.[15]

In the sermon we have been drawing on above ("Praying for the Spirit") Edwards notes the way his people were quick to pray for the pouring out of rain when in a physical drought, but slow to pray for the pouring out of the Spirit in a spiritual drought.

---

[14] *WJE*, 23:582.
[15] *WJE*, 16:174.

If rain be withheld and there be a drought, everybody is concerned. It is spoken of and lamented how the grass withers, and how the corn dies, and what a poor crop there is like to be; and there is, it may be, a great deal of praying for rain. But there may be a spiritual drought year after year, and not only in their crop, but no harvest at all in spiritual respects. Souls may be generally withering and drying up. And God is not very earnestly sought to, not because God is not as ready to bestow these blessings as the other—for he is, as has been shown, more ready to bestow them.

Edwards goes on to say that if there is any chance of God giving us spiritual blessings, we would be wise "to seek them with vastly greater earnestness and diligence than we do temporal things, they being infinitely more necessary for us and will be so much more profitable to us."[16] But not only is there a chance of God pouring out the greatest gifts on us—he is delightedly eager to do so. The importance of this blessing and the eagerness of God to give it therefore expose "the absurdity of such a negligence" in failing to ask for it.[17]

In all this I do wonder if Edwards may have diminished the validity and value of ordinary, earthy, human life in the day to day. Jesus taught his disciples that God's care for his children calms their fears not only about questions such as "How is the state of my soul?" and "Where shall I be for all eternity?" but also "What shall we eat?" and "What shall we drink?" and "What shall we wear?" (Matt. 6:31). God cares about our everyday living and the circumstantial needs that are built in to it. In the same way that a healthy masculinity can morph into unhealthy machismo, so healthy spirituality can morph into an unhealthy superspirituality (a problem addressed in the Bible itself: Col. 2:16–23). Taken in an unhealthy direction, in other words, Edwards may encourage a sort of asceticism that emphasizes the doctrine of redemption to the neglect of the doctrine of creation, the eternality of the Christian life to the neglect of the physicality of the Christian life. We will return to this criticism in the final chapter.

But we will be slow to fault him. For even though "your heavenly Father knows that you need" the material things of everyday life (Matt. 6:32), a deeper priority exists: "But seek first the kingdom of God and his righteousness" (Matt. 6:33). And we live in an age today—which surely typifies all ages—that generally errs not in the direction of heavenly minded asceticism but earthly minded worldliness.

---

[16] *WJE*, 22:218; see also 25:203.
[17] *WJE*, 22:218.

Private Prayer

Second, Edwards reawakens us to the importance of secret, individual praying.

It is tempting at this point to trot out the usual statistics on how little time evangelicals actually spend praying. But that would do little more than evoke guilt and comparison of our own lives with the evangelical population. And anyhow, isn't prayer more than raw time spent? I can imagine a Christian without a prayer journal or prayer list or even a set time for prayer nevertheless spending much of the day in spontaneous prayer, moving through the day in a spirit of constant, brief utterances toward heaven. In short, spending the day communing with God, walking with Jesus.

But Edwards wasn't into guilt and statistics anyway. He was after the cultivation among his people of true communion with God. As far as Edwards was concerned, authentic praying takes place as the beauty of Christ is seen in quietness with God away from the eyes of the world, in "secret prayer and communion."[18] Edwards had felt the value of private prayer ever since he was a boy. A few friends and he built a private prayer booth out in the woods when he was young, and young Jonathan had a few other places in the woods where he alone would retire to pray.[19] Note what he would say years later in *Religious Affections*:

> Some are greatly affected from time to time, when in company; but have nothing that bears any manner of proportion to it, in secret, in close meditation, secret prayer, and conversing with God, when alone, and separated from all the world. A true Christian doubtless delights in religious fellowship, and Christian conversation, and finds much to affect his heart in it: but he also delights at times to retire from all mankind, to converse with God in solitary places. And this also has its peculiar advantages for fixing his heart, and engaging its affections. True religion disposes persons to be much alone, in solitary places, for holy meditation and prayer.[20]

Edwards goes on to ransack the Bible, bringing forth instances of God's people experiencing God most deeply, most truly, when alone.[21]

Edwards's point is that what takes place when no one else is around is

---

[18] *WJE*, 19:121.
[19] See *WJE*, 5:35; 6:7.
[20] *WJE*, 2:374.
[21] *WJE*, 2:374–76.

the truest gauge of where we are spiritually. Anyone can perform for others, including in prayer. But what do we do when alone? Who are we, in solitude? Edwards thus views secret prayer as definitive of authentic Christian living: "gracious affections"—that is, true Christian experience—"are of a much more silent and secret nature, than those that are counterfeit."[22]

Is this simply Edwards the introvert, to be chalked up to his own personal wiring? It's difficult to say yes in light of Edwards's complementary emphasis throughout his ministry on united, corporate prayer (which we will address below). And no one, extrovert or introvert, can dispute the words of Jesus: "But when you pray, go into your room and shut the door and pray to your Father who is in secret" (Matt. 6:6). Edwards himself retains the value of corporate religious experience in closing this section of *Religious Affections*: "Not but that we have also instances of great privileges that the saints have received when with others; or that there is not much in Christian conversation, and social and public worship, tending greatly to refresh and rejoice the hearts of the saints."[23] But his final word is a reiteration of the supreme value of secret communion with God. "But this is all that I aim at by what has been said, to show that it is the nature of true grace, that however it loves Christian society in its place, yet it in a peculiar manner delights in retirement, and secret converse with God."[24]

Our communion with God outstrips in importance our communion with one another. Reverse the order, and you get neither. If we place fellowship with others above fellowship with God, we lose not only fellowship with God but even the fellowship with others, for human fellowship is itself rooted in and informed by fellowship with God. We see this in Galatians, where Paul addresses Christian disunity with the doctrine of justification by faith. Vertical reconciliation, evidently, fuels horizontal reconciliation.

Private prayer, all alone with God, is the lifeblood of Christian living. Show Jonathan Edwards someone with well-worn knees, not eloquent words, and he will show you a growing, calm, happy Christian.

We need to learn this today. Do we truly believe that it is away from church and conferences, small groups and Sunday morning classes, chats over coffee and dinners with other families, that our sweetest communion with God lies? For all of us, there is an internal bewildering that builds over time when we neglect private communion with God. Who we are and who

---

[22] *WJE*, 2:374.
[23] *WJE*, 2:376.
[24] Ibid.

God is both fade. It is in withdrawal from everything and everyone to be with God that we re-center. It is when we are alone with him that there is least chance for playing games, wearing a mask, hiding our sins, covering our anxieties. It is then that we can most fully open our hearts up to God.

United Prayer

Third, complementing his focus on secret, individual prayer, Edwards serves as a stirring example of the significance of joint, concerted prayer. For all his emphasis on private prayer, he spent much energy and effort trying to get Christians on both sides of the Atlantic to pray together for the reviving and health of the church.

In February 1747 Edwards preached a sermon on Zechariah 8:20–22,[25] the title of which was "Prayer for the Coming of Christ's Kingdom." We have only an outline of the sermon, but it is clear from the notes we have that the burden of that message was the burden of the book he would write later that year: *A Humble Attempt to Promote an Explicit Agreement and Visible Union of God's People through the World, in Extraordinary Prayer, for the Revival of Religion, and the Advancement of Christ's Kingdom on Earth, Pursuant to Scripture Promises and Prophecies concerning the Last Time.*[26] The main point of both the sermon and the book was to generate united global prayer for the advancing of God's redemptive purposes in the world. "How beautiful, and of good tendency would it be, for multitudes of Christians, in various parts of the world, by explicit agreement, to unite in such prayer as is proposed to us."[27]

Edwards had been in touch with various Scottish pastors throughout the 1740s, and it was among his Scottish friends that the idea of a concert of prayer originated. He was in solid and enthusiastic agreement and undertook to advocate for occasional united days of prayer on his side of the Atlantic. Such days were organized from time to time, but Edwards was generally underwhelmed by the response.

All this funneled down into *A Humble Attempt*, a public call to unite in

---

[25] "Thus says the LORD of hosts: Peoples shall yet come, even the inhabitants of many cities. The inhabitants of one city shall go to another, saying, 'Let us go at once to entreat the favor of the LORD and to seek the LORD of hosts; I myself am going.' Many peoples and strong nations shall come to seek the LORD of hosts in Jerusalem and to entreat the favor of the LORD" (ESV).

[26] For more on the background of the writing of this book, see *WJE*, 5:30–89; Marsden, *Jonathan Edwards*, 333–35. It was not unusual for Edwards to set aside whole days for prayer and fasting, including a sermon exhorting the people to prayer. See, e.g., the 1741 sermon "Importunate Prayer for Millennial Glory" (*WJE*, 22:365–77).

[27] *WJE*, 5:364.

prayer for the outpouring of the Spirit and the advancement of the church's mission in the world. The preface to the book was signed by five prominent Boston pastors, but they were rather tepid in their endorsement of the book. This is apparently because of Edwards's controversial interpretation of some matters in Revelation, a point that generated mixed feelings about the book in George Whitefield too (ministers in Scotland were generally more positive). [28]

What can be undisputedly agreed upon and received wholeheartedly by Christians today, however, is the point of commonality Whitefield himself identified: that we "can heartily join with all those who pray for the coming of the latter day glory."[29] Jonathan Edwards defies the tired stereotype of the brilliant theologian holed up in his "ivory tower," aloof to the concerns of the world and real people. He *was* brilliant, but he wasn't aloof. For him, theology was for the sake of the church. Without the church, there was no need for theology. The notion of a gifted Christian pursuing *either* a career in academic theology *or* a lifetime devoted to the health of the church through preaching was, for him, a false disjunction. Edwards, the greatest philosopher-theologian America has produced, was also a great father to evangelical activism.

Edwards was introverted, no doubt. You don't spend thirteen hours a day in the study when you get your energy from being with people. But one aspect of the beauty of his life is that his introversion did not cause him to be withdrawn from the cares of thousands of ordinary human beings on both sides of the Atlantic. He followed intently, for example, the military happenings of the day, a concern uppermost in the minds of Americans in the early decades of the eighteenth century. Indeed, his February 1747 sermon on corporate prayer itself, cited above, as well as *A Humble Attempt*, arose in part out of not only spiritual but also political and military events. Edwards was not averse to aligning the French (and their Indian allies) with the antichrist, since France was a Catholic nation. British defeats of the French were not infrequently recorded by Edwards as possible indications of the advancement of Christ's kingdom.

That's a bit strange to evangelicals today, who tend to function with a strong separation between church and state. Yet what must not get lost in all of this is the simple observation of Edwards's commitment to corpo-

---

[28] See *WJE*, 5:86–87.
[29] Quoted in *WJE*, 5:87.

rate prayer. Flagging spiritual tenacity and fewer conversions across New England in the mid-1740s did not fundamentally require more sophisticated evangelistic techniques or more effective dissemination of Christian literature or more financial resources or more clever homiletical strategies, but prayer. Edwards wrote to a friend in Scotland, "It is apparent that we can't help ourselves, and have nowhere else to go, but to God." Therefore, "how fit is it that God's people, under such circumstances, should go to God by prayer." Edwards then added a poignant remark about how God's people should do this: "Oh that this duty might be attended with real meekness towards our opposers, lifting up holy hands without wrath; and that we may go to God, self-empty, brokenhearted, looking to God only through Christ, and without making any righteousness of our performances."[30]

Conclusion

What, then, we might ask in closing, *is* prayer? Is it the perfunctory obligation of bored Christians? Is it a superstitious ritual performed so that life will turn out the way we want it? Is it an attempt to change God's mind? Is it a means of personal psychological healing?

There are varying degrees of truth to all of these. But centrally, for Jonathan Edwards—as was emphasized especially by John Owen before him—prayer is the communion of the Christian life. Praying is fellowshipping. It is delighting in Another. We do not pray to a vague, hazy power. We pray to a Person. We commune with the triune God—speaking to the Father, through the Spirit who assists us, on the merits of the Son who has wiped away every reason for God to plug up his ears to us. Prayer is spiritual breathing; it is what we do spontaneously to survive, without which we suffocate.

Jonathan Edwards's contribution to the church regarding prayer is that it is seeing God, not commending spiritual discipline, that nurtures the Christian's prayer life. Edwards shows us that what we do in prayer only happens truly in the broader context of who God is.

Defibrillated back to life with a reminder of who God is and the access that has broken open to us in prayer, we turn to him once more, child to Father. "Of the more excellent nature any blessing is that we stand in need of, the more ready God is to bestow it in answer to prayer."

---

[30] *WJE*, 16:181.

CHAPTER 8

PILGRIMAGE

The Flavor of the Christian Life

Christianity is hard. One reason for this is the jarring tension between what we say is true of us now that we belong to God and what we experience day in and day out emotionally, relationally, physically, and all the rest. If we are God's children, we wonder, why is there so much senseless adversity in our lives? Such pain is disorienting for those seeking to walk faithfully with God.[1] The difficulty is not just that life is painful, but that life is painful despite the spectacular redemptive realities we believe have washed over us.

One answer Jonathan Edwards would give to this disconcerting experience is the believer's pilgrim status. A Christian is someone who has undergone a transfer of citizenship. We now belong somewhere else. Before new birth, we were at home in the world and strangers to God. After new birth, we are strangers in the world and at home with God. While this exchange results in new joy for the next life, it also results in new pain for this life. We are suddenly aliens here. Ambassadors, as Paul says—that is, someone who represents the king in a foreign land while their homeland lies elsewhere (2 Cor. 5:20). This world is not our home.

Edwards felt this keenly. In befriending him through his writings one gets the sense that he never really felt at home in this world. His somewhat

---

[1] As Edwards once put it, "we see that in this world the greatest prosperity don't always attend virtue, nor the greatest adversity always attend vice, but that it very often happens contrariwise" (*WJE*, 23:160).

idiosyncratic personality may have contributed to his sense of alienation, but does not exhaust it. He simply walked with God. His mind was fixed on things above. He exulted in this world no further than such exultation brought his mind to rest on another world. Edwards was out of place: blessedly out of place. Getting to know him helps us loosen the anchors of our desires from this world and lodge them in the next.

From one angle, pilgrimage is not a major theme of Edwards's theology of the Christian life. Most of his explicit references to Christians as pilgrims come in a single sermon and a smattering of letters.[2] Yet from a broader angle, the nature of the Christian life as one of pilgrimage informs his entire preaching and writing ministry. His words are soaked with a sense of exile.[3] This is why we are calling pilgrimage the "flavor" of the Christian life.

The Christian as pilgrim is an especially helpful theme to dwell on as believers because it brings together in a single metaphor two opposite but equally true realities of Christian living: misery and hope. We'll take them in this order.

The Misery of Christian Pilgrimage

On the one hand, our pilgrim status acknowledges openly the adversity we face in this life. "The saint all the while he is in this world, is like a pilgrim in a dark wilderness."[4]

To be a pilgrim is by definition to be a stranger. One does not pilgrimage through one's homeland. And as those making our way through a foreign land, we are beset with all the difficulties pilgrims in the ordinary sense face—being misunderstood by those at home in the world around us, getting lost at times, feeling out of place, suffering a sense of bewilderment. Ridicule, restlessness, longing. To be a pilgrim is deeply disorienting. It is social vertigo.

In short, there is a misery in being a pilgrim. "The going of long journeys is attended with toil and fatigue," preached Edwards, "especially if

---

[2] The sermon is "The True Christian's Life a Journey Towards Heaven" and is found in *WJE*, 17:427–47. See also the 1743 sermon "Saints Dwell Alone," in *WJE*, 25:51–52, and the 1747 sermon preached at Brainerd's funeral service, "True Saints Are Present with the Lord," in *WJE*, 25:227–28. Edwards also references the Christian life as a pilgrimage in *Religious Affections* (*WJE*, 2:114).
[3] I draw this language from a letter from J. R. R. Tolkien to his son Christopher in *The Letters of J. R. R. Tolkien*, ed. Humphrey Carpenter (n.p.: HarperCollins, 2012), 110.
[4] *WJE*, 19:730.

the journey be through a wilderness."[5] Jesus was speaking to this aspect of discipleship in Luke 9.

> As they were going along the road, someone said to him, "I will follow you wherever you go." And Jesus said to him, "Foxes have holes, and birds of the air have nests, but the Son of Man has nowhere to lay his head." To another he said, "Follow me." But he said, "Lord, let me first go and bury my father." And Jesus said to him, "Leave the dead to bury their own dead. But as for you, go and proclaim the kingdom of God." Yet another said, "I will follow you, Lord, but let me first say farewell to those at my home." Jesus said to him, "No one who puts his hand to the plow and looks back is fit for the kingdom of God." (Luke 9:57–62)

The life of an unbeliever is unavoidable acquiescence to the inertia of this world, like a jellyfish in the current. For, as Edwards would teach, we can only do what we love to do. Before new birth, we love sin and self. The life of a disciple of Jesus, on the other hand, having been granted a new love, is constant swimming against the tide.

Picture two descending escalators, side by side. One is filled with people standing still, slowly descending. These are those who belong to the world. The other is dotted with people running up the descending escalator, strenuously trying to go faster *up* than it wants to take them *down*. These are the pilgrims who now belong to Christ. Edwards spent his life warning unbelievers of the dangers of the first and exhorting believers to the striving of the second. "The way to heaven is ascending; we must be content to travel up hill, though it be hard, and tiresome, and contrary to the natural tendency and bias of our flesh, that tends downward to the earth."[6]

Christian pilgrimage therefore is filled with toils and trials. The very minor daily disappointments and frustrations of life take their toll. Small challenges have a tendency to slowly beat out of us a sense of destiny, the radiant beauty into which every disciple of Christ will one day be swept up. The faithful pilgrim refuses to let this happen. Christian pilgrims set their faces like flint toward the heavenly city and weather the ten thousand little adversities that wash into their life as the years roll on.

---

[5] *WJE*, 17:433; similarly, 17:439.
[6] *WJE*, 17:433.

When Life Implodes

It is not only, however, the general feeling of strangeness and being out of place, and the many little pains, that make the pilgrim's life so hard. What makes this pilgrimage especially difficult is that single adversity above all others that seems to befall most of those who walk with God.

Thomas Gillespie was a Scottish pastor who, like Edwards, had been rejected by his church. Edwards carried on a correspondence with Gillespie and from time to time spoke of their pilgrim status on earth. Shortly after being dismissed from his church, Edwards remarked to Gillespie, "I have much to teach me to behave as a pilgrim and stranger on the earth."[7] God was teaching both men that our pilgrim status is soberly reinforced by adversity. Indeed, the two elements of our pilgrimage, misery and hope, are mutually reinforcing. Our hardships compel us to place our longings elsewhere than in this world. "Men, if they would have Christ, must be cut down as to their worldly happiness," preached Edwards in 1741. "Men naturally place their happiness in the things of the world," with the result that "to part with all the world and sell all for Christ, is like death to them."[8]

"All your breakers and your waves have gone over me," says the psalmist (Ps. 42:7). It is striking how many seasoned saints who walk deeply with God have been through a very distinct experience. We might call the experience "adversity" or "suffering," and that would be true but perhaps too vague. I have in mind the experience of God's children when they are forced to embrace their status as pilgrims. This embrace is thrust upon them as they walk through the deep valley of a single instance of adversity or suffering so great that it cannot be handled in the same way as the various disappointments and frustrations of life. This particular adversity passes a threshold that the garden variety trials do not reach.

Consider visiting the beach. When we wade out into the ocean water, we immediately feel the waves beginning to come against us. First our ankles, then knees, waist, and so on. As we continue out into the water, though, inevitably a wave comes that cannot be out-jumped. It washes over us. We become completely submerged, and there is no way to avoid it.

That total-submersion wave is what Edwards knew God sends to his

---

[7] *WJE*, 16:387. As Lewis put it, "The world is so built that, to help us desert our own satisfactions, they desert us. War and trouble and finally old age take from us one by one all those things that the natural Self hoped for at its setting out" (C. S. Lewis, "Three Kinds of Men," in *Present Concerns* [London: Fount, 1986], 22; see also Lewis, "On Living in an Atomic Age," in *Present Concerns*, 78–79).
[8] *WJE*, 22:308.

children to drive home their pilgrim status and the hope that flourishes only on the other side of such pain. I do not have in mind bad grades, failed dating relationships, rejected applications for school or jobs, the flu, or resentment over being sinned against. These are certainly forms of adversity that can reinforce our pilgrim status. But they are waves that hit us in the knees or the waist. We lose our balance, but quickly get it back. We keep moving on, weathering the trial but essentially unchanged. We aren't *forced* to acknowledge that we are pilgrims. We can continue funneling our hopes and dreams into the things of this world. We are not compelled to change. Such trials wash into all of our lives with some regularity.

But those who live into their later years and are quietly walking with the Lord from a posture of fundamental trust have often weathered something deeper. At some point in their lives a wave washed over them that could not be out-jumped. And somehow they survived emotionally. They softened rather than hardened. Someone who has become a Christian and truly believes what he or she confesses to believe comes to a point in life where they must suddenly, for the first time, bank all that they are on that professed belief. Their true trust must be proved. It is not as though they didn't believe before. They did, with sincerity. But their belief to that point had been tested only by the gently lapping waist-high waves of garden-variety adversity.

To switch metaphors: it's the difference between saying you believe a parachute will float you safely to the ground and actually jumping out of the plane. It's the difference, Edwards would say, between merely professed affections for God and truly gracious affections. At that moment of life meltdown we are forced into one of two positions: either cynicism and coldness of heart or true depth with God as we welcome our pilgrim status. Either we remain citizens of this world psychologically or we embrace a citizenship above.

Saints like Edwards who exhale that depth of trust that makes them almost otherworldly have weathered a wave of adversity that has gone over their heads. Abraham is told to slit the throat of his only son. Jacob, at just the moment when he, about to meet Esau, needs God most, wrestles with God and is crippled for life. Moses kills a man and loses everything the world holds dear. David ruins his life through an afternoon's indulgence. Job reaps the nightmare of all nightmares. Or Jonathan Edwards, before he becomes a revered theologian, is publicly humiliated as he is rejected by his church by a vote ratio of ten to one while he has a large family to support and the prospect of extended unemployment.

When that moment comes looking for us, sent by the hand of a tender Father, we will either believe that what we said we believe has just been disproved, or we will believe that what we said we believe will sustain us. The two lines of professed belief and heart belief, to this point parallel, are suddenly forced either to align completely or to move further apart. We cannot go on as before.

Edwards prepares us for that over-the-head wave by instilling in us our pilgrim status. We do not belong here. There is nothing wrong with comfort, nice vacations, a good tan, and being liked. But we dare not give our hearts' deepest loyalty to such things. Jesus did not say we cannot have mammon, but he did say we cannot serve mammon (Matt. 6:24). If we do, we will never be compelling, magnetic, radiant people—people of *beauty*. We will be wispy, not solid. Our citizenship is in heaven. We are pilgrims.

The Hopefulness of Christian Pilgrimage

And yet the life of a pilgrim has hope built in alongside the misery. More than this, the Christian pilgrim has a hope that ever outstrips the misery. However deep adversity digs, the calm hope of Christian pilgrims digs deeper still. Edwards's reflections on the Christian life as a pilgrimage capture both of these elements, the hardship and the hope—and the supremacy of the hope.

After all, a pilgrim is—to state the obvious—on a pilgrimage. A destination is in mind. Our status as strangers in the world is not perpetual displacement, ceaseless wandering. We are journeying from point A to point B. "He that is on a journey, he is often thinking of the place that he is going to, and 'tis his care and business every day to get along, to improve his time to get towards his journey's end."[9]

And our destination is no temporary rest but final rest. It is paradise, Eden restored. One illustration Edwards uses is to point out that the sane traveler is not tempted to make even the nicest hotel his permanent home. He is simply passing through.[10] Amid all the "waves and breakers" that sweep over us in this life, small and great, we who belong to Christ have planted our hope elsewhere. It is invincible.

---

[9] *WJE*, 17:434.
[10] *WJE*, 17:431.

In the meantime, we enjoy here and now a foretaste of what we will enjoy fully and perfectly hereafter. In John 14:27 Jesus tells his disciples that he is giving them peace, but not as the world does. After all, they are pilgrims. Reflecting on this text while candidating at a church following his dismissal from Northampton in 1750, Edwards preached that Christ "had no earthly estate to leave to his disciples . . . but he had peace to give them."[11] Edwards had been forced in 1750 to grapple more deeply than ever with his pilgrim status. We have no home here, Edwards preached that day. But we do have peace.

By the standards of Hollywood and Wall Street, Christians are of all people most to be pitied. But bank accounts and social standing are not the truest measuring bar. Life in this fallen world often feels like walking through a tornado; but even in a tornado there is a calm eye of the storm. The eye of life's tornado is the calm hope of our final destination. Only this delivers true peace. We therefore remain calm and stayed on God when life upends us. We come to echo the sentiment expressed in a journal entry by David Brainerd, who stayed in Edwards's home for a time and whose journal Edwards read and published: "I hoped that my weary pilgrimage in the world would be short, and that it would not be long before I was brought to my heavenly home and Father's house."[12]

We cannot drive to work or go through the line at the grocery store without being bombarded by the flashy efforts of the multibillion-dollar advertising industry to plant our hopes in this life. Edwards reorients us to soul sanity. "Have you had that divine comfort," he preached, "that has seemed to heal your soul and put life and strength into you and given you peace after trouble and rest after labor and pain? Have you tasted that spiritual food, that bread from heaven, that is so sweet and so satisfying, so much better than the richest earthly dainties?"[13] In the course of our pilgrimage, there is a food that Hollywood does not know of (John 4:32). Not only can money not buy it; money may be a hindrance to the enjoyment of it.

Pilgrimage Is Not Ultimately a Sacrifice

One of the key contributions Edwards makes at this point is his penetrating insight that the final end of our pilgrimage includes the good things of

---

[11] *WJE*, 25:539.
[12] *WJE*, 7:172.
[13] *WJE*, 22:315.

earth. This is part of what makes heaven *heaven*. We do not trade in the good of earth for the better of heaven. We lose nothing. Our final destination is not heaven *minus* the joys of earth but heaven *including* the joys of earth.

Consider his application of this insight to personal relationships, for example, in his personal reflection on heaven: "When a saint dies, he has no cause at all to grieve because he leaves his friends and relations that he dearly loves, for he does not properly leave them." How so? "For he enjoys them still in Christ; because everything that he loves in them and loves them for, is in Christ in an infinite degree; whether it be nearness of relation, or any perfection and good received, or love to us, or a likeness in dispositions, or whatever is a rational ground of love."[14] To grieve that we are leaving behind earthly joys in gaining heavenly ones, then, is like the student grieving that he is leaving behind Poetry 101 for an elective on Shakespeare. The lesser joy is itself included in and heightened in the greater joy. There is no trade-off.

Or as he would put it in his famous sermon on Christian pilgrimage, "The True Christian's Life a Journey Towards Heaven"—

> God is the highest good of the reasonable creature. The enjoyment of him is our proper happiness, and is the only happiness with which our souls can be satisfied. To go to heaven, fully to enjoy God, is infinitely better than the most pleasant accommodations here: better than fathers and mothers, husbands, wives, or children, or the company of any or all earthly friends. These are but shadows; but God is the substance. These are but scattered beams; but God is the sun. These are but streams; but God is the fountain. These are but drops; but God is the ocean. Therefore, it becomes us to spend this life only as a journey towards heaven.[15]

How can a regenerate man or woman not be changed when reading that? Just a little bit? We know such a statement is true. But after days upon days simply living life—paying the bills, working through the marital arguments, fighting and sometimes succumbing to various temptations, worrying about the future, picking up meds from Walgreens—heaven fades from view. Left in neutral, our hearts slide away from enjoyment of God, and toward enjoyment of this world. Psychologically we slowly transition from being pilgrims through this world to being citizens of this world.

---

[14] *WJE*, 13:167.
[15] *WJE*, 17:437–38.

And then we read a paragraph like that. We read, "To go to heaven, fully to enjoy God, is infinitely better than the most pleasant accommodations here." Suddenly the lake home we have been dreaming of owning one day grabs us a little less forcefully. We are liberated. This life, we are brought to feel once more, is not our one shot at joy. We are pilgrims. Our true home, a home better than any that money could buy here, is coming—"an inheritance that is imperishable, undefiled, and unfading" (1 Pet. 1:4). So why not sacrifice the shadow for the substance, the drop for the ocean? Why not invest where it matters?

As Jesus himself taught, we're all amassing wealth; it's only a question of where (Matt. 6:19–21).

Conclusion

In the final sentence of an October 1753 letter to Thomas Gillespie, Edwards movingly wrote, "Let us thus endeavor to help one another (though at a great distance) in traveling through this wide wilderness, that we may have the more joyful meeting in the land of rest, when we have finished our weary pilgrimage."[16] Unlike most of us, when great pain swept into Edwards's life, he didn't become cynical and hard. He leaned into his pilgrim status. He coaches us in doing the same.

---

[16] *WJE*, 16:610.

CHAPTER 9

OBEDIENCE

The Fruit of the Christian Life

Of all the ways Jonathan Edwards can help us today, understanding true obedience may be the most pressing. And yet my guess is that when scanning the table of contents at the front of this book, readers would not be drawn most readily to the chapter on obedience. It wouldn't be my first choice. But Edwards is helping me here. Maybe he can help you too.

What is obedience? Doing what we love to do, out of a heart alive to beauty.

Sin is doing what we love to do out of an unregenerate heart; obedience is doing what we love to do out of a regenerate heart. Sin is living out of our natural impulse; obedience is living out of our new impulse, what Edwards calls the new sense of the heart.

This is why Edwards overlays the heart and the will.[1] We tend to think of these as distinctive elements in our behavior—what the heart loves, and what the will chooses. Edwards's great insight regarding true obedience is that the will only chooses what the heart loves. The two—heart and will—operate in tandem and cannot do otherwise.

The trouble is that we reflexively think of obedience as doing what we don't want to do. Ponder the word *obedience* for a moment. Don't you

---

[1] E.g., *WJE*, 2:255.

immediately think of that as submitting to what another wants us to do? I can either obey God, we think, or I can do what *I* want to do.

C. S. Lewis exposed this way of thinking with remarkable clarity in a little 1940s essay entitled "Three Kinds of Men." He points out that there are not two ways to conceive of obeying God but three. It is not so simple as merely obeying or disobeying. For even "obeying" can be done from a wrong heart. So Lewis explains that there are three sorts of people. The first live totally for themselves. The second know they should live a certain way, and they sincerely try to do so, but only after they have first ensured their own security and happiness. Lewis compares this kind of obedience to paying a tax—they pay it all right, "but hope, like other taxpayers, that what is left over will be enough for them to live on."[2] In other words, their time is divided, so that every action is either for their own sake or for the sake of this other, higher power, whether God, some ethical code, the government, their own conscience, or whatever.

The third kind of person, however, no longer has this divide. These people have killed their old self. They aren't trying to balance their internal desires and the external claim on them. The external claim has become their internal desire. As Lewis says, "The will of Christ no longer limits theirs; it is theirs. All their time, in belonging to Him, belongs also to them, for they are His."[3] Lewis then draws the following conclusion:

> And because there are three classes, any merely twofold division of the world into good and bad is disastrous. It overlooks the fact that the members of the second class (to which most of us belong) are always and necessarily unhappy. The tax which moral conscience levies on our desires does not in fact leave us enough to live on. As long as we are in this class we must either feel guilt because we have not paid the tax or penury because we have. The Christian doctrine that there is no "salvation" by works done to the moral law is a fact of daily experience. Back or on we must go. But there is no going on simply by our own efforts. If the new Self, the new Will, does not come at His own good pleasure to be born in us, we cannot produce Him synthetically.
>
> The price of Christ is something, in a way, much easier than moral effort—it is to want Him.[4]

[2] C. S. Lewis, "Three Kinds of Men," in *Present Concerns* (London: Fount, 1986), 21.
[3] Ibid., 22.
[4] Ibid. I reflect at greater length on this insight from Lewis in connection to Edwards in Dane Ortlund, *A New Inner Relish: Christian Motivation in the Thought of Jonathan Edwards* (Fearn, UK: Christian Focus, 2008), 100–103.

Others have picked up on this same idea that true obedience is doing what we love to do, when we love virtue and beauty and God. One sees this in Thomas Aquinas, Martin Luther, Blaise Pascal, Søren Kierkegaard, F. B. Meyer, Karl Barth, and Herman Ridderbos.[5] All these church leaders of the past have pointed out that there are not two ways to live (obedient and disobedient) but three: disobedient, sullenly obedient, and joyfully obedient. And, of course, since we are commanded to obey joyfully, sullen obedience is in fact disobedience.

Along with Lewis and others, Edwards understood that it is easy and natural for Christians to slip into a kind of obedience akin, as Lewis puts it, to tax paying—we'll pay it, all right, but we hope after we've done so we can finally do what *we* want to do. Edwards returned to this theme time and again in his preaching and writing: real obedience is living out of a new sense of the heart, in which God and holiness now appear beautiful rather than ugly. This is the basic point of Edwards's treatise *The Nature of True Virtue*[6]—namely, that anyone can behave in a morally upright way out of self-love, but true virtue behaves a certain way out of a heart that is drawn to God and his beauty. There are two ways to obey God: false virtue and true virtue. "There are two kinds of persons among God's professing people," Edwards opens one 1740 sermon. "The one are the truly godly . . . and the other are the sinners in Zion, or hypocrites."[7]

Will the church today allow itself to be instructed by Jonathan Edwards at this point? If so, many who are not born again at all will come to see their true situation. And many who are born again but treating obedience like tax paying will settle into the soul joy for which they were saved in the first place.

Many of the themes already treated in this book could easily be brought to bear on Edwards's theology of obedience. Joy, gentleness, prayer, and, above all, love are all important elements of Edwards's thinking on obeying God. Indeed, this whole book, really, is a book on obedience. To avoid unnecessary repetition, then, we will highlight here some aspects of Christian obedience that have not been developed to this point.

[5] A. M. Fairweather, ed., *Aquinas on Nature and Grace: Selections from the Summa Theologica* (Louisville: Westminster John Knox, 2006), 144; Martin Luther, "The Three Kinds of Good Life for the Instruction of Consciences," in *Luther's Works*, vol. 44, *The Christian in Society I*, ed. James Atkinson (Philadelphia: Fortress, 1966), 235–42; Blaise Pascal, *Pensées* (Middlesex, UK: Penguin, 1995), 52; Claire Carlisle, *Kierkegaard: A Guide for the Perplexed* (London: Continuum, 2006), 77–83; F. B. Meyer, *The Directory of the Devout Life* (London: Morgan & Scott, 1904), 148–51; Karl Barth, *Church Dogmatics*, ed. G. W. Bromiley and T. F. Torrance (Edinburgh: T&T Clark, 1961), IV/3:461–62; Herman Ridderbos, *Paul: An Outline of His Theology*, trans. John Richard de Witt (Grand Rapids: Eerdmans, 1975), 137–40.
[6] *WJE*, 8:537–628.
[7] *WJE*, 22:265; see also 22:268, 278–79.

Obedience Is Fruit

What is fruit? Some of our favorite foods, of course—apples, oranges, and all the rest. But how does the Bible speak of fruit? Not simply as the juicy reproductive body of various seed plants found in warmer climates of the world. The Bible uses the metaphor of fruit, rather, to speak of the positive visible result of internal health. "You will recognize them by their fruits," Jesus said (Matt. 7:16, 20). Recognize whom? False teachers, "who come to you in sheep's clothing but inwardly are ravenous wolves" (Matt. 7:15). A hungry wolf, Jesus is saying, can look like a sheep only in terms of clothing—not in terms of actions. Elsewhere Jesus returns to the fruit metaphor: "Either make the tree good and its fruit good, or make the tree bad and its fruit bad, for the tree is known by its fruit" (Matt. 12:33). As goes internal health, so goes external result.

This, for Edwards, gets to the essence of Christian obedience.[8] This is why I am calling this chapter the fruit of the Christian life. The heart of obedience is not summoning the will to do what it loathes. Rather, obedience is fruit—it is the outward manifestation of internal health. We naturally blossom because we are planted in the soil of the gospel with the sun of divine grace shining down on us. Obedience does not come out of a new raw power to now do what we don't want to do; obedience comes because we now delight to do what we hated before. To obey is thus not to mechanically force our behavior into line with God's moral law so much as it is living out of a new delight in God. Burgeoning bank accounts, lavish vacations, orgasmic pleasure, celebrity-like fame—such things have lost their luster. We have God. We have seen real beauty.

A further implication of viewing obedience as fruit is that the fruit of a tree is not the root. The root is cause; the fruit is effect. A truth that was precious to Jonathan Edwards is that authentic obedience does not cause our salvation but is the fruit of salvation. In 1734 Edwards began a sermon series on justification by faith. Looking back years later, he said that this series was the cause for the local revival of those years. The key text was Romans 4:5, and especially the bit about God justifying the ungodly. Edwards preached that there is nothing whatsoever in the believer that contributes to his justification (being legally declared just or righteous in the divine courtroom). Not even human faith justifies us, for that would still make

---

[8] E.g., *WJE*, 2:185. At times Edwards used "fruit" as a virtual replacement synonym for obedience (e.g., *WJE*, 2:422, 424).

justification dependent on us. Rather, we are justified by being united to Christ, and while faith connects us to Christ, faith is not itself a work, but simply the apprehending of Christ. Faith is not working; it is looking. Obedience does not contribute to, validate, strengthen, or in any other way help our standing.[9] Edwards had made the same point in *Religious Affections*.[10] Obedience is fruit, not root.

Obedience Is Required for Salvation

And yet there is a tension built into Edwards's understanding of obedience at this point, and it is a tension he does not add to the Bible but which he takes from the Bible itself.

While we are not saved by our obedience, we are not saved without it. Obedience is necessary for salvation. "There is a keeping of God's commands that the Scripture from time to time speaks of as necessary to salvation, and always accompanying a title to salvation."[11] The twelfth and final sign of authentic spirituality in *Religious Affections* is given to the necessity of "practice" (actual obedience) in the life of the Christian, and this is by far the longest treatment of the twelve signs.[12]

The Bible says that we are not saved by our works (Eph. 2:8–9; 2 Tim. 1:9; Titus 3:5) and also that we are not saved without them (Heb. 12:14; James 2:14–26). Letters such as Galatians and Colossians were written to those who thought they could be saved by their works, while letters such as 2 Peter and Jude were written to those who thought they could be saved without obedience. Both assumptions were wrong.

The necessity of obedience for salvation may be disconcerting at first sight to evangelicals standing in the historic stream of the Reformation (as I do). And yet we are familiar with this logic in everyday life. A baby is not given life by her breathing. She is given life by her mother and father. But she cannot live without breathing. Flowers do not exist because they blossom. They exist because someone (such as a gardener) or something (such as a gust of wind) placed a tiny seed in the earth. But a healthy flower will necessarily blossom.[13] An airplane doesn't exist because of its wings, but

---

[9] *WJE*, 19:234–35.
[10] *WJE*, 2:456.
[11] *WJE*, 25:529.
[12] *WJE*, 2:383–461.
[13] Cf. Edwards: "The external heaven surrounds Christ not merely as an house surrounds an inhabitant, or as a palace surrounds a prince, or as stones and timber encompass a land; but rather as plants and flowers are before the sun, that have their life and beauty and being from that luminary" (*WJE*, 20:494–95).

because of a group of engineers and mechanics. But it will never get off the ground without wings. We understand that something can be necessary to the existence of an object but not causative of the object's existence.

Here's how Edwards puts it:

> We are said to be justified by faith alone: that is, we are justified only because our souls close and join with Christ the Savior, his salvation, and the way of it, and not because of the excellency or loveliness of any of our dispositions or actions that moves God to it. And we are justified by obedience or good works only as a principle of obedience or a holy disposition is implied in such a harmonizing or joining, and is a secondary expression of the agreement and union between the nature of the soul and the gospel, or as an exercise and fruit and evidence of faith.[14]

Translation: Yes, in some far-off way we might say we are justified by our obedience. But only in this way—we are freely justified by being graciously united to Christ, yet it is this very union from which authentic obedience springs.[15] Therefore we are not justified by our works, but no one in a justified state will be found without them.

Here's another way to understand the necessity of obedience from Edwards's point of view. When we obey, we are simply carrying out what we say we believe to be true. If we truly believe that Christ is our greatest treasure, and sin our greatest danger, and God the loveliest beauty, then we will live a certain way. It is the person who actually jumps out of the airplane who believes his parachute will carry him safely to the ground. What we do reveals what we believe. "To depend upon the word of another is so to believe it as to dare to act upon it as if it were really true."[16] The obedience of our hands reflects the doctrine of our hearts.[17]

Consider what Edwards is saying in light of the state of the evangelical church today. Something of a gospel renaissance has been taking place in

---

[14] WJE, 13:476.
[15] Note, similarly, Turretin: "As faith is the instrument of justification by receiving the righteousness of Christ, so it is the root and principle of sanctification, while it purges the heart and works through love. Justification itself (which brings the remission of sins) does not carry with it the permission or license to sin (as the Epicureans hold), but ought to enkindle the desire of piety and the practice of holiness. . . . Thus justification stands related to sanctification as the means to the end" (Francis Turretin, *Institutes of Elenctic Theology*, ed. James T. Dennison Jr., trans. George Musgrave Giger, vol. 2 [Phillipsburg, NJ: P&R, 1994], 692–93). Michael J. McClymond and Gerald R. McDermott briefly compare Edwards's moral vision to Turretin's in *The Theology of Jonathan Edwards* (New York: Oxford University Press, 2012), 547.
[16] WJE, 21:426.
[17] Cf. Conrad Cherry, *The Theology of Jonathan Edwards: A Reappraisal*, rev. ed. (Bloomington, IN: Indiana University Press, 1990), 127–28.

recent years across evangelicalism. I happily consider myself part of it. As must happen in every generation, the utter gratuity of the gospel of grace is enjoying widespread reassertion. I love what I am seeing.

But I am asking myself and my readers: Will we allow ourselves to be instructed by Jonathan Edwards's vision of authentic obedience?

On the one hand, Edwards perceived as well as any of today's "gospel-centered" preachers and thinkers that we are all inveterate legalists—the natural human impulse to earn our internal okayness is deeply hard-wired into us, and only regular bathing in the gospel of free grace to us failures can begin to calm down our works-oriented hearts. "'Tis inexpressible, and almost inconceivable," says Edwards in *Religious Affections*, "how strong a self-righteous, self-exalting disposition is naturally in man; and what he will not do and suffer, to feed and gratify it."[18] He goes on to say:

> There are some that are abundant in talking against *legal doctrines*, *legal preaching*, and a *legal spirit*, who do but little understand the thing they talk against. A *legal spirit* is a more subtle thing than they imagine, it is too subtle for them. It lurks, and operates, and prevails in their hearts, and they are most notoriously guilty of it, at the same time, when they are inveighing against it.[19]

Edwards knew how law-ish we really are, deep inside. I use the word "law-ish" because that is roughly how Paul speaks, in texts such as Galatians 3:10, of those who are simply "of works" (similarly Rom. 9:32). Paul seems to be speaking not simply of what we do or what we believe, but of what we are *of*. As the gospel sinks in more and more deeply as we walk with God, one of the first outer shells of our old life that the gospel pierces is the *doing* of works unto approval. But there is another, deeper level—instinct level, "of-ness" level—that must be gradually deconstructed and shed too. This is what Edwards means by "a legal spirit." One can go through the whole day trumpeting the futility of doing works to please God, all the while saying the right thing from an "of works" heart. Jonathan Edwards understood the dangers of legalism.

Yet, at the same time, he could never be accused of the moral laxity that some of today's gospel preachers seem to be encouraging. The way some are preaching and writing these days, it sounds as if the gospel of grace *replaces*

---

[18] *WJE*, 2:315.
[19] *WJE*, 2:317; similarly, 2:173.

the pursuit of holiness rather than *fuels* it. Edwards rejected any either–or when it comes to earnest obedience and gospel centrality. So should we. The Christian life is "the single-minded pursuit of holiness," he wrote.[20] And yet this is a pursuit of personal holiness that is the flowering of one who has already been fully "holy-fied," sanctified, made clean, by a work of divine grace. The pursuit of personal holiness without a heart-sense of positional holiness is legalism.

Adopted children, when they realize what's happened to them, *want* to please their magnanimous father. Not all attempts to please God are moralistic. When we communicate that they are, we are being reductionistic and one-dimensional. A one-to-one correspondence between seeking to please God and works-righteousness simply cannot be sustained if we submit to the New Testament in its entirety.

Obedience is required for final salvation.

Obedience Is Universal

For Jonathan Edwards, obedience is not selective. It is universal.[21] To seek to yield ourselves to God in every area of life except one is proof that we are still in love with sin. We are making a deal with our conscience. A trade-off. We agree to surrender in these areas over here, as long as we can retain and coddle this cherished selfism over there.[22] Such a strategy feels virtuous, perhaps, but it is self-deception. Trade-off morality is not morality; it is immorality because it exposes what we really want: self and sin. Thus Edwards spoke repeatedly of "universal obedience," by which he meant a consistent pattern of holiness.[23]

True Christian obedience does not bargain like this. Such bargaining indicates that our moral life is still largely externalized rather than internalized. However we're behaving on the outside, our *desire* is still to sin. In Lewis's terms, we are the second kind of person. But it is Lewis's third kind of person that describes an Edwardsian theology of Christian obedience.

Thus even good intentions are not enough if they do not issue in obedience. For good intentions without the follow-through of actual deeds simply expose the true state of the heart. Edwards creates a delightful word at

---

[20] *WJE*, 13:44.
[21] In this Edwards echoes a major theme in the writings of John Owen on the mortification of sin. See, e.g., Sinclair Ferguson, *John Owen on the Christian Life* (Edinburgh: Banner of Truth, 1987), 150.
[22] *WJE*, 14:260.
[23] E.g., *WJE*, 2:384–90; 13:460.

this point—"wouldings." "That religion which God requires, and will accept, does not consist in weak, dull and lifeless wouldings."[24] True obedience issuing from new birth is not intention, but action; not *would*, but *will*.

All this is not to say that a "besetting" sin is a sign of being unregenerate. We are all weak in different ways, the regenerate as well as the unregenerate. While we may *be* more sinful before new birth, we generally *feel* more sinful after new birth.[25] Though we sin less, the sin that remains throbs more painfully within the soul.

How then do we make sense of repeated falling into sin, even as believers? What would Jonathan Edwards say to that?

We don't need to wonder. Edwards directly addresses this. He himself was accused in his day of promoting a view of the Christian life which, because of its high view of new birth and the new inclination toward holiness accompanying it, fails to allow for the moral messiness of our lives even as believers. Edwards acknowledged openly that "true saints may be guilty of some kinds and degree of backsliding."[26] But in the wake of sin they are convicted. Their hearts do not remain hard, but eventually soften. Sin is mourned.

The key here is this: the truly regenerate are dismayed over their sins, while the unregenerate go on untroubled. There is a profound pastoral point here for all of us. The real question for us is not whether we sin or not. We do, and we will. The question is whether we are bothered by our sin or not.

What we are saying in all this is that Christian obedience is not a list to be checked off the way Ben Franklin sought to build morality into his life one virtue at a time—acquire patience, then move on to temperance; once that is achieved, proceed to generosity, and so on. Rather, we are either inclined toward holiness or we aren't.[27] Obedience is universal. This is why Paul called obedience "the fruit of the Spirit" and not "the fruits of the Spirit." Love, joy, peace, patience, kindness, and all the rest are not disconnected virtues to be cultivated one by one. They are rather all manifestations of a single reality: new birth, having been made alive to the beauty of God. It is one thing to fall into a sin, even repeatedly. It is another thing to *live* in sin contentedly.

---

[24] *WJE*, 2:99.
[25] Cf. *WJE*, 2:172–73.
[26] *WJE*, 2:390.
[27] Cf. McClymond and McDermott, *Theology of Jonathan Edwards*, 546–47.

Obedience Is Beautiful

Obedience, then, is a matter of beauty. Apprehending divine beauty, we move toward what we see. We are pulled, not pushed. Just as a man who has been living in darkness is naturally drawn toward the light, a sinner who has been regenerated is naturally drawn toward obedience.

Sin is false beauty. It is ugliness masquerading as loveliness. In the ancient Greek myth *The Odyssey* by Homer, the sirens' song is enchantingly beautiful, so beautiful that sailors passing by in their boats would jump into the water, dashing themselves upon the rocks, to try to get close to that beauty. This is what sin is. It is an enchanting song that kills. Ulysses therefore has his men plug their ears as they row by and strap him to the mast so that he can hear their song without endangering himself.

When Jason (of Jason and the Argonauts) sails by, he employs a different strategy. Instead of being tied to the mast like Ulysses, Jason brings with him a harp-player whose music is so lovely, even more beautiful than the sirens' song, that the sirens' enticement is emptied of its power. A superior beauty has inoculated Jason against deadly temptation.[28]

This is precisely Jonathan Edwards's vision of obedience. We do not obey out of willpower, restraining ourselves from doing what we want to do by tying ourselves to the mast of self-control. Rather, our true affections have been directed to something much less deadly and much more beautiful: Christ. The issue once more is what we love. We can only do what we delight to do, whether that is quietly sending an anonymous check to a family in need or viewing pornography in the darkness of a solitary dorm room.

This is not to say that the Christian life is devoid of struggle. On the contrary, new birth is the beginning, not the ceasing, of real struggle. And many times we will fail. In the final chapter of this book I will criticize Edwards for neglecting the need *Christians* have for the gospel. Nevertheless, when we do obey truly, it is not the result of forcing the will, but of delighting in Christ.

To draw together many of the themes of this book, consider the conclusion to the early and programmatic sermon "The Way of Holiness":

> Holiness is a most beautiful, lovely thing. Men are apt to drink in strange
> notions of holiness from their childhood, as if it were a melancholy, mo-

---

[28] I am grateful to Sam Storms for first introducing me to this illustration in a systematic theology class at Wheaton College in 2001.

rose, sour, and unpleasant thing; but there is nothing in it but what is sweet and ravishingly lovely. 'Tis the highest beauty and amiableness, vastly above all other beauties; 'tis a divine beauty, makes the soul heavenly and far purer than anything here on earth—this world is like mire and filth and defilement compared to that soul which is sanctified—'tis of a sweet, lovely, delightful, serene, calm, and still nature.

Edwards goes on to speak of holiness as "above all the heathen virtue, of a more bright and pure nature, more serene, calm, peaceful, and delightsome. What a sweet calmness, what a calm ecstasy, doth it bring to the soul. . . . How doth it change the soul, and make it more pure, more bright, and more excellent than other beings."[29] The holiness of obedience is not raw duty; it is beauty. Holiness gentle-izes us. The RPMs of our frantic hearts calm down.

Notice how Edwards speaks here of holiness as a matter of the soul. This is critical to understand about authentic obedience: it is centrally about what is happening in our souls, not by our hands. To be sure, if beauty is alive in our souls, our hands will work. But hands can work apart from anything beautiful taking place inside us—as Jesus made clear when he said to the scribes and Pharisees, "You are like whitewashed tombs, which outwardly appear beautiful, but within are full of dead people's bones and all uncleanness" (Matt. 23:27).[30]

Obedience, then, is inside-out. In a strange verse in Titus, Paul tells the younger pastor, "To the pure, all things are pure, but to the defiled and unbelieving, nothing is pure; but both their minds and their consciences are defiled" (Titus 1:15). One of the marks of the moralism infecting our hearts is viewing Christian growth as outside-in rather than inside-out. Rules are set up to avoid TV and alcohol and laziness and yelling and certain films, and to demand certain amounts of giving and service and time spent at church and Sabbath observance and daily reading large chunks of Scripture (rather than however much it takes to commune with God) and daily praying at set times (rather than to enjoy and admire God, whether that takes five minutes or an hour) and so on. In all of these examples, an object (rule) is expected to transform the subject (person), the external shaping the internal. According to Paul's words to Titus, the subject is meant to transform

---

[29] *WJE*, 10:478–79.
[30] Cf. *WJE*, 2:172–73.

how he views objects. The internal determines how we view the external. To the one who has been made pure and is being made pure, and for whom such purity is the dominant chord of life, all things are pure (cf. Titus 1:15). The point is not, fundamentally, what one views. The point is what kind of eyes are used to view it.

Certainly there is godly wisdom in avoiding certain domains of worldliness. There are certain films we simply must not watch. And much TV is spiritually numbing. That's not the point. The point is that abstinence from such things will not transform us. You can train a chimpanzee to act in certain ways, but it will still be a chimp on the inside. True Christian obedience is inside-out. When a Guinness TV commercial stated, "The choices we make reveal the true nature of our character," these beer marketers were making an Edwardsian statement.

A final point. Part of the beauty of obedience is that it is thrilling. Skydiving is a pallid substitute for an act of genuine love for our next-door neighbor. This is not to say obedience is free of all resistance in the way skydiving is. Obedience is messy and difficult much of the time. But the point is that for many, obedience may not seem distasteful so much as boring. According to Edwards, however, holiness is not "dull and lifeless."[31] It is the greatest thrill to be enjoyed by human beings in this fallen world. It is sin that is boring.

I recently read a story about three teenagers in Oklahoma City who were sitting on a front porch when a twenty-two-year-old man jogged by. They followed him in a car and shot him in the back, killing him. When asked about their crime, one said: "We were bored and didn't have anything to do, so we decided to kill somebody."[32] This is where sin ultimately takes us: boredom and the empty quest to fill that boredom with anything, even horrific acts of evil.[33]

We will do anything to fill the hunger for glory that bubbles up within every human being made in God's image. Many who confess addiction to pornography articulate boredom as a key factor fueling their actions—the need for a thrill, for excitement, overwhelmed them.

Obedience is where this excitement—paradoxically, a calming excitement—lies.

---

[31] WJE, 2:99.
[32] "Baseball Player Killed in Oklahoma," at espn.com, accessed August 20, 2013, http://espn.go.com /college-sports/story/_/id/9583091/baseball-player-killed-kids-were-bored.
[33] See WJE, 2:396–97.

Conclusion

Both sin and obedience consist in doing what we want to do. What makes the difference is whether we are alive to the beauty of God or not. If we are, we will delight to obey. Sin and obedience are fundamentally distinguished not by outward behavior but by the state of the heart. Anyone can conform outwardly. Only by divine grace can we be changed at the level of what we desire. Sovereign, regenerating grace does not force us to do what we don't want to do. More deeply, it brings us to want to do what we should want to do, through a vision of divine beauty. Grace gets underneath even our felt levels of desire.

I can get my three-year-old Nathan into bed by picking him up, as he kicks and screams, and carrying him. Or I can get him into bed by promising him that Where's Waldo and castle Legos await him in his bed.

For Jonathan Edwards, surprisingly, *neither* of these reflects true obedience. Even strategy 2 doesn't quite capture it. Even there Nathan is getting into bed not out of a delight to obey but because I've dangled something else in front of him. His desire to look for Waldo and play Legos passes the threshold of his desire to stay downstairs. But he still doesn't delight in obedience. The will remains untouched. It is toys, not me, that he wants.[34]

Edwards teaches us that true obedience is wrought by grace that softens us way down deep at the core of who we are. Taste-bud transformation. In a miracle that can never be humanly manufactured, we find ourselves, strangely, delighting to love God. We have seen, and begun to participate in, beauty. For Edwards, ethics and aesthetics are bound up with one another.[35]

If this is authentic obedience, then many of us (Christians) are living deeply disobedient lives without realizing it. We are saying the right things, praying the right prayers, tithing the right amounts, wearing the Christian mask externally. But we view obeying as squelching our wills for the sake of submitting to another's will. To be sure, in our fallen state at times we do have to simply grit our way forward without delighting in God. But authentic obedience is external *as a reflection of* what is internal, not external *in conflict with* what is internal. Real obedience is freely doing what we now love to do, not forcing our wills to do something we are loathe to do.

The real question is not whether we obey God. The question beneath that question is, What do we love?

---

[34] Luther draws out the way true obedience is rendered freely and willingly, not out of compulsion, in his *Bondage of the Will*, in *Luther's Works*, vol. 33, *Career of the Reformer III*, ed. Philip S. Watson (Philadelphia: Fortress, 1957), 64–65.

[35] Cf. McClymond and McDermott, *Theology of Jonathan Edwards*, 528–48.

CHAPTER 10

SATAN

The Enemy of the Christian Life

To be a Christian is to be loved and loathed. New birth introduces a new and powerful love from heaven that defies our categories. And new birth introduces a new and powerful loathing from hell that makes human hatred look tame in comparison.

Christianity is therefore not only a journey and a worldview and a religion. It is also combat. A battle. And Satan is our great enemy. This is the way Jonathan Edwards consistently spoke of the Devil—"the grand enemy of mankind,"[1] "that proud and potent enemy,"[2] "our mighty, proud, and cruel enemy."[3]

This is one reason for the difficulty many believers seem to express about living the Christian life. Life seems to get harder once they are Christians. Yet wasn't Jesus supposed to ease our burdens? If we are really now the recipients of so many lavish blessings, how could life be harder?

There are many reasons for this, but one is heightened hatred from God's ancient enemy. Though born into darkness and enslavement to hell, we have now sworn allegiance to Satan's bitter foe. We have defected. We are either on Satan's side or God's; there is no spiritual Switzerland, a neutral no-man's land.[4] Given our reversal of loyalties, is it surprising life gets

---

[1] *WJE*, 14:418; similarly, 9:130.
[2] *WJE*, 18:151.
[3] *WJE*, 13:419. Edwards identifies pride as the chief sin of Satan (e.g., *WJE*, 22:531).
[4] *WJE*, 22:361.

harder? A snake lashes out all the more if you step on its tail. We shouldn't be surprised if Satan lashes out all the more if we aggravate him by committing mutiny against him.

Jonathan Edwards fortifies us against our great enemy. Edwards wrote much on the Devil and his demons, and is an insightful teacher.[5] Surface-level wisdom might teach that it is only those who befriend the Devil who really get to know him, but this is untrue. It is by walking in light that one sees the danger and misery of darkness. Edwards pursued holiness, and it was in this pursuit that his understanding of Satan deepened. It is satanists, not Christians, who are most blind to who Satan actually is.

Satan is the great enemy of the Christian life. In this chapter we will consider four themes in Edwards: Satan the accuser, Satan the tempter, Satan the puppet, and Satan the defeated.

The Accuser

Satan is the great finger pointer. He is "the accuser of our brothers" (Rev. 12:10). "The devil is the accuser of the brethren," reflects Edwards, quoting the King James Version rendering, "and accuses them before God day and night."[6] When God's people are under the accusing tongue of a hostile person, this is only a taste of the awful work of Satan himself, the king of accusation.[7]

What does Satan accuse believers of? Our sins, of course—sins that have justly been placed under the blood of Christ and emptied of their power to condemn us. Here we come to one of the great paradoxes of Christian living. The unregenerate stand justly under accusation for their sin, but live generally oblivious to the sting of accusation. The regenerate have been exonerated of all accusation for their sin, but live generally sensitized to the justice of such a charge. Because of the work of the Son, Christians are the only ones not deserving ultimate indictment; but because of the work of the Spirit, Christians are the only ones aware of how just such an indictment, but for mercy, would be.

---

[5] In this chapter we will largely subsume Edwards's comments on the devils (Edwards did not call them "demons") within his comments on Satan, since the two (Satan and the devils) largely overlap in his theology. Also, Edwards tended to lump together the devils of hell with unregenerate men (e.g., WJE, 2:202, 210; 5:101, 149); Satan tends to be treated in his own category, and also receives more pungent treatment from Edwards than the devils.

[6] WJE, 18:517; also 20:190.

[7] Cf. Edwards's comments in this regard in the Blank Bible, on Ps. 120:3–4 (WJE, 24:532).

When Satan launches what Edwards calls "vexatious accusations of conscience" against believers, he is playing upon the believer's resensitized conscience (awakened by the Spirit) while muting the believer's full and free forgiveness (won by the Son). The way to combat these accusations from hell is therefore not to deny the first, but to remember the second. We should not downplay the reasonableness of our condemnation. We do deserve to be condemned. But another reality transcends our condemnation: the atoning work of Christ. This work not only frees us from accusation (negatively) but also renders us righteous (positively).[8]

The gospel has defanged Satan. His bite is all gums and no teeth. When Satan accuses believers covered by the blood of Christ, he is (to switch metaphors) firing empty cartridges—his gun makes a bang, but it can't ultimately hurt us. "Satan cannot hurt" true believers, Edwards preached. "All the powers of darkness, with all their spite and malice, can do them no harm, and the flames of hell cannot reach them."[9]

The Tempter

The Devil not only accuses believers after they sin but also tempts them before they sin. The reason he tempts is so that he has something of which to accuse.

Satan tempts people to be spiritually lazy,[10] to neglect prayer,[11] and to keep their problems to themselves instead of confiding in another.[12] He tempts with glory, pleasure, and money.[13] In short, he lures us into spiritual apathy and imperceptibly creeping misery. One of the great reliefs of heaven is that the Devil's temptings will cease once and for all.[14] On that day, says Edwards, heaven will more than compensate for all earthly self-denial of pleasurable temptations.[15] Therefore to resist temptation is not to forgo pleasure but to delay it. We can have candy now or steak later.

Edwards frequently draws out the *sneakiness* of Satan in his temptations—what Edwards calls the Devil's "subtlety."[16] The reason Satan is so effective in tempting is that he flies in under the Christian's radar; he is

---

[8] *WJE*, 14:60.
[9] *WJE*, 10:458; similarly, 24:128.
[10] *WJE*, 10:444.
[11] *WJE*, 19:126, 130.
[12] *WJE*, 19:126.
[13] *WJE*, 10:554.
[14] *WJE*, 25:596.
[15] *WJE*, 10:606.
[16] E.g., *WJE*, 2:119; 13:324–25; 20:505.

quietly crafty in his strategies. This subtlety has been honed with centuries of experience in tempting the people of God.

How does he sneak in so subtly in tempting us? By presenting us with what appears to be beautiful and delightful. If to be a Christian is fundamentally to be alive to beauty, temptation is in essence the masquerading of ugliness as beauty. Temptation is the result of the magician-like sleight of hand the Devil exercises on sin to make it look appealing instead of what it really is, repulsive. Sin looks attractive, but it is a counterfeit beauty.[17] To call Satan the tempter is therefore simply to call him the deceiver. To tempt is to seek to deceive. The Devil is the "great deceiver, who makes it his whole business to deceive."[18]

All this is not to say temptation is uniform in the way it is presented by Satan to believers. As he explains in a 1747 letter to Thomas Gillespie, Edwards understood that the Devil is to be resisted in different ways by different people. Those who have what Edwards called a more "melancholic" disposition, for example, should not try to engage the Devil head-on in combatting temptation; rather they should divert their minds by simply occupying themselves with whatever lies ahead of them in the course of life.[19] And so on.

While Satan is the great tempter, even hell's temptations come to us ultimately from the hand of God.[20] God does not himself tempt anyone in such a way that makes God the promoter of sin (James 1:13). Yet nothing takes place outside the sovereign will of God. Consider this beautiful reflection from Edwards:

> Though it is to the eternal damage of the saints, ordinarily, when they yield to, and are overcome by temptations, yet Satan and other enemies of the saints by whom these temptations come, are always wholly disappointed in their temptations, and baffled in their design to hurt the saints, inasmuch as the temptation and the sin that comes by it, is for the saints' good, and they receive a greater benefit in the issue, than if the temptation had not been, and yet less than if the temptation had been overcome.[21]

---

[17] Edwards speaks of Satan as "counterfeiting" authentic spirituality, in *Religious Affections* (*WJE*, 2:86, 146, 158) and elsewhere (e.g., 5:218; 19:127–28). On Edwards's developed understanding of the way spirituality can be counterfeited, see Samuel T. Logan Jr., "Justification and Evangelical Obedience," in *Jonathan Edwards and Justification*, ed. Josh Moody (Wheaton, IL: Crossway, 2012), 104–109, 115.
[18] *WJE*, 14:86. See Edwards's thoughts on Satan as a deceiver, in *WJE*, 2:288–89.
[19] *WJE*, 2:482.
[20] Temptation does not *only* come from Satan; our own sinful inclinations are also a cause of temptation (James 1:14). Not all temptation is satanic. We are simply dealing here with that which is.
[21] *WJE*, 2:488–89.

That is worth reading carefully a second time. Is this your theology? You will be a stronger Christian if it is. Consider what Edwards is saying. He is asserting that when Satan presents a temptation to a Christian, at that moment—whether the Christian succumbs to it or not—the Christian is guaranteed to wind up better off for having faced the temptation. If the temptation is overcome, the Christian avoids sinning and is all the stronger. But even if the temptation is not overcome, God in his inscrutable wisdom and grace will invariably cause that temptation and sin to net out for the believer's final good. Satan cannot win. (If one wonders why Satan, for all his cunning, does not see this and therefore desist, Edwards's answer is that "although the devil be exceeding crafty and subtle, yet he is one of the greatest fools and blockheads in the world. . . . Sin is of such a nature that it strangely infatuates and bewitches persons.")[22]

To be sure, anyone who embraces temptation and sin with the excusing thought that it will work for his good is flaunting God's sovereignty, is welcoming misery, and may prove himself not to be born again. But for the struggling believer who is distraught at his failures and wondering how his life can be useful to the kingdom in light of so many repeated moral failures, Jonathan Edwards has something to say: Relax. You cannot lose. You are invincible. Every darkness that envelops your life will turn out only to brighten your final radiance.

This high view of God's sovereignty even in temptation leads us into our next section.

The Puppet

A key aspect of the beauty of God, for Jonathan Edwards, is God's unmitigated sovereign rule over all that happens. This includes the activity of the Devil. While Satan is the great enemy of God, God and Satan are not locked in an eternal cosmic duel as equal and opposite forces, one of good and one of evil. Satan himself, rather, can do no other than the bidding of heaven. He is both the enemy and the unwilling servant of God at one and the same time.

The key to understanding Edwards at this point is to understand that we can speak of God's "will" in two distinct ways.[23] God's "decretive will" is what he has *decreed* from time immemorial to come to pass, and this in-

---

[22] *WJE*, 13:227.
[23] For what follows in this paragraph see esp. Miscellany no. 170, in *WJE*, 13:323.

cludes all things. God's "preceptive will" is what God desires, as laid down in his *precepts*. One is what will happen, and the other is what God naturally delights in happening. And God's preceptive will is the smaller bubble included within the larger bubble of his decretive will. Or to state it differently, not all that takes place within the decretive will of God is what God delights in. There are some things that, while inscrutably included within the sovereign plan of God, go against what he desires and delights in. In *Freedom of the Will* Edwards takes the crucifixion of Christ as an example of this—God determined this to happen, and yet there was grave evil and disobedience involved.[24]

How does all this relate to Satan? Understanding the two wills of God enables us to comprehend how God can be sovereign over Satan, yet without approving of what Satan does. Is it God's will that Satan work misery and devastation in the world? Yes and no. Yes, in terms of God's will of decree. No, in terms of his will of delight.

Take Job as an example. Was it God's will that Satan wreak havoc on Job's life? A crucial lesson to learn from this book of the Bible is that Satan can act to wreak havoc in the world, yet when the dust settles we can rightly assert, "The LORD gave, and the LORD has taken away" (Job 1:21; cf. also 2:10). The devils too, Edwards thought, can do only what God allows and ever super-ordains.[25]

Satan is therefore a puppet. He is an active puppet, and a malicious puppet, and a never-resting puppet—but a puppet all the same. All that Satan does must finally contribute to the good of God's people and the glory of God's Son. "God suffered Satan to do what he has done in the world, on purpose that his Son might have his glory, to obtain a complete victory over the devil and his armies."[26]

The Defeated

Because Satan is ultimately a puppet in the hands of a sovereign God, his defeat is sure. The outcome is settled. In a miscellany entitled "Satan Defeated," Edwards reflects: "Nothing can more clearly manifest to the heavenly hosts that God is the supreme and absolute disposer of all things than to see God carry on his designs from age to age," even carrying out "his

---

[24] *WJE*, 1:407.
[25] *WJE*, 1:408–10.
[26] *WJE*, 13:419.

great ends by a most powerful and subtle enemy." God thus works "as he doth by Satan, who, in all that he doth," works "to his utmost endeavors to frustrate and counterwork him"—but fails.[27]

If God is sovereign over Satan, what could God possibly *not* be sovereign over? A teacher who can control the most ill-behaved child in the class can control anyone in the classroom.

One notable contribution Edwards makes to our understanding of Satan's defeat is the sheer irony and beauty of *how* Satan was defeated: through shame and weakness. Christ took up the fight against Satan not with outright strength but with the "glory and beauty" of choosing "to become weak, to take upon him the nature of a poor, feeble, mortal man, a worm of the dust, that in this nature and state he might overcome Satan." Thus "the weapons that Christ made use of in fighting with the hellish giant were his poverty, afflictions, reproaches, and death." And Christ's supreme weapon was the cross itself. At the very moment when Satan appeared most decisively victorious, Satan was securing his own demise. In these ways Christ "overthrew all the power and baffled all the craft of hell."[28]

Christ's defeat secured Satan's defeat. Satan won and therefore lost. He was unaware of the deeper magic from before the dawn of time, as C. S. Lewis would say. For his victory was the crushing of a man who deserved not to be crushed. We deserved Christ's defeat, but his defeat has been reckoned as ours vicariously, with the surprising result that Satan can no longer threaten us. As for Christ, he was raised from defeat, because the author of life cannot stay dead (Acts 3:15). Hell's hopes have been marvelously dashed.

Conclusion

A soldier would be greatly heartened in battle if he discovered that the enemy's assault weapons were filled with Nerf darts. Such is the delightful discovery made by those under grace, who have been swept up into safety in Christ.

Satan is real and he is powerful. One could even say he rules this world (Eph. 2:2). But he is ultimately impotent in his ability to harm the souls of believers (Matt. 10:28). He is all bark and no bite. Do not fear him. We have

---

[27] *WJE*, 18:152.
[28] *WJE*, 18:151.

Christ. Whatever Satan does to us in all his raging will only call forth more healing, mercy, and restoration from Christ.

> The sweet beams of [Christ] the Sun of righteousness heal the wounds of believers' souls. When they have been wounded by sin and have labored under the pain of wounds of conscience, the rays of this Sun heal the wounds of conscience. When they have been wounded by temptation and made to fall to their hurt, those benign beams, when they come to shine on the wounded soul, restore and heal the hurt that has been received.[29]

---

[29] *WJE*, 22:56.

CHAPTER II

THE SOUL

The Great Concern of
the Christian Life

In the 1959 novel *A Canticle for Leibowitz*, by Walter Miller, a character utters the well-known words: "You don't *have* a soul, Doctor. You *are* a soul. You *have* a body."[1] Central to Edwards's vision of the Christian life, and foundational to all that is covered in this book, is his agreement with this. Beauty is perceived and enjoyed with the soul; love is expressed and received in the soul; Scripture and prayer feed the soul; and so on. The soul is the organ of beauty.

His relentless preoccupation with the soul is the direct byproduct of his keen sense of eternity. Has anyone ever felt the shortness of life like Jonathan Edwards? "Resolved," he wrote as a young man, "to think much on all occasions of my own dying."[2] Edwards had seen the young people of Northampton die no less abruptly than the elderly. He frequently warned the youth in his Massachusetts church to resist the temptation to brush aside thoughts of eternity, a temptation to which the youth of every generation are prone.

What lasts beyond this life, however, and indeed never dies, is the soul. Human beings are not eternal in both directions, past and future; unlike

---

[1] Walter M. Miller Jr., *A Canticle for Leibowitz* (1959; repr., New York: Eos, 2006), 293. The statement is often wrongly attributed to C. S. Lewis, who would agree with, but did not originally utter, these words.
[2] *WJE*, 16:753.

God, we have a fixed starting point. But we are immortal, because we have no ending point.

In a modern world that floods us with an exaggerated sense of the importance of this earthly life through advertisement, media, and our own natural fixation on the present, Jonathan Edwards has something to say to us: the soul is the great concern of the Christian life. "Consider," he preached in 1740, "that the good of the soul is of infinitely the greatest concern."[3]

What Is the Soul?

The soul is not the bottom of your foot. That's your sole. The soul is what makes you *you* and what will remain when your body dies. It overlaps with what the Bible calls the "heart," which in biblical usage does not mean feelings or emotions more narrowly (as we often use the word *heart* today) but the entire feeling, thinking, and willing being—the animating center of the human that drives all we do.[4] The soul is close to this but with the added emphasis on human immortality, to which we will come in a moment.

The soul, according to Edwards, is not passive but active. Today we tend to view the soul as the latent part of us that will pass on into the next life. Life happens to us, and the soul is duly affected, we tend to think. Edwards deconstructs this way of thinking in his penetrating reflection in *Freedom of the Will*. There his basic point is to argue that the soul is active, but this does not mean the soul is able to choose various moral paths from a state of neutrality; rather, the soul actively chooses what it loves, and cannot do otherwise.[5]

The soul is not a part of the human, then; the soul *is* the human, viewed comprehensively and spiritually. In a miscellany Edwards compares the omnipresence of God throughout the universe to the presence of the soul in the body.[6] While it is true that the soul and the body are distinct realities,[7] there is nowhere in the body that the soul does not reach, just as there is nowhere in the universe that God does not exist. And looking to the future

---

[3] *WJE*, 22:164.
[4] Edwards commonly uses *soul* and *heart* interchangeably (e.g., *WJE*, 14:408–9). The close biblical association between the heart and the soul is evident in texts such as Deut. 4:29; 6:5; 10:12; 30:6; 1 Sam. 14:7; Ps. 94:19; Prov. 24:12; Luke 10:27; Acts 4:32.
[5] *WJE*, 1:186–89, 207–9. Edwards makes the same point about the soul in Miscellany 830, in *WJE*, 18:540.
[6] *WJE*, 13:335.
[7] *WJE*, 13:394.

judgment and the new heavens and the new earth, we could say that as goes the soul, so goes the body: either to destruction or glory.

The soul, then, is the entire person as viewed from the perspective of heaven. Think of a heat-sensing machine that shows on a screen different colors representing degrees of heat, thus helping military leaders, for example, identify human beings from a distance. When God and the angels look down from heaven, they view humans the way a military officer views humans through a heat-sensing machine. What matters to the officer is the location of the heat. What matters to heaven are human souls.[8] This is not to say that bodies do not matter. The point rather is that non-soul matters— what you or I wore to work today, for example—matter only to the degree that they affect the soul. There is simply nothing else. The soul is what is united to Christ.[9] It is the soul that is regenerated.[10] It is the soul that has its very nature changed.[11] It is the soul that is renewed into the image of Christ.[12] It is the soul that rejoices and grieves.[13]

We do not have a soul. We are a soul.

The Priority of the Soul

The soul is therefore of the utmost priority. When Edwards taught this, however, he was not advocating for a conviction abstracted from his own experiences. In 1704 Eunice Williams, Edwards's cousin who was one year younger than he, was captured by Indians and taken to Canada, where she was converted to Roman Catholicism. Edwards seems to allude to this at the close of the 1740 sermon "God's Care in Time of Public Commotion." After exhorting his people to nurture their children's souls, he says, "How will your consciences hereafter accuse you, if your children should be taken from you to be instructed in the popish religion, or if they should be carried captive to Canada. *Therefore don't neglect their souls.*"[14]

In the sermon "Praying for the Spirit," Edwards begins his application by identifying the two kinds of blessing God gives: what Edwards calls "temporal" and "spiritual."[15] The temporal blessings include

---

[8] Cf. *WJE*, 25:572–73.
[9] *WJE*, 13:219–20.
[10] *WJE*, 14:295.
[11] Ibid.
[12] *WJE*, 17:135.
[13] *WJE*, 2:98.
[14] *WJE*, 22:363–64, emphasis added. Edwards again exhorts parents to care for their children's souls in the sermon "The Importance of Revival among Heads of Families," in *WJE*, 22:453.
[15] *WJE*, 22:216.

- food,
- clothing,
- a home,
- friends,
- wood for the fire,
- fodder for the farm animals.

The spiritual blessings Edwards lists are

- the sanctification of our natures,
- participating in the divine nature,
- having God's love poured into our hearts,
- union with Christ,
- adoption by God,
- enjoying fellowship with God,
- living in divinely granted peace and joy,
- the promise of heaven and perfect bliss forever.

He goes on to explain that our heavenly Father knows that we need both. Edwards's first point in juxtaposing these two kinds of blessings is to point out that the first kind is enjoyed in vastly different degrees—for example, a prince enjoys worldly goods to a vastly greater degree than a poor beggar. Yet as great a difference as this is, Edwards then says, even greater is the difference between an ordinary person who is enjoying the life of the soul and the richest prince who isn't. For the spiritual blessings of the soul "are infinitely the most necessary, the most profitable, the most honorable, the most pleasant and delightful and satisfying, and the most durable" of the two kinds of blessing.[16]

Strangely, however, the vast difference in importance between temporal and spiritual matters is not reflected in our pursuits in life. We seek earthly, circumstantial comforts "with much the greatest earnestness," says Edwards.[17] He puzzles over the fact that people do not need preaching to stir them up to seek a greater salary or more plush vacations. Yet we do need preaching to stir us up to pursue that which far outstrips any amount of money or comfort in degree of pleasure and delight. Edwards speaks of "the absurdity of such a negligence" in that when we undergo a small drought of literal rain, we cry out to God with tears; yet when we undergo a

---

[16] *WJE*, 22:217; see also 22:164, 295.
[17] *WJE*, 22:217.

large drought of spiritual rain, we are hardly bothered and do not even ask God to do something about it.[18]

The soul is our great priority. Strange is the drowning man who ignores the need for air in his lungs because he is captivated by the colors of the fish around him. If he does not care for his lungs, he will die. If we do not care for our souls but fixate on the good but transient things of this world, we will die eternally.

The Immortality of the Soul

As to the future, the soul is eternal. It has a beginning, but no ending. A moment's reflection recognizes our inability to truly take this in, owing to our finitude. We can think in terms of great lengths of time, but not of time that extends forever out in front of us. As soon as our minds have stretched as far out into the distant horizon as we can fathom, millennia upon millennia, we are brought short by the thought that even our greatest mental conception of time is a speck compared to forever.

But this is what Jonathan Edwards insists that we reckon with. We are finite in our mental horizon, but not in the length of time that the soul will live. Indeed, we know tacitly that we were made for more. Because we are made in the image of God, death feels unnatural. It feels like an intrusion. Mortality would not feel wrong without our knowing we were made to be immortal. Haunted by our mortality, we cram our daily lives with distractions and amusements to deal with the pain of what we know, consciously or subconsciously, is coming: our own funeral. Ernest Becker famously drove this point home from a secular perspective in 1973 in his Pulitzer Prize–winning *The Denial of Death.*[19] Becker was no follower of Edwards, but it was the very awareness of our mortality, felt so keenly by Edwards, that Becker exposed, arguing that all of human civilization across the centuries is ultimately an ornate effort to squelch our innate sense of mortality and unavoidable death.

The biblical answer that Edwards provides to this painful reality is that it is care for the soul, not the body, that alleviates this pain. Yes, we must care for the body—"bodily training is of some value" (1 Tim. 4:8). But it is soul training in godliness that "holds promise for the present life and also

---

[18] *WJE*, 22:218. He makes the same point elsewhere (e.g., *WJE*, 14:502; "I Know My Redeemer Lives," in *The Sermons of Jonathan Edwards: A Reader*, ed. Wilson H. Kimnach, Kenneth P. Minkema, and Douglas A. Sweeney [New Haven, CT: Yale University Press, 1999], 148–49).

[19] Ernest Becker, *The Denial of Death* (New York: Free Press, 1973).

for the life to come" (1 Tim. 4:8). As Jesus taught, building bigger barns is foolish if it serves as a replacement for soul concern (Luke 12:13–21). Awareness of death ought not to lead us to cover it over with the medication of television, sexual stimulation, fat bank accounts, or anything else. Awareness of death ought to lead us into sober concern for that which will last beyond death and never die.

Edwards's first pastoral charge was a congregation in New York City. There he preached a sermon with this main point: "The salvation of the soul is of vastly more worth than the whole world."[20] Here is a representative and typically elegant statement from this sermon by the nineteen-year-old Edwards:

> The soul is immortal and shall certainly endure forever and ever. We have heard that all worldly things shall certainly be destroyed at the end of the world, and besides that, they will certainly be at an end with respect to every particular man at death, and oftentimes come to an end before death; and there [is] not the least certainty of their enduring till that time.
>
> And if man live to old age, the enjoyment of them will certainly be at an end before death; and if he don't live to old age, then they will certainly be at an end before that time comes.
>
> But none of these things are so with respect to the soul: when heaven and earth shall be destroyed, when everything upon the face of the earth shall be burnt up, when the sea shall [be] dried up, when the sun, moon and stars shall come to an end, the soul shall endure still. When the body shall die and return to dust, the soul shall remain; when worldly good things shall have an end by accidents, by diseases or old age, the soul will remain. The world shall continue but a few moments, but the soul shall remain throughout all eternity. . . . Worldly profits and pleasures shall last no longer than the body, and many times not half so long, but the soul shall last as long as God lasts. Surely that which lasts forever, if it be worth anything, if it lasts always, must be worth vastly more than that which lasts but a little while: that good which lasts millions of ages must be worth more than that which lasts but a minute.[21]

Edwards is not exaggerating for the sake of effect if we take seriously Jesus's words in Matthew 10:28: "Do not fear those who kill the body but cannot kill the soul. Rather fear him who can destroy both soul and body in hell."

---

[20] WJE, 10:313.
[21] WJE, 10:316.

On the morning of his execution, an inmate on death row does not wake up concerned that he might forget to take his multivitamin that day. He wakes up praying. He is confronted with the eternal significance of the soul because he is forced to reckon with what the rest of us generally ignore or mute: death is coming, it is unavoidable, and it will kill the body but not the soul. The soul is eternal.

The Happiness of the Soul

The soul is our great concern not only in the next life, but also in this life. The state of the soul determines the degree of joyfulness in the Christian life.

It is not what happens *to* us but *in* us that makes us truly happy. Edwards understood this. Our natural tendency as believers is to receive the gospel as a way to save our souls for the next life and then to go on funneling all our old fleshly desires into the way we live this life in the meantime. To Edwards this is like sick people receiving from the doctor medicine that will cure them now, but putting it in the cupboard for the future. Soul joy will be perfected in the future, but it is to be imperfectly experienced here and now. The state of the soul—not the state of the body, or one's financial situation, or one's reputation, or anything else—is what determines joy.

Edwards often used a food metaphor to describe soul happiness. In a 1734 sermon to the youth of his church, he said:

> They that walk in a way of holiness, do obtain in this world the gratifica-
> tions of those spiritual appetites in a degree for the discoveries of God's
> glory, and the views of Christ's beauty, and in the incomes of the holy
> spirit, whereby the soul is filled with joy of the Holy Ghost. They feed on
> angel's food, on the bread which came down from heaven and have the
> foretastes of heaven's dainties.[22]

Circumstances are not the authoritative determiners of joy. Indeed, it is often in adverse circumstances that our joy seems to be more fresh, more real, than in ease. In *Some Thoughts concerning the Revival*, Edwards reflects on the way the outpouring of God's Spirit manifested itself among those who were suffering. He spoke of the revival as "fortifying the heart under great trials, such as the death of children, and extreme pain of body." And yet these very same people were at the very same time "wonderfully

---

[22] *WJE*, 19:84.

maintaining the serenity, calmness, and joy of the soul, in an immovable rest in God, and sweet resignation to him."[23]

Pain outside us and joy inside us are not two sides of a seesaw, fluctuating in inverse proportion to one another. Pain and joy, in a heart alive to the beauty of God, often rise and fall together. To the soul at ease due to circumstantial prosperity, suffering seems to threaten joy; yet when suffering comes, the Christian often in hindsight recognizes that it was shallowness and emptiness and misery that the pain was squeezing out, not joy.

A Caution

Care must be exercised as we zero in on the supreme value of the human soul. We might express this truth in such a way that undercuts the biblical teaching on the goodness of human physicality. The statement from Walter Miller's novel early in this chapter, and Edwards's statements throughout this chapter, while true, could reinforce a widespread Christian misunderstanding that the physical body is inherently bad.[24] Two reminders help us avoid this mistake.

First, the human body is a good creation of God. The fall into sin recounted in Genesis 3 does indeed affect every dimension of human living, including the physical. But our physicality is not itself the problem. Our bodies are not a result of the fall; our *corruptible* bodies are a result of the fall. The first chapter of the Bible calls created, embodied humanity "very good" (Gen. 1:31).

The idea that the human body is inherently bad is a mistaken view that goes back to the second century AD and a defective cluster of teachings known as Gnosticism, with roots even further back in Platonism. Gnosticism had distinct emphases in different times and places, but the common thread running through all forms of Gnostic teaching was the inherent inferiority of physical matter and the inherent superiority of the immaterial world. Some letters in the New Testament, such as 1 John, seem to be directed against an early form of just such a denigration of the body.[25]

---

[23] WJE, 4:330.

[24] Lewis himself spoke against the denigration of the body. E.g.: "God never meant man to be a purely spiritual creature. That is why He uses material things like bread and wine to put the new life into us. We may think this is rather crude and unspiritual. God does not: He invented eating. He likes matter. He invented it" (C. S. Lewis, *Mere Christianity* [New York: HarperCollins, 2001], 64).

[25] Edwards himself engaged a form of "Gnosticism" in his interaction with John Taylor in Edwards's treatise on original sin. Taylor was suggesting that the human soul was created pure, but joined to a fallen body; see WJE, 3:126–27.

One reason Christians through the ages and today have mistakenly thought the Bible to teach the body to be naturally inferior in some way is the apostle Paul's references to "the flesh," especially in Romans. But while Paul uses this word in different ways, and sometimes does indeed refer to the physicality of human existence, his negative use speaks of the fallen *soul*. This is evident by the way he sets "the flesh" opposite not the spirit—that is, the immaterial part of the human, but "the Spirit," meaning the Holy Spirit. And even here, the point is not that the Holy Spirit is immaterial but that he is the producer of godliness—thus the works of the flesh in Galatians 5 are matters not of physicality but of ungodliness, and the fruit of the Spirit are matters not of immateriality but of godliness. In 1 Corinthians 15, the great chapter on the resurrection of the body, Paul even uses "spiritual" to refer to our future resurrection *body*.

Second, the final, permanent state of every human being is an embodied one. The possession of a body is not a temporary reality, one day to be shed as we fly off to a better immaterial world. To be sure, death before Christ's return ushers one into a spiritual, disembodied existence. But it is *this* that is ultimately temporary, not our physicality. Our final state is fully physical.

Edwards himself was thoroughly orthodox in his anthropology (doctrine of humanity), but his emphasis on the soul should not allow us to denigrate the goodness of the body.

Conclusion

"Religion is our great business."[26] Edwards never shifted from the rock of that conviction. In an age that bombards us with the message that our circumstances, not our souls, deliver happiness, he has a pungent word in season. The billboards along I-355 in the western suburbs of Chicago where I live do not encourage me to store up treasure in heaven. The constant hand-wringing of the media amid economic anxiety and political unrest, the multibillion-dollar global advertising industry, and my own natural worldliness—all this conspires to hypnotize me into the false thinking that this world and the circumstances of this life are where my greatest concerns lie. Jonathan Edwards defibrillates my heart back into health by reminding me of what I know to be true in my sanest moments: it is the soul that matters.

---

[26] *WJE*, 25:203.

True Christian beauty is found in the soul. When a sinner is made alive to beauty, it is the soul that is brought to life. It is the soul that is beautified. And this is all from the God of beauty. "All the beauty of the soul is wholly and only divine light reflected."[27]

The soul is the great concern of the Christian life.

---

[27] *WJE*, 15:52.

CHAPTER 12

HEAVEN

The Hope of the Christian Life

It's my life
It's now or never
I ain't gonna live forever

—BON JOVI, "IT'S MY LIFE"

If the tent that is our earthly home is destroyed, we have a building from
God, a house not made with hands, eternal in the heavens.

—PAUL THE APOSTLE, 2 CORINTHIANS 5:I

Each of us rolled out of bed this morning in pursuit of one of these visions of reality or the other. Either this life is my shot at joy and glory, or the next is. No third option.

And yet it is easy to contrast Bon Jovi's expression of the world's pursuit of glory with the Bible's without recognizing what is so right about what he sang. Jon Bon Jovi is made in the image of God. There is a quest for glory in him that in his fallenness is diseased and thus self-directed, but the healing of that fallen impulse does not cut off all pursuit of glory (note Rom. 2:7) but redirects it from self to Christ.

Bon Jovi doesn't want to sludge his way through life. He wants to matter. As he should. Life is frighteningly short and he wants to seize the moment. He even, in his own twisted way, wants to redeem the time. He eschews normalcy. Those of us in the church who want more than any-thing to play it safe—just make it through life offending as few people as possible, being liked, not stepping on toes, not bothering anyone and not being bothered—have something to learn from Bon Jovi. Regeneration is a change from glory-in-self pursuit to glory-in-Christ pursuit, not a change from glory-in-self pursuit to no pursuit of glory at all.

And yet my main reason for setting Bon Jovi alongside 2 Corinthians 5 is that Jonathan Edwards's biblically saturated vision of reality and the future is diametrically opposed to what we hear when we turn on the radio. Even as followers of Christ we tend to fixate strangely on this life to the ne-glect of the next, like a vacationer fixating on a few moments of turbulence before the plane touches down in Hawaii.

In this chapter we will enjoy Jonathan Edwards's depiction of what awaits all true believers in heaven.

Heaven and Joy

In 1993 I was a freshman at Libertyville High School on the north side of Chicago. My American literature teacher, Mrs. Arbiture, was excellent. So when she told us of the misanthropic preacher from New England, Jona-than Edwards, who delighted to preach hellfire sermons and torment his listeners by gleefully reminding them that God holds them squirming over the pit of hell ready to drop them at any moment, I believed her. What she didn't tell me, because she had neither read much of Edwards nor (more importantly) shared his taste of the beauty of God, was that he reflected far more on the delights of heaven than on the horrors of hell.[1]

The joy that will be experienced by Christians in heaven, says Edwards,

---

[1] On Edwards's greater focus on heaven than on hell, see the comments of Philip F. Gura, *Jonathan Edwards: America's Evangelical* (New York: Hill and Wang, 2005), 237–38. On the legitimacy of Edwards's doctrine of hell, consider the words of contemporary theologian Oliver Crisp, defending Edwards's un-derstanding of hell: "The traditional doctrine of hell seems terrible to our modern ears because it is out of step with our modern intuitions about how God should behave. But our intuitions about these matters are hardly a reliable guide, given what Scripture says about the noetic effects of sin. To put it another way, the fact that an infinite punishment for sin seems an appalling, even disproportionate, punishment to contemporary human beings does not necessarily mean it is an appalling, disproportionate punishment. It may be that this is simply testimony to our failure to take with sufficient seriousness the idea of sinning against a being of infinite beauty and value" (Oliver Crisp, "Karl Barth and Jonathan Edwards on Reproba-tion," in *Engaging with Barth: Contemporary Evangelical Critiques*, ed. David Gibson and Daniel Strange [London: T&T Clark, 2008], 316–17). Translation: the fact that an eternal hell seems disproportionately cruel as a punishment for sinners—that very sense of disproportion—is itself one manifestation of the sin that deserves eternal punishment.

"is exceeding great and vigorous; impressing the heart with the strongest and most lively sensation, of inexpressible sweetness, mightily moving, animating, and engaging them, making them like to a flame of fire."[2] We tend to view the joy of heaven in abstract and unappealing ways, but Edwards squeezes all that he can out of the language at his disposal to upend this mistake. In 1747 Jonathan Edwards preached the funeral sermon for the now-famous missionary David Brainerd. Brainerd lived in Edwards's home for a time and today is buried next to Edwards's daughter Jerusha, with whom Brainerd was apparently in love. Preaching on 2 Corinthians 5:8, Edwards reflected: "O how infinitely great will the privilege and happiness of such be, who at that time shall go to be with Christ in his glory." He went on to say that it is

> the privilege of being with Christ in heaven, where he sits on the right hand of God, in the glory of the King and God of angels, and of the whole universe, shining forth as the great light, the bright sun of that world of glory, there to dwell in the full, constant, and everlasting view of his beauty and brightness, there most freely and intimately to converse with him, and fully to enjoy his love, as his friends and spouse, there to have fellowship with him in the infinite pleasure and joy he has in the enjoyment of his Father, there to sit with him on his throne, and reign with him in the possession of all things, and partake with him in the joy and glory of his victory over his enemies, and the advancement of his in the world, and to join with him in joyful songs of praise, to his Father and their Father, to his God and their God, forever and ever.[3]

This quote picks up many of the distinctly Edwardsian themes of heaven. Heaven is a place of supreme beauty. It is a place of infinite happiness. This happiness is the joy of the Father and the Son delighting in one another. There we are with Christ in open fellowship, as his own bride. Christ exudes a light and a brightness. We participate in Christ's own glory and happiness. This joy is expressed in glad praise—Edwards says many times throughout his writings that the chief joy of heaven will be that we will finally be able to *express* our love to God. All this will never end. And perhaps most important and distinctive to Edwards's vision of heaven, our joy there will be the joy of love. The full and free exercise of love, to God and to other saints, is what makes heaven *heaven*. More on that in a moment.

---

[2] *WJE*, 2:114.
[3] *WJE*, 25:243–44.

Edwards often reflected on heaven in his private musings. In one miscellany he ponders the unrestrained delight of God in providing for his people's full joy in heaven, as unrestrained as will be his wrath on his enemies. On the one hand, "God will have no manner of regard to the welfare of the damned, will have no pity, no merciful care, lest they should be too miserable. . . . There will be no merciful restraint to God's wrath." Yet as unrestrained as his wrath will be on the impenitent, his delight over the penitent will be equally unrestrained: "with respect to the saints, there will be no happiness too much for them. God won't begrudge anything as too good for them. There will be no restraint to his love, no restraint to their enjoyment of himself; nothing will be too full, too inward and intimate for them to be admitted to."[4]

There will be nothing tepid in the joy God sweeps his people up into as they enter heaven. Nothing hindered, nothing held back. Christ has purchased all. His atoning work has swept away every reason for God to be restrained toward us. Drooping, anxious hearts may take refuge in the joy that must one day, invincibly and irreversibly, envelope us.

Edwards also rightly teaches that the joy experienced by those currently in heaven pales in comparison with what Christians will enjoy upon Christ's return. Edwards compares the happiness of those in heaven now with the happiness a young man enjoys on the day before his wedding—he is experiencing joy, but it is the joy of anticipation. True and final and fullness of joy still awaits.[5]

Finally, heavenly joy will grow and never stop growing. This is perhaps the most remarkable aspect of Edwards's theology of heaven, and worth pondering. Edwards believed that joy in heaven will not only be full but also expand eternally. At first sight this may seem contradictory. If our joy grows, does that not imply that earlier experiences of heavenly joy were incomplete? Edwards says no—for it is not the perfection of joy that increases but the capacity for joy that increases. A one-gallon jug and a ten-gallon can might both be perfectly full of water, yet the capacity of the larger container means that it has ten times the water. Similarly, in heaven we will always have perfect joy, but our capacity for that perfect joy will always be expanding.

Heaven will not be disappointingly boring. All our latent longings will finally be satiated as we bask in the fellowship with God for which we

---

[4] WJE, 18:371.
[5] WJE, 18:338.

were created and which, often without our knowing it, has been our hearts' deepest desire.

Heaven and Love

Heaven's joy is not an isolated benefit but is itself, in the thought of Jonathan Edwards, deeply intertwined with *love*. Many times in his preaching and writing he refers jointly to "the love and joy" of heaven.[6] There is no joy in heaven without love, and there is no love in heaven without joy. Heaven is heaven because of love. Love is not one ingredient of heaven; it is what makes heaven *heaven*. "There love shall flourish in everyone's breast, as a living spring perpetually springing, or as a flame which never decays. And the holy pleasure shall be as a river which ever runs, and is always clear and full."[7]

Nowhere in the writings of Jonathan Edwards, and perhaps nowhere in twenty centuries of church history, is the *love*liness of heaven clearer than in Edwards's final sermon in his "Charity and Its Fruits" series on 1 Corinthians 13. The title of the sermon was, simply, "Heaven Is a World of Love."

Edwards makes five points. First, heaven is a world of love because God is there. "Heaven is the palace, or presence-chamber, of the Supreme Being who is both the cause and source of all holy love."[8] The point is not that heaven is a lovely place and God is there too; heaven is lovely *because* God is there. Because God is "a full and overflowing and an inexhaustible fountain of love," God fills heaven with love the same way the sun fills a cloudless day with light. Second, there is nothing unlovely there, and everything in this world that is a mixture of loveliness and unloveliness will be purged of the unloveliness so that only what is beautiful and pure remains.[9] Third, moving from the objects of heavenly love to its subjects, the love that is in heaven pours forth from God himself, especially to his own dear Son and then also to the saints.[10] Believers are caught up into the never-ending, calm explosion of love transpiring between the Father and the Son, love that is itself the Holy Spirit.[11]

---

[6] E.g., *WJE*, 2:113-14; 4:232, 434; 8:713; 13:260; 18:371; 23:503; 24:870, 1020; 25:184, 243.
[7] *WJE*, 8:383.
[8] *WJE*, 8:369.
[9] *WJE*, 8:370–73.
[10] *WJE*, 8:373–74 .
[11] On the Trinitarian nature of the love expressed in heaven, see the good discussions of William J. Danaher Jr., *The Trinitarian Ethics of Jonathan Edwards*, Columbia Series in Reformed Theology (Louisville: Westminster John Knox, 2004), 235–38; and Steven M. Studebaker and Robert W. Caldwell III, *The Trinitarian Theology of Jonathan Edwards: Text, Context, and Application* (Farnham, UK: Ashgate, 2012), 222–23.

Edwards then, fourth, considers the love itself.[12] Here we find some of the most beautiful reflection on heaven the church has ever been given. Edwards explains that while the saints will have different degrees of glory, this will be no problem—for heaven is a world of love. Those in lower places in glory will not envy those in higher places, but due to their perfect love those in lower stations will actually be perfectly delighted on behalf of those above them. They would have it no other way. And those above them will know no condescension, because they too will be perfectly full of love, looking with exquisite joyous delight on those in lower stations. The beauty of this confounds us because we do not have a category for such a sin-free delight in one another. Yet this love for one another is what makes heaven *heaven*. Fifth and finally, Edwards reflects on the "circumstances in which love shall be expressed and enjoyed"—such as the way in which perfect love is always mutual: the saints expressing their love for Christ to their hearts' content, and Christ himself opening up to them "the great fountain of love in his heart far beyond what they ever saw before."[13] Love is inherently reciprocal. In a perfect world—which heaven will be—love is always returned.

In all of this Edwards's basic point is that love is not a slice of heaven but the whole pie. Love is in heaven not as a tree in a prairie but as the light in which the prairie is bathed on a bright summer morning. Indeed, the light of the sun is the pervasive metaphor for heavenly love throughout this sermon, as well as a favorite metaphor for divine things throughout his writings. In one miscellany Edwards even surmised that Christians in their glorified bodies will be able to see from one side of the universe to the other, since the light by which they see will not be that of the sun but something infinitely more bright and glorious—the glorified Christ.[14]

Made in God's image yet fallen and disfigured, we long for what Edwards describes. This is what we were created for. We all know the sick hollowness of vented selfishness. We were not made to self-fixate but to delight in others, in God and neighbor, outside of ourselves. This is what it means to be truly human. In heaven we will be in love—not in romantic attraction as Hollywood uses the phrase "in love," but actually *in love*. In it.

[12] *WJE*, 8:374–76.

[13] *WJE*, 8:376–77.

[14] *WJE*, 20:170. See also Robert W. Jenson, *America's Theologian: A Recommendation of Jonathan Edwards* (New York: Oxford University Press, 1988), 182.

Swimming endlessly, in ever-increasing delight, in the ocean of divine love into which cleansed sinners have been drawn.[15]

Heaven and Christ

Heaven is only a place of joy and love because Christ is there. Edwards calls Christ "the darling of heaven," enjoying unfiltered delight from the Father and from the angels.[16] There we will see him face to face and finally achieve unfiltered expression of love and adoration to him, and unfiltered reception and enjoyment of his love for us. As Edwards put it in David Brainerd's funeral sermon, "The souls of departed saints with Christ in heaven, shall have Christ as it were unbosomed unto them, manifesting those infinite riches of love towards them, that have been there from eternity."[17]

In various places among his writings Edwards considers the Christ-centeredness of heaven. By that I mean that Edwards viewed Christ's presence in heaven as a summing up of all possible joys one might experience. Christ in heaven is not one joy among many, like the best ride at an amusement park. Christ in heaven is the one in whom all earthly joys find their full and final expression. *Christ is not a part of the joy of heaven; every joy in the universe is a part of Christ.* Sound strange? Consider what Edwards says, in his first ever published sermon, about God generally:

> The glorious excellencies and beauty of God will be what will forever entertain the minds of the saints, and the love of God will be their everlasting feast. The redeemed will indeed enjoy other things: they will enjoy the angels, and will enjoy one another; but that which they shall enjoy in the angels, or each other, or in anything else whatsoever, that will yield them delight and happiness, will be what will be seen of God in them.[18]

In a miscellany written later in life Edwards gets more specifically Christ-focused in making this point about heaven:

> When a saint dies, he has no cause at all to grieve because he leaves his friends and relations that he dearly loves, for he doth not properly

---

[15] In heaven the saints "shall eat and drink abundantly, and swim in the ocean of love, and be eternally swallowed up in the infinitely bright, and infinitely mild and sweet beams of divine love" (*WJE*, 25:233).
[16] *WJE*, 14:417; 22:172.
[17] *WJE*, 25:233.
[18] "God Glorified in Man's Dependence," in *WJE*, 17:208.

leave them. For he enjoys them still in Christ; because everything that he loves in them and loves them for, is in Christ in an infinite degree; whether it be nearness of relation, or any perfection and good received, or love to us, or a likeness in dispositions, or whatever is a rational ground of love.[19]

Consider what this means if Edwards is right (and based on texts such as Psalm 84:11 and 1 Corinthians 3:21, I believe he is). Whatever you love in your spouse, your children, a sunset, an accomplishment, a hilarious joke—it will all be recapitulated in Christ. Summed up, perfected. You will leave *nothing* behind when you die. You have everything to gain, nothing to lose. It is impossible to make a sacrifice in leaving earth for heaven. Christ is there.

Scott Oliphint and Sinclair Ferguson relate a radio program they heard some years ago in which several famous people were asked what they envisioned when they thought about heaven. Oliphint and Ferguson note with interest a consistent three points articulated by those being interviewed:

1. They all believed in heaven.
2. They all assumed they would be there.
3. When asked to describe heaven, not one of them mentioned that God was there.

Oliphint and Ferguson then make that point that "it is the presence of God in holy, loving majesty that makes heaven what it is."[20] This is the heart of Jonathan Edwards's contribution to our understanding of heaven. Heaven is heaven because of who God is in all his beauty, manifested specifically in the love of Christ to sinners. Heaven is heaven because the triune God is there, in love. Hell is hell not because God is absent, but because he is present—in wrath. But heaven will be an eternal swim in the ocean of God's love.

"Edwards spent his whole life preparing to die," writes George Marsden.[21] That is not morbidity; it is sober realism, and our only sanity. In a world doing all it can to fixate our minds on the present, let us follow Edwards's example.

---

[19] *WJE*, 13:167.
[20] K. Scott Oliphint and Sinclair B. Ferguson, *If I Should Die before I Wake* (Grand Rapids: Baker, 1995), 44; quoted in Dan C. Barber and Robert A. Peterson, *Life Everlasting: The Unfolding Story of Heaven* (Phillipsburg, NJ: P&R, 2012), 185.
[21] George M. Marsden, *Jonathan Edwards: A Life* (New Haven, CT: Yale University Press, 2003), 490.

Conclusion

In the next chapter we will identify a weakness in Edwards's vision of heaven. But this ought not to detract from the profound and powerful vision of our future that Edwards leaves us with—a vision of heaven exquisite beyond imagining, in joy and love, unceasingly, increasingly, with the Friend of Sinners. So horrible is hell, and so delightful heaven, that Edwards believed that to those in hell, this life will seem to have been heaven, and to those in heaven, this life will seem to have been hell.

Miscellany "FF" in Edwards's private rumination has been for me one of the most powerful statements God has used in my own life to peel back my fingers from clutching onto the empty pleasures of the world. Edwards is reflecting on what heaven will be like if we have actually been united to Christ. We close this chapter with this:

> By virtue of the believer's union with Christ, he doth really possess all things. That we know plainly from Scripture. But it may be asked, how doth he possess all things? What is he the better for it? How is a true Christian so much richer than other men?
>
> To answer this, I'll tell you what I mean by "possessing all things." I mean that God three in one, all that he is, and all that he has, and all that he does, all that he has made or done—the whole universe, bodies and spirits, earth and heaven, angels, men and devils, sun, moon and stars, land and sea, fish and fowls, all the silver and gold, kings and potentates as well as mean [low, common] men—are as much the Christian's as the money in his pocket, the clothes he wears, the house he dwells in, or the victuals he eats; yea more properly his, more advantageously his, than if he could command all those things mentioned to be just in all respects as he pleased at any time, by virtue of the union with Christ; because Christ, who certainly doth thus possess all things, is entirely his: so that he possesses it all, more than a wife the share of the best and dearest husband, more than the hand possesses what the head doth; it is all his. . . .
>
> Every atom in the universe is managed by Christ so as to be most to the advantage of the Christian, every particle of air or every ray of the sun; so that he in the other world, when he comes to see it, shall sit and enjoy all this vast inheritance with surprising, amazing joy.[22]

See you there.

---

[22] *WJE*, 13:183–84.

CHAPTER 13

FOUR CRITICISMS

"Remember your leaders, those who spoke to you the word of God. Consider the outcome of their way of life, and imitate their faith" (Heb. 13:7). Jonathan Edwards is worthy of imitation. Not replication; there is only one Edwards. But imitation—building into our lives the "faith" that drove him, producing a certain "way of life" and a certain "outcome." I have written this book to commend to you Jonathan Edwards's life and theology as guidance to your own walk with God. Such imitation will manifest itself uniquely in each reader's life, different as we all are. But there is much for each of us to learn from him. Read him. Befriend him. Get to know him.

But even the writer to the Hebrews knew the limits of human exemplars. In chapter 12 he had exhorted believers to "run with endurance the race that is set before us, *looking to Jesus*, the founder and perfecter of our faith" (Heb. 12:1–2). Only one human life guides infallibly. Only one "is the same yesterday and today and forever" (13:8).

In this final chapter I want to reflect on a few ways we ought not to imitate Jonathan Edwards. With Edwards, as with every historical hero, we must swallow the meat and spit out the bones. We should not uncritically swallow everything he says simply because of the man's genius and godliness, both of which he undoubtedly had.[1] We will focus in this chapter especially on one question—whether Edwards sufficiently brought the gospel to bear on the hearts of his people. We will then more briefly consider three

---

[1] An example of a work succumbing to hagiography regarding Edwards is Steven J. Lawson, *The Unwavering Resolve of Jonathan Edwards* (Orlando: Reformation Trust, 2008).

more weaknesses: his neglect of the doctrine of creation and the goodness of an embodied human existence, his use of Scripture, and his view of the regenerate as compared with the unregenerate.

Jonathan Edwards is way out ahead of me, and probably you, both in living and in theologizing on the Christian life. But the student, standing on the teacher's shoulders, may on occasion glimpse something the teacher doesn't. Cautiously, we proceed.

Failure to Apply the Gospel

Jonathan Edwards's greatest weakness may have been a failure to adequately apply the gospel to the hearts of Christians. Lest I overstate this criticism, let me put it this way: the Christian church has much to learn from Edwards about the gospel, but Edwards has a little to learn from us.

Twenty-first-century evangelicalism has seen a steady rise in voices calling for reform toward a more "gospel-centered" way of personal and church life. I consider this reform, in general, cause for rejoicing. The movement has found its voice especially among younger evangelicals. It has been spread to a large degree through digital means such as websites, blogs, and podcasts.[2]

By "gospel-centered" I mean a view of the Christian life that sees the gospel not only as the womb that gave new birth to us but also as the oxygen we now breathe every day as believers. If a Christian's life is a line on a piece of paper, the gospel of grace—that sinners are accepted and loved by God on the basis of Christ's work instead of their own—is not one point on that line, but the paper on which it is drawn. The gospel is a home, not a hotel; it is to be lived in, not passed through. Christians still sin. Therefore Christians need the gospel. To be sure, Edwards clearly believed in the objective truth that the gospel is crucial and foundational for ushering one into the Christian life. But what about the ongoing relevance subjectively, psychologically, for Christians who, however godly, still sin?

Numerous passages of Scripture make particularly explicit the relevance of the gospel to every day of the Christian life. In John 6, when the crowds ask Jesus what they must do to be doing the works of God, Jesus's surprising response is, "This is the work of God, that you believe in him whom he has sent" (John 6:29). The work they need to do is: don't work.

---

[2] See Collin Hansen, *Young, Restless, and Reformed: A Journalist's Journey with the New Calvinists* (Wheaton, IL: Crossway, 2008).

Believe. In 1 Corinthians 15, Paul calls the gospel that which is "of first importance" and says that the Corinthians are presently standing in this gospel and are being saved by it. He thus draws attention to the present power of the gospel. Paul tells the Colossians to "continue in the faith, stable and steadfast, not shifting from the hope of the gospel" (Col. 1:23) and that they are to walk now in Christ in just the same way they have received him in the first place—with the empty hands of faith (2:6). And so on.

So, was Jonathan Edwards sufficiently centered on the gospel as a resource for Christians? I want to answer with a carefully qualified no.

I believe that Edwards is among the top few most beneficial writers from which Christian readers today could possibly profit. That conviction fueled the writing of this book. And yet, I think he missed the functional centrality of the gospel in his preaching and writing. Please do not hear something I am not saying. I don't mean he misunderstood what the gospel was, or that he misread the Bible, or that he was a closet legalist, or that he promoted works' righteousness.[3] It was Edwards's extended sermon series on justification by faith alone from Romans 4:5 that sparked the local revival in Northampton in 1734. He was a profound (if debated) theologian of justification.[4] And one does occasionally find in Edwards statements such as, "The gospel is the main instrument by which the influences of this Sun of righteousness [Christ] are derived on the hearts of men."[5]

Yet as we view his entire corpus as a whole, this is not the dominant theme in his theology of the Christian life. His focus is on the subjective much more than the objective aspect of Christian living: Christ in us more than Christ for us. In two specific ways Edwards failed to bring the gospel to bear on the hearts of believers. One, he missed opportunities to startle his hearers and readers into wonder and worship through the wonder of free grace to God's own children amid their daily faults and failures. Two, he was overly introspective. Let me give a few examples of each.

Missed Opportunities to Bring the Gospel Home

First, Edwards missed the opportunity to bring his sermons home with the gospel. One example is the sermon "A Glorious Foundation for Peace"—

---

[3] David Vaughan makes a good distinction between legalism and Edwards's pursuit of holiness in David Vaughan, *A Divine Light: The Spiritual Leadership of Jonathan Edwards* (Nashville: Cumberland House, 2007), 155.
[4] See most recently, e.g., Josh Moody, ed., *Jonathan Edwards and Justification* (Wheaton, IL: Crossway, 2012).
[5] *WJE*, 22:54.

a sermon crying out for gospel clarity if ever there was one. The point of the sermon is that Christ has brought peace into the world. Edwards concludes like this:

> Surely it would be a glorious thing if God should send down some extraor-
> dinary messenger from heaven to the earth to be a peacemaker among
> men and to reconcile them one to another. This God has done. He has sent
> his own Son on this errand, and he restores peace to men in these ways:
>   1. He has set a wonderful example of love and a peaceable Spirit. . . .
>   2. Christ abundantly insisted on His doctrine and commands upon
> the exercise of love and peace. . . .
>   3. Christ restores peace to men one with another by giving them his
> Spirit which is the spirit of love and peace.[6]

All this is right and true and wise. Jesus came as an example of peace, to command peace, and to give the Spirit to enable peace. But Edwards should have added a clinching fourth point: Jesus came and in his own death broke down the wall of hostility between people (Eph. 2:11–22). Or as Paul puts it later in Ephesians, it is in view of Christ's saving work that we act a certain way toward one another (Eph. 4:31–5:2). Christ not only helps us do the right thing; he has also emptied the threat of accusation when we do the wrong thing. Peace with my neighbor blossoms in the rays of a rich awareness of peace with God through the gospel. When I know God has laid down his gun that was justly aimed at me, I can lay down my gun that is (even if justly) aimed at another.

This is only one example. But it is representative. Edwards did not have well-developed gospel instincts when it came to bringing his sermons home to his people. For all that he said about the beauty of Christ, he could have been clearer on what precisely it is that makes Christ so beautiful—namely, his grace toward sinners, including regenerate sinners.[7] Others down through church history provide better examples at this point, such as the Scottish pastor Thomas Chalmers (1780–1847), himself steeped in Edwards. Take Chalmers's well-known sermon "The Expulsive Power of a New Affection," which is often misunderstood. His basic point is not simply that

---

[6] Jonathan Edwards, "A Glorious Foundation for Peace," in *The Glory and Honor of God: Volume 2 of the Previously Unpublished Sermons of Jonathan Edwards*, ed. Michael D. McMullen (Nashville: Broadman & Holman, 2004), 182–84.

[7] J. I. Packer has made a criticism of Henry Scougal similar to the one that I am making of Edwards: see Packer's introduction to Henry Scougal, *The Life of God in the Soul of Man* (Fearn, UK: Christian Focus, 1996), esp. 12–14.

godliness comes by replacing sinful pleasures with the greater pleasures of holiness. His basic point is that it is the grace of the gospel that is itself the greatest power in expelling sinful desires. "The freer the gospel, the more sanctifying the gospel; and the more it is received as a doctrine of grace, the more will it be felt as a doctrine according to godliness. This is one of the secrets of the Christian life."[8]

Unhealthy Introspection

Second, Edwards was very introspective. Healthy, occasional self-examination is one thing. But Edwards went beyond this into an unhealthy preoccupation with his own spiritual state, encouraging the same preoccupation among his people.[9]

Speaking of the Great Awakening in his 1742 work *Some Thoughts concerning the Revival*, he wrote: "There are things that must be done directly to advance it. And here it concerns everyone, in the first place, to look into his own heart and see to it that he be a partaker of the benefits of the work himself, and that it be promoted in his own soul."[10] An occasional exhortation along these lines would be one thing. But this is not an isolated statement. It is representative of the tenor of entire works, such as *Religious Affections* and *The Distinguishing Marks of a Work of the Spirit of God*. Jonathan Edwards was the premier theologian of revival. Perhaps teaching others how to assess the state of their souls was unavoidable. And certainly, there was much excess amid the eighteenth-century revivals, excess that required the wise and careful assessment of a Jonathan Edwards. But Edwards could have made clearer that reviving comes to those who fix their eyes on Christ, not those who fix their eyes on whether their eyes are fixed on Christ.

It is a biblical imperative to examine ourselves (2 Cor. 13:5). But it is a rare biblical imperative. The Scottish preacher Robert Murray McCheyne famously said that for every one look at self, the believer should take ten looks at Christ. This is closer to the biblical rhythm than the Edwards corpus is. For all his talk about seeing the beauty of Christ, Edwards did not consistently follow this advice in the overall flavor of his writing and preaching.

---

[8] Thomas Chalmers, *The Expulsive Power of a New Affection* (Minneapolis: Curiosmith, 2012), 27–28.
[9] A similar point is made in passing by Sean Michael Lucas, *God's Grand Design: The Theological Vision of Jonathan Edwards* (Wheaton, IL: Crossway, 2011), 214–15.
[10] *WJE*, 4:502.

In *Religious Affections* he writes: "'Tis not God's design that men should obtain assurance in any other way, than by mortifying corruption, and increasing in grace, and obtaining the lively exercises of it." Remember that by "grace" here Edwards has in mind (as he normally does) not grace as pardon but grace as power: not the objective but the subjective aspect to grace. I wish Edwards had called this a valid but secondary means of assurance, and had said instead, for primary assurance, "'Tis not God's design that men should obtain assurance in any other way, than by looking to the cross and the empty tomb." We kill sin and gain assurance of God's favor fundamentally by enjoying the truth that Christ was killed for sin and lost God's favor on the cross. Edwards did not make assurance as clear to his people as he could have. In a 1733 sermon (re-preached three times over the next twenty years), Edwards counseled his people that "seeking and serving God with the utmost diligence is the way to have assurance, and to have it maintained."[11] No, seeking and serving is not the main recipe for assurance. The gospel is.

We see this instinct to turn inward in the young Edwards too. Consider a diary entry from December 1722, as he wrestles with whether God truly loves him or not:

> The reason why I, in the least, question my interest in God's love and favor, is, 1. Because I cannot speak so fully to my experience of that preparatory work, of which divines speak; 2. I do not remember that I experienced regeneration, exactly in those steps, in which divines say it is generally wrought; 3. I do not feel the Christian graces sensibly enough, particularly faith. I fear they are only such hypocritical outside affections, which wicked men may feel, as well as others. They do not seem to be sufficiently inward, full, sincere, entire and hearty.[12]

Contrast the young Edwards here with David Brainerd at about the same age, and note especially how the young Brainerd concludes this journal entry:

> Sept. 19 1747. Near night, while I attempted to walk a little, my thoughts turned thus; how infinitely sweet it is to love God, and be all for him! Upon which it was suggested to me, "You are not an angel, not lively and active." To which my whole soul immediately replied, "I as sincerely desire to love and glorify God, as any angel in heaven." Upon which it was suggested again, "But you are filthy, not fit for heaven." Hereupon instantly appeared

---

[11] *WJE*, 17:442.
[12] *WJE*, 16:759.

the blessed robes of Christ's righteousness, which I could not but exult and triumph in. I viewed the infinite excellency of God.[13]

Edwards questioned the state of his soul and turned to the intensity and sequence of his own experience. Brainerd questioned the state of his soul and turned to the comfort of imputation—Christ's righteousness was his. In this instance Brainerd and not Edwards is the healthier model for us (though Brainerd, too, could be quite introspective at times).

Consider a few others from another era of history than that of Edwards and Brainerd—one from two hundred years before Edwards (Martin Luther) and one from two hundred years after (C. S. Lewis).[14] Each coaches us away from unhealthy Edwardsian introspection.

Take Luther first. The irascible Reformer stayed at the Coburg Castle during the Diet of Augsburg. During these meetings Luther received word that his father had died. Amid the tumults both theological and personal, Luther wrote out Bible texts and thoughts about them on the wall of his room so that they were always before his eyes. Twenty years later Luther's physician visited the room where Luther had stayed and discovered many sayings littering the walls to help the Reformer fight for internal peace and sanity, sayings such as:

1. Our cause rests in the hand of him who distinctly tells us, "No one can snatch them out of my hand." (John 10)

4. It is true that God gave up his own Son for us all, Romans 8:32. If that be true, why do we falter, or worry, or hang our heads?

19. God himself says, "I show mercy to thousands of those who love me and keep my commandments." We ought rightfully to believe these exalted and comforting words of the Divine Majesty. Though our faith be weak, we rely on God, that he can and will do what he promises.[15]

---

[13] *WJE*, 7:465.

[14] Others could be added, such as Archibald Alexander, *Thoughts on Religious Experience* (Philadelphia: Presbyterian Board of Publication, 1844), 201–2; Charles Spurgeon, *Faith* (New Kensington, PA: Whitaker House, 1995); Herman Bavinck, *Reformed Dogmatics*, ed. John Bolt, trans. John Vriend, 4 vols. (Grand Rapids: Baker, 2003–2008), 3:528; 4:245, 248, 257; G. C. Berkouwer, *Faith and Sanctification*, Studies in Dogmatics (Grand Rapids: Eerdmans, 1952), esp. 64, 77–78, 84, 93, 96, 193; Berkouwer, *Faith and Justification* (Grand Rapids: Eerdmans, 1954), 100. I have explored at length Bavinck's and Berkouwer's applications of the gospel of grace to Christian living in Dane C. Ortlund, "Sanctification by Justification: The Forgotten Insight of Bavinck and Berkouwer on Progressive Sanctification," *Scottish Bulletin of Evangelical Theology* 28 (2010): 43–61.

[15] Martin, Luther, "Sayings in Which Luther Found Comfort," in *Luther's Works*, vol. 43, *Devotional Writings II*, ed. Gustav K. Wiencke (Philadelphia: Fortress, 1968), 171–76.

A close equivalent to what Luther did is Jonathan Edwards's famous "Resolutions." In his late teens Edwards wrote down a series of seventy-some self-exhortations. Here are a few:

4. Resolved, never to do any manner of thing, whether in soul or body, less or more, but what tends to the glory of God.

20. Resolved, to maintain the strictest temperance in eating and drinking.

30. Resolved, to strive to my utmost every week to be brought higher in religion than I was the week before.

44. Resolved, that no other end but religion, shall have any influence at all on any of my actions.

Edwards reflected later in life that he had perhaps been a bit too rash and overoptimistic in his early zeal for godly behavior.[16] But throughout his ministry he had little trouble insisting that "if persons do but truly resolve and make it their true and faithful wish and endeavor" to follow through on their covenant obligations, they will succeed.[17] My point is that Luther's "Sayings" reflect a healthier, more realistic, more gospel-mindful, and ultimately more biblical expression of Christian living than Edwards's "Resolutions." Luther's list looked out. Edwards's list looked in.

Next, consider a strikingly relevant statement from C. S. Lewis. In a 1949 letter he wrote:

Everyone who accepts the teaching of St. Paul must have a belief in "sanctification." But I should, myself, be chary of describing such operations of the Holy Ghost as "experiences" if by experiences we mean things necessarily discoverable by introspection. And I should be still more chary of mapping out a series of such experiences as an indispensable norm (or syllabus!) for all Christians. I think the ways in which God saves us are probably infinitely various and admit varying degrees of consciousness in the patient. Anything which sets him saying "Now . . . Stage 2 ought to be coming along . . . is this it?" I think bad and likely to lead some to presumption and others to despair. We must leave God to dress the wound and not keep on taking peeps under the bandage for ourselves.[18]

---

[16] *WJE*, 16:795.
[17] *WJE*, 22:516.
[18] Walter Hooper, ed., *The Collected Letters of C. S. Lewis*, vol. 2, *Books, Broadcasts, and the War 1931–1949* (San Francisco: HarperOne, 2004), 914.

Lewis diagnoses as problematic here precisely how Edwards handles himself in his 1722 diary entry, quoted above—namely, analyze and fret over (the two generally go together) one's spiritual experience. Lewis's no-nonsense approach to the Christian life provides a dose of realism that is at times lacking in Edwards. At the same time (as indicated in chapter 9 on obedience), we must say that Edwards gives a good splash of cold water in the face of those who, in the name of Christian liberty, are careless in how they live. Edwards speaks of those who "flatter themselves with [the gospel] and make use of the glorious and joyful tidings it brings of God's infinite mercy and readiness to pardon as a pillow on which they may indulge their sloth and quiet their consciences in ways of sin."[19] That is not an empty set.

Nevertheless, the point in all this is that Edwards ought not to have been so introspective himself, and he ought not to have encouraged others to be so introspective. There is a place for introspection. This is not an absolute either–or. It is a matter of degree and thus wisdom. But Edwards should have encouraged his people to look inside themselves less and to look outside to Christ more. It is natural to look within, in assessing how we are doing spiritually. And there is a place for this. But it is nearly impossible to look inside yourself and assess accurately; we tend to exaggerate our strengths and others' weaknesses, and to minimize others' strengths and our weaknesses. And even if we assess ourselves accurately, we naturally slide into either smugness in success or despondency in failure. Traps and dangers lurk at every turn when we look mainly within. Simplicity and clarity and gospel freedom await us when we look outside to Christ. An outstanding example of a healthy outward-looking impulse is John Owen, who in (for example) *Communion with God* repeatedly calls his readers to look outside themselves to Christ.[20]

The Goodness of Creation

Though we will treat them more briefly for the sake of space, let's consider three other weaknesses in Edwards's theology of the Christian life. The first is that Edwards did a poor job of fully appreciating the doctrine of creation and the everyday delights that are mediated through our five senses. Edwards emphasized the sense of the heart, what Marsden calls the "sixth

---

[19] *WJE*, 22:58.
[20] John Owen, *Communion with the Triune God*, ed. Kelly M. Kapic and Justin Taylor (Wheaton, IL: Crossway, 2007).

sense,"[21] to the neglect of the five senses. He pursued enjoyment of the Giver but at times neglected enjoyment of the gifts.

We will quickly forgive this, because for every one Christian today who fails to enjoy God's gifts, another twenty fail to enjoy God himself. But the point should stand nonetheless. Edwards had a theology in which Christians are to enjoy and glorify God by enjoying God's gifts, but he seems not to have lived and taught that theology very consistently. Specifically, when we read Edwards, he sometimes sounds like a latter-day Gnostic—implicitly commending the spiritual world to the neglect of the material world.[22] He does at times focus on the material world, but generally only so far as the material world itself points to the spiritual world.[23] Edwards's teaching could easily promote a false asceticism that needlessly denigrates the good things of life—food, sex, sleep, play, laughter, and so on. (Perhaps the gaunt Edwards himself erred in this direction.) What we need is to receive and be duly convicted by Edwards's radical God-centeredness, which refused to make much of a created thing if it did not cause our eyes to run up to the Creator from whom it comes. But we must complement this crucial insight with a healthy dose of the goodness of the created order—fallen, but *good*.

The same apostle who wrote that he counts everything a loss for the sake of Christ (Phil. 3:8) also wrote that it is "the teachings of demons" not to enjoy sex and sushi, because "everything created by God is good" (1 Tim. 4:1–4). Paul appeals here not to the doctrine of redemption but to the doctrine of creation. Yet Edwards so emphasized redemption that creation was sidelined[24]—despite the fact that redemption itself, as the Dutch Reformed tradition has articulated more clearly than we Americans, is the restoration of creation. This seems to be a peculiarly evangelical imbalance. In his recent book on the arts, Jerram Barrs reflects on this passage from 1 Timothy 4 and wisely writes:

> Repeatedly in the history of the church, Christians have been tempted to devalue the richness of creation . . . as if it would be somehow more "spiritual" to live a life devoid of beauty, of good things, of music, of literature, of painting, of color, and so forth. It is as if bare simplicity, barren-

---

[21] George M. Marsden, *Jonathan Edwards: A Life* (New Haven, CT: Yale University Press, 2003), 96.

[22] A better teacher in this regard is Herman Bavinck. I contrast Edwards and Bavinck on this point in Dane C. Ortlund, "'Created Over a Second Time' or 'Grace Restoring Nature'? Edwards and Bavinck on the Heart of Salvation," *The Bavinck Review* 3 (2012): 9–29.

[23] Cf., e.g., his "Images of Divine Things."

[24] See Edwards's comments in *WJE*, 4:344.

ness, and even ugliness were somehow more pleasing to God. Behind this idea is the conviction that the "spiritual" is all that matters, and that the physical, therefore, is at best only of secondary value. . . . But this belief is nonsense and, according to Paul, a heresy of the most serious kind, for in the end it is a denial of the goodness of creation and the goodness of its Creator.[25]

To be sure, all that we saw in our earlier chapter on "the soul" should stand. It is the Christian's soul that will live on into eternity. It is the soul that finally matters.

But no one will be in heaven forever. Heaven—if by that word we mean the disembodied state of glory into which believers will be transferred when they die—is temporary. The true and final state is one of resurrected bodies on a restored planet earth.

George Marsden writes at the end of his biography:

Edwards challenges the commonsense view of our culture that the material world is the "real" world. Edwards' universe is essentially a universe of personal relationships. Reality is a communication of affections, ultimately of God's love and creatures' responses. Material things are transitory and ephemeral.[26]

Marsden's depiction of Edwards's thought here is right. And yes, the universe is essentially about relationship and love. But this does not mean it is essentially immaterial. The immaterial state in heaven is what is ephemeral. Our final material state on the new earth is permanent.

Not only the goodness of the material body, then, but also the goodness of the material world, is neglected by Edwards. In a miscellany Edwards even defines the new heavens and the new earth as located in heaven and not on this globe.[27] In his famous sermon on Christian pilgrimage Edwards says things like, "It was never designed by God that this world should be our home."[28] That is of course true in one sense. We are sojourners and exiles here because sin has infected everything in this world since the fall (1 Pet. 2:11). Our citizenship is now in heaven (Phil. 3:20). There is truth when

---

[25] Jerram Barrs, *Echoes of Eden: Reflections on Christianity, Literature, and the Arts* (Wheaton, IL: Crossway, 2013), 18.

[26] Marsden, *Jonathan Edwards*, 503.

[27] *WJE*, 18:514. See also the editorial comments regarding this point of Edwards's as articulated in this miscellany in *WJE*, 22:23; also Glenn R. Kreider, *Jonathan Edwards's Interpretation of Revelation 4:1–8:1* (Lanham, MD: University Press of America, 2004), 164.

[28] *WJE*, 17:436.

Edwards says later in this sermon: "Our present state, and all that belongs [to it], is designed by him that made all things to be wholly in order to another world. This world was made for a place of preparation for another world."[29]

But in another sense it is not true that God never designed this world to be our home, and Edwards did not sufficiently acknowledge this other sense. At the end of the Bible, in the final and climactic depiction of the end of all things, believers do not leave earth and go to heaven; rather, heaven comes down to earth. God's work of redemption does not leave his work of creation behind but restores his work of creation. Our final state will be not Heaven 1.0 but Eden 2.0. God *did* design this world to be our home.

An uncritical reading of Edwards by modern evangelicals could easily reinforce a vision of our final state as disembodied, shadowy, ethereal, ghost-like. The result is that we are left to conclude that this present life is our only chance to enjoy peach cobbler, a beautiful sunset, a game of basketball with the kids in the driveway, a hug from a friend, sleeping in, skiing, the beach, back rubs, the smell of a rose, and Pachelbel's "Canon in D." We tend to think God created the world in Genesis 1 and 2, we screwed it up in Genesis 3, and God is tolerating the whole thing till one day he scraps it all and brings us to heaven. Yet when we consider the three instances of human life without sin—Adam and Eve before the fall, Jesus, and the new earth in Revelation 21–22—none of these is disembodied, and none of them takes place in heaven. None is ethereal. Final redemption will not eradicate our need for a body; final redemption will restore our bodies right along with our souls, all in a restored planet earth.[30]

Use of Scripture

Among all the saints who have gone before us, it is difficult to imagine a greater love for, knowledge of, and delight in the Bible than that of Jonathan Edwards. This is why I have given a chapter to Edwards's exemplary cherishing of the Bible as the greatest earthly treasure of the Christian life.

And yet one wishes Edwards had at times stayed closer to the biblical text as that which provides not only the starting point for a sermon

---

[29] *WJE*, 17:438.

[30] As a superior alternative to Edwards at this point, readers are encouraged to explore the writings of Herman Bavinck, esp. vol. 2 of his *Reformed Dogmatics*. The best brief articulation of the goodness of creation and bodily human existence from a Reformed perspective of which I am aware is Michael D. Williams, "The *Imago Dei* and the Order of Creation—Part I," *Presbyterion* 39, no. 1 (2013): 30–44.

but also the end point and everything in between. To be sure, we ought to be measured in our criticisms of Edwards's use of Scripture. Many today are too quick to write off his preaching strategy, dismissing him as a pre-Enlightenment thinker and thus an unsophisticated student of the Bible.

Yet Edwards's use of Scripture leaves something to be desired. His sermonic strategy was to take a text, usually a single verse, and use it as a launching point for a sermon. The verse would provide a starting point for, but not the boundaries of, the sermon. This is not necessarily a problem, because what Edwards said, even if not the main point of the passage preached on, was invariably theologically rich and true and penetrating. And at times we do find stark exceptions to his usual method, such as in the sermon "They Sing a New Song," where he considers each word of this phrase, taken from Revelation 14:3, always mindful of the text's context.[31]

But Edwards's normal method sometimes caused him to import meaning into rather than export meaning out of the text. In *Religious Affections*, for example, Edwards quotes Jesus's words in Luke 10:3, "I send you forth as lambs, in the midst of wolves," and then makes the following connection: "The redemption of the church by Christ from the power of the devil was typified of old, by David's delivering the lamb, out of the mouth of the lion and the bear."[32] Such a whole-Bible connection is intriguing, but Edwards's creativity in putting the Bible together led at times to connections that are less than fully convincing.

A related weakness in his use of Scripture is his fondness for lining up biblical prophecy with contemporary events in a way that now looks strained. Edwards surmised that the return of Christ was imminent and gave America a pivotal role in the playing out of end-time events. Such statements are unfortunate.[33] And yet one also wonders what commonly held beliefs today will look strained to believers three hundred years from now. We are all children of our times.

Edwards also tended toward allegory.[34] Like many of the Puritans before him, for example, he interpreted Song of Solomon in a way that jumped over the plain and literal meaning of the text (as speaking about male-female romantic love) to get to the spiritual meaning of the text (as speaking about Christ-church redemptive love). To be sure, from a whole-Bible

---

[31] *WJE*, 22:224.
[32] *WJE*, 2:348.
[33] See E. Brooks Holifield, "Edwards as Theologian," in *The Cambridge Companion to Jonathan Edwards*, ed. Stephen J. Stein (Cambridge: Cambridge University Press, 2007), 154–56.
[34] Cf. editor's comments in *WJE*, 22:490–91.

perspective, the romantic love of Song of Solomon finds its true and final expression in Christ's love for his bride, the church. But the jump from the plain meaning of the text to the ultimate, whole-Bible meaning ought to be made with a bit more restraint than Edwards (and many other Puritans) exercised.

In these ways Edwards ought to be followed cautiously. And yet, despite all this, one has to say that while his methods ought not always to be replicated, few of us will ever attain the encyclopedic knowledge of the Bible that Edwards had and, more importantly, the heart-instincts as to who God is as presented in the Bible. It is astonishing to observe Edwards's pervasive quoting and referencing of Scripture when one considers that he had nothing but a Bible to help him track down texts—no electronic search capabilities, and so forth, and little more than what he had stored up in his own mind and the notes he had created in his "blank Bible." It is fairly commonplace for Edwards scholars to attribute his theological framework to the philosophical categories of the day, such as the Cambridge Platonists and John Locke and other empiricists.[35] Yet never once in his writings does Edwards appeal to any philosopher over the text of Scripture. The Bible was all-trumping for him. He was a man of the Word.

Even if some of us wish, then, that Edwards were a step closer to expositional preaching, even today's most faithful expositors will nevertheless find much to learn from him for their own preaching. For the Bible is to be read and understood and preached not only line-by-line but also as a grand, synthetic whole. It is to be read not only as a human book rooted in history but also as a divine book giving us the very words of God from heaven. It is to be studied not only grammatically and historically but also spiritually and theologically. Edwards helps us in these crucial ways, even if we must be cautious about replicating his methods. Let us follow him carefully, then, but never deflect his use of the Bible simply because of the century in which he lived.

View of the Regenerate and the Unregenerate

Finally, Jonathan Edwards tended toward an overly negative view of the unregenerate and an overly positive view of the regenerate. One wishes he had retained a robust sense of the image of God even in those who are not

---

[35] E.g., Philip F. Gura, *Jonathan Edwards: America's Evangelical* (New York: Hill and Wang, 2005), 66–69, 227–38.

born again, and of remaining sin in those who are. Unbelievers are not as bad as they might be, and believers are not as good as they might be.

The second chapter of this book focused on a major theme in Edwards: regeneration. This is the ignition of the Christian life. I wish to take nothing away from the rich theology of new birth in that chapter. We are a people today with an immature understanding of the new birth, and Jonathan Edwards has something to teach us. Yet one wishes he explored at greater length the complexity of fallen-yet-redeemed human beings.

In a letter to Edwards, Thomas Gillespie argued this very point against him, and I think his point lands squarely and fairly. Gillespie noted that believers often meet grave temptations and adversities after regeneration, and that we ought to be wary of facile or overly optimistic views of the Christian life.[36] He suggested that people sometimes seem even more sinful after new birth! In short, Edwards is of course right that we *are less* sinful after regeneration. But he should have explained that we often *feel more* sinful after regeneration. The very regenerating reality that fundamentally changes us also hypersensitizes us to remaining indwelling sin.

As for the unregenerate, conversely, Edwards could have done more justice to the fact that the image of God is a transcendent reality marking all human beings, regenerate and unregenerate. For example, we find him saying things such as:

> What is born in the first birth of man, is nothing but man as he is of himself, *without anything divine in him*; depraved, debased, sinful, ruined man, utterly unfit to enter into the kingdom of God, and incapable of the spiritual divine happiness of that kingdom: but that which is born in the new birth, of the Spirit of God, is a spiritual principle, and holy and divine nature, meet for the divine and heavenly kingdom.[37]

There is truth to this, but it is not the whole truth. The first, natural birth of every human being does indeed mark them with something divine: the divine image. Edwards of course acknowledges and believes this. But it is one thing to acknowledge a theological truth occasionally, and it is another to build a truth into the warp and woof of one's overall theological vision. It would not be unfortunate that Edwards made little of the image of God in the unregenerate but for the fact that he makes such a big deal about

---

[36] *WJE*, 2:475–76.
[37] *WJE*, 3:279–80, emphasis added.

the radical newness of the regenerate. Given the tenor of his writing and preaching as a whole, the conclusion is inescapable that Edwards's anthropology (theology of human beings) was somewhat lopsided.

When human beings are savingly converted by sovereign grace, two parallel changes wash into their lives. One is objective, one is subjective. The objective is the pardon that grace brings; the subjective is the power that grace brings. One is legal, the other transformative. One is external, the other internal. The objective is the main message of Romans 1–4; the subjective is the main message of Romans 5–8. And so on.

Edwards's theology of the Christian life tended to emphasize the subjective to the neglect of the objective—by which I mean that the ongoing need for justification in the believer's life was not a strength of Edwards's ministry. If some in the history of the church have emphasized the objective to the neglect of the subjective (Luther or some Lutherans?), others have done the opposite, and Edwards was in this latter camp. Had he brought both justification and regeneration equally to bear on the Christian life, he would not have neglected the image of God in the unregenerate and remaining sin in the regenerate as it is met by their justification.

CONCLUSION

J. I. Packer once remarked that it was the Reformers who recovered our doctrine of justification and the Puritans who recovered our doctrine of sanctification. If Edwards can be labeled a late Puritan—even though his birth in 1703 came two generations after the age of the Puritans (1560–1660)—this rings true for his own ministry.[1] He helps us to live the Christian life.

This is not to say Edwards neglected the forensic, legal, justifying aspect of salvation, what both Luther and Calvin considered the key to the health of both the church and the individual Christian life. True, we have been critical of Edwards for not bringing the gospel to bear in all its fullness on the lives of his people. But this criticism should not be exaggerated.

Nevertheless, the great legacy Jonathan Edwards has left the church lies not in the realm of the objective but in the subjective side of salvation. The Reformers' legacy above all else has been the conviction that justification is outside-in and we lose it if we make it inside-out. Our status before God comes to us as an alien righteousness, utterly external to us, and we dare not seek to supplement it by what we bring to the table.

Edwards's legacy, on the other hand, was that sanctification is inside-out and we lose it if we make it outside-in. Transformation occurs as the heart is changed within, not as we seek to crowbar our behavior into alignment with an external moral code or set of rules or even our conscience. For Edwards, we do not become beautiful centrally by obeying. We obey as we see and taste beauty. In *Religious Affections* Edwards memorably remarked

---

[1] Cf. Conrad Cherry's comments along these lines in *The Theology of Jonathan Edwards: A Reappraisal*, rev. ed. (Bloomington, IN: Indiana University Press, 1990), 126–27; also Harry S. Stout, "The Puritans and Edwards," in *Jonathan Edwards and the American Experience*, ed. Nathan O. Hatch and Harry S. Stout (New York: Oxford University Press, 1988), 142–59.

that even washed pigs still like to roll in the mud.[2] They must be changed on the inside if they are to act differently on the outside.

The Christian life is a life of beauty. This is Edwards's legacy. Love, joy, gentleness, prayer, obedience—all these Edwardsian emphases are spokes extending from the hub of a soul alive to beauty. All are diverse manifestations of this single, fundamental reality. They are what healthy Christians exhale, having inhaled the loveliness of God.

Amid all the good activity of God's people today—all the books and blogs, conferences and coalitions, education and training—may God give the church a fresh awakening to divine beauty in the twenty-first century. Such an awakening will be the difference between our energies being spent in the flesh or in the Spirit, with corresponding significance either transient or eternal.

---

[2] WJE, 2:341.

SELECT BIBLIOGRAPHY

Primary Sources

Bailey, Richard A., and Gregory A. Wills, eds. *The Salvation of Souls: Nine Previously Unpublished Sermons on the Call of Ministry and the Gospel by Jonathan Edwards.* Wheaton, IL: Crossway, 2002.

Grosart, Alexander B., ed. *Selections from the Unpublished Writings of Jonathan Edwards of America.* Ligonier, PA: Soli Deo Gloria, 1992. Reprint from 1865.

Haykin, Michael, ed. *A Sweet Flame: Piety in the Letters of Jonathan Edwards.* Grand Rapids: Reformation Heritage, 2007.

Kimnach, Wilson H., Kenneth P. Minkema, and Douglas A. Sweeney, eds. *The Sermons of Jonathan Edwards: A Reader.* New Haven, CT: Yale University Press, 1999.

McMullen, Michael D., ed. *The Blessing of God: Previously Unpublished Sermons of Jonathan Edwards.* Nashville: Broadman & Holman, 2003.

———, ed. *The Glory and Honor of God: Volume 2 of the Previously Unpublished Sermons of Jonathan Edwards.* Nashville: Broadman & Holman, 2004.

Miller, Perry, John E. Smith, and Harry S. Stout, eds. *The Works of Jonathan Edwards.* 26 vols. New Haven, CT: Yale University Press, 1957–2008.

Secondary and Other Sources

Alexander, Archibald. *Thoughts on Religious Experience.* Philadelphia: Presbyterian Board of Publication, 1844.

Aquinas, Thomas. *Summa Theologica.* Translated by Fathers of the English Dominican Province. 3 vols. New York: Benziger Brothers, 1947–1948.

Barrs, Jerram. *Echoes of Eden: Reflections on Christianity, Literature, and the Arts.* Wheaton, IL: Crossway, 2013.

Bavinck, Herman. *Calvin and Common Grace.* Translated by Geerhardus Vos. New York: Westminster, 1996.

———. *Reformed Dogmatics.* Edited by John Bolt. Translated by John Vriend. 4 vols. Grand Rapids: Baker, 2003–2008.

Bombaro, John J. "Dispositional Peculiarity, History, and Edwards's Evangelistic Appeal to Self-Love." *Westminster Theological Journal* 66 (2004): 121–57.

———. *Jonathan Edwards's Vision of Reality: The Relationship of God to the World, Redemption History, and the Reprobate.* Princeton Theological Monograph Series. Eugene, OR: Pickwick, 2011.

———. "Jonathan Edwards's Vision of Salvation." *Westminster Theological Journal* 65 (2003): 45–67.

Byrd, James. *Jonathan Edwards for Armchair Theologians.* Louisville: Westminster John Knox, 2008.

Calvin, John. *Institutes of the Christian Religion.* Edited by John T. McNeill. Translated by Ford Lewis Battles. 2 vols. Louisville: Westminster John Knox, 1960.

Carlisle, Claire. *Kierkegaard: A Guide for the Perplexed.* London: Continuum, 2006.

Carpenter, Humphrey, ed. *The Letters of J. R. R. Tolkien.* New York: Houghton Mifflin, 2000.

Cherry, Conrad. *The Theology of Jonathan Edwards: A Reappraisal.* Rev. ed. Bloomington, IN: Indiana University Press, 1990.

Cho, Hyun-Jin. *Jonathan Edwards on Justification: Reform Development of the Doctrine in Eighteenth-Century New England.* Lanham, MD: University Press of America, 2012.

Dallimore, Arnold A. *George Whitefield: The Life and Times of the Great Evangelist of the Eighteenth Century Revival.* 2 vols. Edinburgh: Banner of Truth, 1970–1980.

Danaher, William J. *The Trinitarian Ethics of Jonathan Edwards.* Louisville: Westminster John Knox, 2004.

Fairweather, A. M., ed. *Aquinas on Nature and Grace: Selections from the Summa Theologica.* Louisville: Westminster John Knox, 2006.

Ferguson, Sinclair. *John Owen on the Christian Life.* Edinburgh: Banner of Truth, 1987.

Flieger, Verlyn, and Douglas A. Anderson, eds. *Tolkien on Fairy-Stories.* New York: HarperCollins, 2008.

Gerstner, John H. *Jonathan Edwards: A Mini-Theology.* Wheaton, IL: Tyndale House, 1987.

———. "Outline of the Apologetics of Jonathan Edwards." *Bibliotheca Sacra* 133, no. 1 (1976): 3–10, 99–107.

———. *The Rational Biblical Theology of Jonathan Edwards.* 3 vols. Orlando: Ligonier Ministries, 1991–1993.

Gura, Philip F. *Jonathan Edwards: America's Evangelical.* New York: Hill and Wang, 2005.

Hansen, Collin. *Young, Restless, and Reformed: A Journalist's Journey with the New Calvinists.* Wheaton, IL: Crossway, 2008.

Hart, D. G., Sean Michael Lucas, and Stephen J. Nichols, eds. *The Legacy of Jonathan Edwards: American Religion and the Evangelical Tradition.* Grand Rapids: Baker, 2003.

Haykin, Michael A. G. *Jonathan Edwards: The Holy Spirit in Revival.* Darlington, UK: Evangelical Press, 2005.

Holbrook, Clyde A. *The Ethics of Jonathan Edwards: Morality and Aesthetics.* Ann Arbor, MI: University of Michigan Press, 1973.

Holmes, Stephen R. *God of Grace and God of Glory: An Account of the Theology of Jonathan Edwards.* Grand Rapids: Eerdmans, 2000.

Hooper, Walter, ed. *The Collected Letters of C. S. Lewis.* Vol. 3, *Narnia, Cambridge, and Joy.* San Francisco: HarperCollins, 2007.

Hunsinger, George. "Dispositional Soteriology: Jonathan Edwards on Justification by Faith Alone." *Westminster Theological Journal* 66 (2004): 107–20.

Jenson, Robert W. *America's Theologian: A Recommendation of Jonathan Edwards.* New York: Oxford University Press, 1988.

Keyes, Dick. *Chameleon Christianity: Moving beyond Safety and Conformity.* Grand Rapids: Baker, 1999.

Lane, Belden C. *Ravished by Beauty: The Surprising Legacy of Reformed Spirituality.* New York: Oxford University Press, 2011.

Lewis, C. S. *The Pilgrim's Regress.* Grand Rapids: Eerdmans, 1958.

———. *Present Concerns.* London: Fount, 1986.

———. *Surprised by Joy.* Orlando: Harcourt, 1955.

Lloyd-Jones, Martyn. "Jonathan Edwards and the Crucial Importance of Revival." In *The Puritan Experiment in the New World.* Huntington, UK: Westminster Conference, 1976.

Logan, Samuel T. "The Doctrine of Justification in the Theology of Jonathan Edwards." *Westminster Theological Journal* 46 (1984): 26–52.

Lucas, Sean Michael. *God's Grand Design: The Theological Vision of Jonathan Edwards.* Wheaton, IL: Crossway, 2011.

Marsden, George M. *Jonathan Edwards: A Life.* New Haven, CT: Yale University Press, 2003.

———. *A Short Life of Jonathan Edwards.* Grand Rapids: Eerdmans, 2008.

McClymond, Michael J., and Gerald R. McDermott. *The Theology of Jonathan Edwards.* New York: Oxford University Press, 2012.

McDermott, Gerald R. *Jonathan Edwards Confronts the Gods: Christian Theology, Enlightenment Religion, and Non-Christian Faiths.* Oxford: Oxford University Press, 2000.

———. "Jonathan Edwards on Justification: Closer to Luther or Aquinas?" *Reformation & Revival Journal* 14, no. 1 (2005): 119–38.

———. *One Holy and Happy Society: The Public Theology of Jonathan Edwards*. University Park, PA: The Pennsylvania State University Press, 1992.

Miller, Perry. "Jonathan Edwards on the Sense of the Heart." *The Harvard Theological Review* 41 (1948): 123–45.

Minkema, Kenneth P. "Jonathan Edwards in the Twentieth Century." *Journal of the Evangelical Theological Society* 47 (2004): 659–87.

Moody, Josh, ed. *Jonathan Edwards and Justification*. Wheaton, IL: Crossway, 2012.

Murray, Iain H. *Jonathan Edwards: A New Biography*. Edinburgh: Banner of Truth, 1987.

Nichols, Stephen J. *An Absolute Sort of Certainty: The Holy Spirit and the Apologetics of Jonathan Edwards*. Phillipsburg, NJ: P&R, 2003.

———. *Heaven on Earth: Capturing Jonathan Edwards's Vision of Living in Between*. Wheaton, IL: Crossway, 2006.

———. *Jonathan Edwards: A Guided Tour of His Life and Thought*. Phillipsburg, NJ: P&R, 2001.

Nichols, William C., ed. *Seeking God: Jonathan Edwards' Evangelism Contrasted with Modern Methodologies*. Ames, IA: International Outreach, 2001.

Oberman, Heiko. *The Reformation: Roots and Ramifications*. Translated by Andrew Colin Gow. London: T&T Clark, 2004.

Old, Hughes Oliphant. *The Reading and Preaching of the Scriptures in the Worship of the Christian Church*. 5 vols. Grand Rapids: Eerdmans, 1998–2004.

Oord, Thomas Jay. *The Nature of Love: A Theology*. St. Louis: Chalice, 2010.

Ortlund, Dane C. "'Created Over a Second Time' or 'Grace Restoring Nature'? Edwards and Bavinck on the Heart of Salvation." *The Bavinck Review* 3 (2012): 9–29.

———. *A New Inner Relish: Christian Motivation in the Thought of Jonathan Edwards*. Fearn, UK: Christian Focus, 2008.

———. "Sanctification by Justification: The Forgotten Insight of Bavinck and Berkouwer on Progressive Sanctification." *Scottish Bulletin of Evangelical Theology* 28 (2010): 43–61.

Packer, J. I. *A Quest for Godliness: The Puritan Vision of the Christian Life*. Wheaton, IL: Crossway, 1990.

Patten, William. *Reminiscences of the Late Rev. Samuel Hopkins*. Boston, 1743.

Piper, John, and Justin Taylor, eds. *A God-Entranced Vision of All Things: The Legacy of Jonathan Edwards*. Wheaton, IL: Crossway, 2004.

Plantinga, Cornelius. *Engaging God's World: A Christian Vision of Faith, Learning, and Living*. Grand Rapids: Eerdmans, 2002.

Rutherford, Samuel. *The Letters of Samuel Rutherford*. Edinburgh, 1891.

Simonson, Harold. *Jonathan Edwards: Theologian of the Heart*. Grand Rapids: Eerdmans, 1974.

Smith,, John E. *Jonathan Edwards: Puritan, Preacher, Philosopher*. Notre Dame, IN: University of Notre Dame Press, 1992.

Stein, Stephen J., ed. *The Cambridge Companion to Jonathan Edwards*. Cambridge: Cambridge University Press, 2007.

———. "The Quest for the Spiritual Sense: The Biblical Hermeneutics of Jonathan Edwards." *Harvard Theological Review* 70 (1977): 99–113.

Storms, Sam. *Signs of the Spirit: An Interpretation of Jonathan Edwards' Religious Affections*. Wheaton, IL: Crossway, 2007.

Sweeney, Douglas A. *The American Evangelical Story: A History of the Movement*. Grand Rapids: Baker, 2005.

———. *Jonathan Edwards and the Ministry of the Word: A Model of Faith and Thought*. Downers Grove, IL: InterVarsity, 2009.

Turretin, Francis. *Institutes of Elenctic Theology*. Edited by James T. Dennison Jr. Translated by George Musgrave Giger. 3 vols. Phillipsburg, NJ: P&R, 1992–1997.

Veenhof, Jan. *Nature and Grace in Herman Bavinck*. Translated by Albert M. Wolters. Sioux Center, IA: Dordt College Press, 2006.

Wainwright, William. "Jonathan Edwards and the Sense of the Heart." *Faith and Philosophy* 7 (1990): 43–62.

Warfield, B. B. "Edwards and the New England Theology." In *Biblical and Theological Studies*, edited by Samuel G. Craig, 515–38. Philadelphia: Presbyterian & Reformed, 1952.

Williams, Michael D. "The *Imago Dei* and the Order of Creation—Part I." *Presbyterion* 39, no. 1 (2013): 30–44.

Wilson, Stephen A. *Virtue Reformed: Rereading Jonathan Edwards's Ethics*. Brill's Studies in Intellectual History 132. Leiden: Brill, 2005.

Winiarski, Douglas L. "Jonathan Edwards, Enthusiast? Radical Revivalism and the Great Awakening in the Connecticut Valley." *Church History* 74, no. 4 (2005): 683–739.

Zaspel, Fred. *The Theology of B. B. Warfield: A Systematic Summary*. Wheaton, IL: Crossway, 2010.

GENERAL INDEX

presence of, 174
promises of, 114–17
sovereignty of, 113
  and Christian gentleness, 92
  and human responsibility, 114–15
  over Satan, 153–55
God-centeredness, 77–78, 114, 186
gospel
  beauty of, 28
  centrality of, 141–42, 178–79
  defangs Satan, 151
grace, 39, 43, 147
  ordinary and extraordinary, 64
  as pardon and power, 182, 192
  restores nature, 49–50
gracious affections, 67, 84, 121
  vs. professed affections, 129
  as true Christian experience, 121
Great Awakening, 51, 82
Gura, Philip F., 168n1

Hall, David, 36
happifying, 26
happiness, 26, 170
Harnack, Adolf von, 107n18
heart, 158, 185
  as fallen, 97
  and will, 135
heaven, 167–75
  ascent to, 127
  and Christ, 173–74
  as hope of Christian life, 18
  and joy, 85, 168–70
  and love, 132–33, 169, 171–73
  supreme beauty of, 169
  as temporary, 187–88
hell, 168n1, 174, 175
hellfire sermons, 109, 168
Helm, Paul, 48n34
Herbert, George, 30
holiness, 42, 142, 144–45, 146
"holy practice," 64
Holy Spirit
  and divine love, 56–57, 58
  neglect of, 116
  pouring out of, 58
  and prayer, 116–17
Homer, 144
hope, in pilgrimage, 130–31
Hopkins, Samuel, 85
Hughes, Kent, 104

humility
  in joy, 83–85
  and love, 70–72

idols, 66
image of God, 190–91
immortality of the soul, 158, 161–63
introspection, 181–85

Jesus Christ
  beauty in, 27–28
  in heaven, 173–74
  as key that unlocks Scripture, 108
  loveliness of, 32
  manhood of, 100
joy, 17, 26–27, 75–87
  and desire, 79–81
  God-centeredness of, 77–78
  of heaven, 85, 168–70
  and humility, 83–85
  and light, 78–79
  and love, 68–69
  of new birth, 46–47
  in obedience, 137
  and pain, 164
  and solemnity, 81–83
judgmental, being, 62
justification, 140, 179, 192, 193
  and new birth, 47–48
  and revival, 138

Kierkegaard, Søren, 137
kindness, 62, 65, 90

laughter, 81–83
legalism, 141–42, 179
legal preaching, 109
levity, 81–83
Lewis, C. S., 23, 46, 58, 77n4, 80–81, 83, 96, 128n7, 136, 142, 155, 164n24, 183, 184–85
light, 78–79
light of sun metaphor, 172
Locke, John, 190
longing, 81–82, 172
long-suffering, 61, 90, 91, 92
looking to Christ, 185
love, 17, 55–73
  and Christian practice, 64–66
  as comprehensive of all virtues, 59–62
  for God, 58–59
  and heaven, 171–73
  as humble, 70–72

SCRIPTURE INDEX

WISDOM FROM THE PAST
FOR LIFE IN THE PRESENT

Theologians on the Christian Life

AUGUSTINE by GERALD BRAY

BAVINCK by JOHN BOLT

BONHOEFFER by STEPHEN J. NICHOLS

CALVIN by MICHAEL HORTON

EDWARDS by DANE C. ORTLUND

LEWIS by JOE RIGNEY

LLOYD-JONES by JASON MEYER

LUTHER by CARL R. TRUEMAN

NEWTON by TONY REINKE

OWEN by MATTHEW BARRETT & MICHAEL A. G. HAYKIN

PACKER by SAM STORMS

SCHAEFFER by WILLIAM EDGAR

SPURGEON by MICHAEL REEVES

WARFIELD by FRED G. ZASPEL

WESLEY by FRED SANDERS

The Theologians on the Christian Life series provides accessible introductions to the great teachers on the Christian life, exploring their personal lives and writings, especially as they pertain to the walk of faith.

For more information, visit **crossway.org**.